Best Sermons 3

CONTRIBUTING EDITORS

Best Sermons 3

James W. Cox, Editor

Kenneth M. Cox, Associate Editor

HarperSanFrancisco
A Division of HarperCollins*Publishers*

Library of Congress Catalog Card Number 88-656297

ISSN 1041-6382

91 92 93 94 HAD 10 9 8 7 6 5 4 3 2

This edition is printed on acid-free paper that meets the American National Standard Institute Z39.48 Standard.

Contents

87443

Preface

Surely everyone has driven past a church that has next Sunday's sermon title displayed on a sign outside, under glass. Often that little preview of the coming attraction can pique the interest of the passer-by, perhaps not enough to come back on Sunday morning, but at least enough to think about the possibilities. We rarely find out whether the sermon delivered is the sermon promised. But what is remarkable in seeing those sermon titles out in front of churches everywhere is that no matter where the church or what the specific beliefs and ideas proclaimed within, many of the themes and concerns addressed from any given pulpit are the same as in another church three miles or three thousand miles away.

As we have read the many sermons preachers have sent us, one striking fact has emerged: Whatever the preacher's nationality, color, gender, or religion, the matters of concern are similar. A preacher in Switzerland is interested in peace; so is an Australian preacher. God, Christ, Holy Spirit; love of God and love of humanity; justice and freedom; suffering and joy; forgiveness and salvation—all of these themes wrap themselves around the issues of the day, woven into the fabric of relevant biblical texts.

The most important criteria in the selection of sermons for *Best Sermons 3* were originality, scriptural and/or Christian basis, relevance, clarity, and interest.

Judges for the contest were:

James W. Cox, Lester Professor of Christian Preaching, Southern Baptist Theological Seminary

A. Leonard Griffith, former minister at St. Paul's Church and Lecturer in Preaching, Wycliffe College, Toronto

Charlene Kammerer, District Superintendent, Tallahassee District, Florida Annual Conference, United Methodist Church

Richard C. Marius, Director of Expository Writing and Senior Lecturer in English, Harvard University

James Earl Massey, Dean of the Chapel and University Professor of Religion and Society, Tuskegee University; now Dean, Anderson University School of Theology

Duke K. McCall, Chancellor, Southern Baptist Theological Seminary; former President, Baptist World Alliance

Allan M. Parrent, Professor of Christian Ethics, Associate Dean for Academic Affairs and Vice President, Virginia Theological Seminary, Alexandria, Virginia

Once again, we thank all those who submitted sermons for the competititon, and we encourage those and others to send us more of your best sermons.

JAMES W. COX
KENNETH M. COX
Louisville, Kentucky

Best Sermons 3

I. EVANGELISTIC

1.   Do You Want to Be Healed?

Raymond Bailey

2 Kings 5:8–19; John 5:1–16

While it is certainly true that the words of Scripture and the presence of God comfort the afflicted, is it not also true that the Word of God afflicts the comfortable? Just when I have God in a corner where I can handle him, boxed up and packaged to suit my taste, squeezed into familiar middle-class modes, a story like this arrests me and brings me back to the reality that he defies all religious stereotypes. He simply will not be a God who is sophisticated, domesticated, and controlled by human standards. Here is Jesus on a religious holiday coming to the holy city of Jerusalem, but does he go into the Temple to worship? Does he seek out the wise men of the town for discourse? No. He goes with haste to this place where the clientele are the blind, lame, or paralyzed. It was a place that would not be beautiful by our standards. The odors of illness and unkept bodies are not pleasant to our noses. The sight of uncared for, broken bodies in their own waste turns weak stomachs. The sounds of pain pound our senses.

Imagine, if you will, Jesus coming to our city for some religious festival or holiday and not showing up at our church but choosing rather to go the slums of our city or to the emergency room of the city hospital where people wait in hope of healing. Simple little notes like this one remind us of the grace of God—the goodness, the holiness, the mercy, the kindness, the self-giving that character-

Raymond Bailey is professor of Christian Preaching at Southern Baptist Theological Seminary in Louisville, Kentucky, where he also serves as director of the National Center for Christian Preaching. Dr. Bailey most recently coauthored *The Bible Alive: The Dramatic Monologue Sermon,* to be published this year.

ize the loving Father, those special traits manifested so clearly in the person of the Lord Jesus Christ. Here is Jesus in this place with all of these sick people lying around waiting for some kind of miracle, desperately hoping for wholeness and a new life. The life they long for is the one most of us take for granted.

Can you see him walking in, looking around the five gates, studying each case, assessing varying degrees of illness, and finally selecting this person who had obviously been there for a very long time? See Jesus turning his attention to this paralyzed person on a mat, walking over to him, and asking, "Do you want to be healed?" Some of the questions that Jesus asked seem a bit silly to me. It ought to be pretty obvious that a person lying on a mat, who has been for thirty-eight years waiting for healing, who knows he is sick, wants to be healed. But Jesus asked him, "Do you want to be healed?" Is it possible that some sick people don't want to be healed? Might it be an appropriate question for us with regard to our spiritual, physical, and psychological conditions? Does the Christ ask of us, "Do you really want to be healed?" Most of us know what is wrong with us. We know what needs to be done in our lives.

In most of my pastoral counseling, I have found that those who come to me have already pretty well diagnosed the problem. Many of them already know the solution. They come looking for a less threatening diagnosis, an easy remedy. We have physical problems, spiritual and emotional problems, of which we are fully aware, but we do not do anything about them. Some of us are part of a sick marriage. We know there is a problem in the relationship. We know that our relationship as husband and wife is not what it ought to be. Some of us live in sick families where relationships between parents and children are not what they ought to be. On the job we know there are relational problems with people with whom we spend hours every day, a sickness in some of those relationships, yet we do nothing to alter our pattern. We do nothing to face the problem, let alone solve it. We cling to the security of the known—even when it is sick.

There are reasons why we do not turn loose of our illness. Look back at the man who had been ill for thirty-eight years. For him, as for us, sickness can become a way of life. All of us have known people who have illnesses, sometimes physical illnesses, who have learned to manipulate and use those illnesses to satisfy some psychological need or maintain a hold on another person. Many parents hold on to children long after they should have set them free. The parents control their life with a constant threat that "if you are not here continually to take care of me, to watch over me, or if you do not build your whole life around me, then you will be contributing to my death." Some children learn that the only way they can get their parent's attention is by being sick. If they simply develop a little temperature or have a bit of a sore throat, then the parent who does not have time to talk with them or time to deal with them in ordinary circumstances will find time if it's nothing more than to put them in the car and drive with them to the doctor's office. We learn to use our illnesses, both physical and psychological—yes, spiritual, too—to manipulate other people and control our world. Illness may be a hiding place from responsibility.

Do you realize that in Jerusalem in his day and time this man had as good a way of earning a living as was to be found? As long as he lay each day on this mat, people would pass by, pity him, and throw a few coins his way. No one expected much of him. He was able to live fairly comfortably off his illness, just as we are sometimes able to live comfortably off our illnesses. It is not uncommon to resist healing because healing would mean an assumption of responsibility for our lives. For this man to be healed would mean that no longer would people look at him as an invalid, no longer would they have pity for him and expect nothing of him. They would demand that he assume a normal role in his society. He would be expected to go to work and earn his own bread. He would be expected to care for others rather than be cared for. So it is with us. There is always some threat, some change called for on our part when we accept healing.

Some time ago I read a newspaper account of a bizarre parole board hearing. A seventy-year-old man who had spent most of his life in prison was offered a parole. In tears, he rejected the offer, explaining that he had lived so long in prison that he would not know how to live in the outside world. He did not want responsibility for his life. Is it possible that an individual can be a prisoner of a life-style that is self-destructive? Are there those who are so religiously institutionalized (as were the Pharisees) that they reject the liberation of the grace of God? Are there not those who prefer the security of ignorance, daily routine, unexamined values, and theology to the challenge of change and independent choice? Do you want to be free?

Illness may be self-indulgence. I read in a book some time ago something about the art of trapping monkeys in India. One technique is to drill a hole in a coconut and place rice in the coconut. A monkey will come along and stick a paw into the coconut, grab a fistful of rice, and then be unable to pull its paw back from the coconut. He is trapped by his greed. All he would have to do is turn loose of the rice, his hand would be free, and he could draw it out. The problem is that he places greater value on the rice that he is holding than he does on his freedom. Some of us place greater value on our weaknesses, our dependencies, greater value on our immorality, than we do upon the freedom that would be possible for us if we would turn loose of a certain style of living, a certain way of life, a certain sickness that binds us. In Shakespeare's play *Hamlet*, a king who has murdered his brother, married his brother's wife, and usurped his brother's kingdom struggles with the results of his wicked acts. Like many of us, in spite of this dreadful behavior he goes through the routine of evening prayers. He struggles to pray. He kneels, casts himself down on the floor, and cries out with great anguish that his prayers seem to bounce off the ceiling. But he knows why his prayers choke in his throat.

> Pray can I not
> Though inclination be as sharp as will;
> My stronger guilt defeats my strong intent . . .

He knows that he clings to the rewards of his sin and thus can find no relief from it. His mind and heart cannot ascend to God while he clings to those things that motivated his wickedness. How often this is true for us. We want to be forgiven of sin; we want to be cleansed; we want to be made whole again. But we are unwilling, like the monkey, like King Claudius, unwilling to turn loose of those things that have brought us into this condition of weakness. Our choices leave us paralyzed in a state of dependency, alienation, and separation.

"Do you want to be healed?" Jesus asked. The man does not answer the question directly but offers instead excuses for not having been healed. Jesus does not bog down in analysis or debate but gives an invitation. No excuses! Here is your opportunity! Act now! "Rise, take up your pallet and walk." It is easy to get so bogged down in the search for excuses for our problems that we have no energy left to solve them. Christ calls for action. When we are set free from sin, free from the false self, free from those things that make us less than we ought to be, immediately we have placed upon us the responsibility to respond to the gift of God. Freedom is freedom to act according to the image of God within us. We should remember that the prayers of Christians always are to be geared to the action of Christians and the responsibility to do that which God has called us to do.

Years ago I came upon a cartoon that captures our morass. In the first panel was a man who looked about college age, a rawboned sort of fellow, kneeling before an altar. There was a cross in the background and a stained-glass window behind it. There before the altar, the young man prayed. The little balloon read, "O Lord, help us feed the starving masses of the world. Feed the hungry." In the next panel, the scene is unchanged: the young man before the altar praying, the caption above reading, "O Lord, we pray for an end of war in the world. Lord give us peace in the world in which we live." And then a third panel: the subject even more intense now, down on all fours before the altar, and the caption in the balloon reading, "O Lord, bring peace among the races and make us to live as brothers, one with another." But then in the fourth panel, a shock; the picture has radically altered. A lightning bolt has pierced the altar, the stones from the altar have fallen all about the young man who is lying back in the rubble of his altar with an expression of astonishment on his face. The caption reads, "Do it yourself, you clod!"

There is so much that we ask God to do, which God has set us free to do. How dare we pray for the hungry when we do nothing for the hungry! How dare we pray for racial and ethnic peace when we do nothing to bring that about! How dare we pray for peace when we are not peacemakers! How dare we pray that God will heal those who are sick when we are unwilling to participate in that healing ourselves! How can we gather week after week to pray for the lonely, the sick, and the hurting, the pained in the convalescent centers and in the various institutions around the world, when we are unwilling to get our hands dirty, to offend our nostrils, to inconvenience our schedules to do anything about it. Jesus said to the man, "Pick up your pallet and walk." Take some responsibility for your life. There will be some risk involved. But being free in God means to assume responsibility for your life. And so it is with all of us. He says to us when he calls us, "Take up your pallet and walk!"

Perhaps the poor fellow's worst fears were realized, because he walked only a short distance into trouble. He took up his pallet and did what Jesus told him to do, and immediately he was identified as a nonconformist, a law-breaker, a sacrilegious person. The religious people confronted him: "Man, what are you doing carrying this pallet around on the Sabbath? You know that is illegal, it's not right, it's unlawful." And the man responded, "The one who healed me told me to take it up, and I did." In his excitement, he had put aside social norms and focused on the one who had demonstrated healing power. That is the challenge for every Christian. We should keep our mind stayed on the one who said, "Rise and walk!"

In Sean O'Casey's play *Within the Gates*, there is a moving scene toward the end of the play as it reaches its climax. A bishop, as an indiscreet youth, fathered a child. Through the years he has done nothing but observe from afar as her life has been corrupted. Discovering that she is in serious crisis, he decides that he will care for her. The bishop's sister says to him, "But you must remember who you are. And you must know that people will talk. What will people say? You can't go." The bishop responds, "It does not matter what people say or what people think. The only thing that matters is what God thinks. And what God says. What does it matter what men think a man to be if God thinks him to be a saint?"

How many of us hide from the suffering of our lost generation? Let us put aside custom, status, and expediency and live our lives according to God's standard. Stop asking, "What will people think?" and ask, "What does God think?" Are we willing to be nonconformist, willing to break some rules, willing to do whatever God has called us to do in the assumption of our responsibility as people healed through the power of God? "Do you want to be healed?" Being healed is an awesome responsibility. The risk is real.

This healing differs somewhat from most of the healings in the New Testament. The difference is a significant one. We have often placed so much emphasis on faith that we have made faith itself a good work that we do. We have made it a point of boasting. "See how faithful I am; therefore, I'm a Christian and I've been forgiven. I'm a good person because I have faith." Do you notice that this man who was healed by Jesus did not seek out Jesus? Jesus sought out him. Note that even after Jesus had healed him the man ran off without asking who it was who had healed him. He didn't know who Jesus was. When the Jews attacked him for carrying his pallet, he said, "*That man* told me." And they said to him, "Who is that man?" And he said, "Gee, I don't know. I never thought to ask his name."

There is so much in our lives that God has done for us that we don't know about. So much that he has done in healing us, in setting us free, in providing for us to become the whole people created in the image of God that he intended for us to become. We do not always have to know the formulas; we do not have to know the religious propositions; we do not have to know the doctrine; we do not have to know the rituals. We must respond to that grace that comes to us, and we must respond to what God is doing in our lives. The man did not care who healed him or how, but he knew that he had been made whole.

How marvelous it would be if some of us could see that God has been working in our lives in ways we did not recognize. He has been working for us even when we didn't pray. God works in our lives outside the church. God heals according to his will. God gives us power and strength. If only we could respond without being able to identify what has happened or to pigeonhole it! When we recognize that we have been healed, that we have been given strength and life, how wonderful it would be if we would act on the gift of God.

Later, Jesus encounters the man in the Temple. That's interesting, isn't it? Having been healed, without any direction from God, without even knowing who Jesus is, without any direction from Jesus, the man went to the Temple, apparently to give thanks. In the Temple Jesus encounters him. Jesus says to him, "Go and sin no more, that nothing worse than your physical illness befall you." The purpose of the admonition not to sin is not payment for the healing but health for the healed. Christian behavior is not a reward to God but a benefit for the believer. "Go and sin no more, that nothing worse befall you." Out of that healing experience, one becomes a disciple, a follower, a worker, a living witness and testimony to the power of God. Have you been healed? In what way does your behavior reflect thanksgiving?

Jesus addresses us and asks, "Do you want to be healed?" Do you want your marriage to be what it ought to be? Then why are you passive and inactive about it? Do something about it! Do you want to be free of depression? Do you avail yourself of God's gifts and opportunities and the counseling possibilities and all of the many ways in which depression can be managed? Accept the gifts of God! Do you want to be healed? Are you willing to give up those things that cause you to be less than what God calls you to be? Turn loose of the rice in the coconut! Do you want to be healed? God is the healer.

Even before you knew his name, before you were born, before you were a thought in your parents' mind, God loved you. God became man and died on the cross for you. God provided for your freedom before you even knew his name. Now that you know, how will you act upon it? This is the invitation. It is always the invitation of God that we be healed, that we be made whole, that we accept the gift that he has offered us and act responsibly upon it. "Do you want to be healed?" "Rise, take up your pallet and walk!"

2. Midwives of Hope

Roger Lovette

Luke 24:1–6

Long before daylight a group of women walked through the darkness to anoint the dead body of Jesus. So the Resurrection begins with the women. The men were not there. They were asleep and hiding in caves and in despair. The women were last at the cross and first at the tomb. And God used them to tell all the others. Someone has called them "midwives of hope"—helping along by their very presence the forces of goodness and grace in the world.[1]

That phrase, *midwives of hope*, has a ring to it. At this time in our history, what we may need more than anything else are men and women who are giving themselves to this very tedious task of bringing hope back into the world.

Mary Magdalene and Joanna and Mary the mother of James and the other women did not know that Easter morning all they were doing. But they were the instruments by which the birth of hope would begin to find its way out into the world once more.

What would we do without this great biblical word *hope?* From the very beginning, all the way through the book, *hope* is on almost every page. "I will give you a land . . . " "I will give you a son . . . " "I will make you a people . . . " "I will lift your chains . . . " "I will be with you . . . " "I will forgive your sins and heal your land . . . " "I will remember your sins no more . . . " "I will send you a prophet and a son . . . " "I will prepare a place for you . . . " "I will not leave you comfortless . . . " "I will give you a new heaven and a new

Roger Lovette received his doctorate from Lexington Theological Seminary and is currently senior minister at Second Baptist Church in Memphis, Tennessee. Dr. Lovette is the author of *A Faith of Our Own, Questions Jesus Raised,* and other books.

earth . . . " The Book of Hebrews called hope the anchor of the soul (Heb. 6:19). And Frederick Buechner has said that if Paul were writing in our time he would probably say that the greatest of these is not love at all, but hope is what we need most.

If we look carefully at this Easter story, what we see emerging are clues and hints to help us become midwives of hope for our time.

We discover, like those first midwives, that *the Resurrection is real and true.* There would be no gospel and no Church without Easter. Even when the women did bring the news back that morning they were met with disciples perplexed, frightened—those who thought it was only an idle tale. Those who first heard did not believe. The cross was too real. The blood had barely dried. Their hearts still ached. They remembered too much.

But the women, Mary Magdalene and the others, believed. And it was their belief that first helped the disciples discover the Resurrection truth for themselves.

Something similar happened in Mason, Tennessee, in 1984. One day Louise Degrafinried was cleaning up her little house. There was a knock at the door, and she went to answer it. Standing before her was a terrible-looking man with a gun. "Open up," he whispered. She opened the door. He looked around to see if anyone was there while Mrs. Degrafinried looked him over. He looked awful. Dirty. Hair matted. Smelly. He had escaped from the state prison and was on the run and very dangerous. She had heard about it on her television. After looking at him for a long time she said, "Are you hungry?" He looked at her as if she were crazy.

"What?"

"Are you hungry?" she asked again.

"Yeah, I am."

"Well," she said, "come on into the kitchen and sit down. I'm gonna fix you some bacon and eggs. Before I do though, I want you to get yourself right down that hall to the bathroom and wash your face and hands. Wash good. You look terrible."

The escaped prisoner was dumbfounded. But he went on down the hall to the bathroom. Mrs. Degrafinried got out the bacon and began to fry.

When he had finished washing up, he came back into the room, and she inspected him. "Well, you look a whole lot better." Then she told him to put his gun down, that it made her nervous. And so he put it down.

She began to talk to him as he ate. She told him about her little Baptist church and about Jesus and how he had come into her life and how it had made such a difference. She talked to him about how God loved everybody and didn't want any of his children breaking into anybody's houses and scaring the wits out of them. She asked him about his own family, and he told her that his father and mother were both dead. He told her she reminded him of his grandmother who had died when he was eight. And she told him more about the Lord Jesus. And when he had finished his eggs and bacon, he did the strangest thing. He picked up the telephone receiver and called the police and gave himself up. The guards came and took him away. And as he was leaving, Mrs. Degrafinried reached over and patted his cheek and said, "Now you be good, you hear?"[2]

If we are going to be midwives of hope, we are going to have to spend some time and energy with the practicality of this faith business.

Another thing we learn from this Easter account is that if we want to be midwives of hope, *we must live the story*. And this may be the hardest part of our task. But it was the living out of the Easter message that changed those first disciples' lives. Resurrection became their story. And they discovered in the empty tomb what Peter would later call "a lively hope" (1 Pet. 1:3–4).

We can't be midwives of hope unless we believe in what we are doing. The job is too messy. It takes enormous patience. We don't always see the results. We cannot do this job long unless we make Easter part of our own story.

This means that we really are the Easter people. We believe that Christ is not dead, that evil did not win, that wrong does not have the last word, that right really does matter, and nothing can separate us from the love of God. This lively hope begins to invade our lives in such a way that we live it out.

Several years ago there appeared a story in the *New York Times* by Samuel R. Ogden, former member of the Vermont legislature and author. He wrote that at noon on one of the happiest Christmases he could remember, his wife of fifty-one years died quite suddenly. From that moment on his life had no meaning for him. At the age of seventy-six, widowed and bereft, he was plunged into a black despair that seemed to have no end. Without his wife, Mamie, nothing mattered. Everything fell apart. His children and grandchildren tried to reach him, but nothing helped.

Seeing no way out, he hooked up a hose to the exhaust pipe of his car, brought the hose around to the car window, caulked all the windows, and started the motor. But a freak thing happened. The hose became disengaged from the exhaust. His housekeeper found him almost unconscious and called the emergency squad.

And he reports:

> It was in the hospital that I made my great discovery. I discovered that all the values which my unbearable grief had twisted into a pattern of evil could be set aright once that I looked at them through Mamie's eyes; and this, by the grace of God, I managed to do. Now I resolved to live with as much joy as I could accomplish, doing the things I knew she would have me to do. I was still capable of work, and there was much that I had left undone. The spirit of my beloved one charged me with the task of fulfilling these, my obligations, and thus I came out of the pit which had seemed so deep and hopeless.
>
> I pray that the hurt that I have caused may be forgiven and forgotten, and I hope for understanding on the part of those whom I had unwittingly distressed. I have now broken through into a new world which I pray will come to some purpose. I shall make peace with everyone, adjust my course to the ways of love, and I know the will of God will prevail.[3]

At the age of seventy-six, Sam Ogden discovered that he can be a midwife of hope even in his last years. We have to live out the story. Easter must be woven into the fabric of our lives. If we are to be midwives of hope there is another task before us. *We must carry the hope.* Midwives work. They come in and roll up their sleeves and tell somebody to boil water and somebody to get some clean towels. They place a cool bath cloth on the patient's forehead and whisper, "Everything is going to be all right." They pass it on.

Midwives of hope are not selfish. They do not keep this hope to themselves. They take it out and pass it on. We all carry germs and burdens and anxiety. Our task is also to carry hope for those who need it the most.

In the city of Amsterdam, not too far from Central Station, you will find the red-light district. Along those narrow, cobblestone side streets there are shops that promise all sorts of sexual ecstasy. The farther you go down those streets, the sleazier they become, until you come to a different kind of a shop. In the window, like mannequins, women sit scantily clad. They sit there, in chairs, day after day, waiting for some man to come along and decide if he wants to buy their favors.

One particular woman sat there for a long time. She often watched, with eyes that managed to conceal and yet attract, the men who stood looking on the other side of the plate-glass window. Some of the men would stand boldly challenging her to acknowledge their desire. She could usually tell who would ring the bell and ask for her services and who would move on. She had been in the business long enough to know this. Some men were nervous and ashamed as they looked. But some of them would ring the bell and then run away ashamed before she answered the door.

After a man had chosen her, she would lead him up the creaking wooden stairs to her room, which was furnished with mirrors and a bed. There he would pay for whatever pleasure he chose. And when it was over, she would return to the display window and sit there waiting for another customer.

One day a man came by and just stood there looking at her face. With her eyes and her sensuous movements, she sought to tempt him. And the man simply walked away. But the next day she looked up, and there he was again, staring at her. This occurred for several days, and she grew afraid. But there was something about his presence that she looked forward to. She found that the coldness way down inside that seemed to be dead began to thaw. This prostitute began to feel, as the man came and stared, like a young girl in love.

One day she wiped the seduction from her eyes and raised them, naked and vulnerable, toward his. She gazed deeply into his eyes and saw something she had not seen before. They were very sad. Those eyes disarmed her. He seemed to see what she was and what she had done with her wasted, sleazy life. And yet, as she looked at him, she thought she saw reflected in his eyes the woman who could have been a teacher, a wife, a friend—somebody who lived next door. Maybe even somebody's mother. She saw reflected in his eyes the woman she thought was dead, who more than anything else longed to love and be loved. And as she watched, those eyes on the other side of the window grew luminous. Tears began to trickle down her cheeks. He smiled. And she smiled back. And then the man was gone.

He came back the next day but the seat behind the plate-glass window was empty. As he looked for her, someone came up behind him and touched his arm. It was the woman from the window. She put her arms around him and held him close, offering him the best she had—a simple embrace from the heart.

Nobody knows what happened after that. But I am told that if you walk down that street today, you'll find a different woman there. The other woman never came back to her job. She found somebody who saw in her what nobody else had ever seen—and it had changed her life.[4]

> But on the first day of the week, at early dawn, they went to the tomb, taking the spices which they had prepared. And they found the stone rolled away from the tomb, but when they went in they did not find the body. While they were perplexed about this, behold, two men stood by them in dazzling apparel; and as they were frightened and bowed their faces to the ground, the men said to them, "Why do you seek the living among the dead? Remember how he told you, while he was still in Galilee, that the Son of man must be delivered into the hands of sinful men, and be crucified, and on the third day rise." And they remembered his words, and returning from the tomb they told all this to the eleven and to all the rest. (Luke 24:1–9, RSV)

NOTES

1. Jim Wallis, "The Door of Hope," *Sojourners* (April 1988):21.
2. Maxie Dunham, *The Sanctuary for Lent 1988* (Nashville, TN: Abingdon), 5.
3. Samuel R. Ogden, "When Mamie Left," *New York Times,* January 23, 1973.
4. Narrative about Amsterdam is based in part on a story by Michael A. King, "The Window-Display Woman," *Christian Century* (October 22, 1986):911.

3. Dinner at the Homesick Restaurant

H. Stephen Shoemaker

Acts 2:41–42, 46; 4:32–37

A recent novel by Anne Tyler tells of Ezra, who ran a restaurant. All life long, feeding people was his way of caring for them. He made friends with Mrs. Scarlotti who owned Scarlotti's Restaurant: He worked for her, and one day she turned the business over to him. Ezra tried various menus and formats. One day this idea came to him:

> He'd cook what people felt homesick for—tacos like those from vendors' carts in California, which the Mexican was always pining after; and that wonderful vinegary North Carolina barbeque that Todd Duckett had to have brought by his mother several times a year in cardboard cups. He would call it the Homesick Restaurant.[1]

Hence the title of the novel: *Dinner at the Homesick Restaurant*. What kind of food do you get homesick for? I read that when Alexander Julian, the fashion designer of the *Colours* label, a North Carolina native, designed the new uniforms for the Charlotte Hornets, he was paid in monthly shipments of North Carolina barbeque. I know a transplanted Texan here in Louisville. When he goes to the Tumbleweed Restaurant, he almost drinks the hot salsa sauce. Mother's milk.

H. Stephen Shoemaker is pastor of Crescent Hill Baptist Church in Louisville, Kentucky. He has written three books, *Re-telling the Biblical Story: The Theology & Practice of Narrative Preaching*, *The Jekyll and Hyde Syndrome: A New Encounter with the Seven Deadly Sins*, and *Strength in Weakness*.

What kind of food are you homesick for? A regional dish? A dish you could only get at home?

I

Are your tastebuds beginning to awaken? Are your memories? Food and memories go together, don't they? And food is more than just food. The food you are homesick for has to do with more than taste; it has to do with place and time and the experience of joy or comfort or love. It tastes like *home.*

When you were growing up and were feeling ill your mother may have served you a special kind of soup. So now when you're feeling weak and low you hunger for that soup and the hands that served it to you.

What was your favorite meal at home growing up? I know one family where, on the birthday of each of the children, the one whose birthday it is gets to pick what Mom or Dad will cook that evening, their favorite meal. What do you cook for your son or daughter when they come home after being away for a while? What do you hope to eat when you go home?

You may be remembering your grandmother's cooking. At my grandparents' home I'd wake up early to the smell of country ham frying in the pan, and I'd walk to a table heaped with mountains of eggs, grits, biscuits, country ham, and "red-eye" gravy to pour over it all. Just thinking about it raises my cholesterol.

One of our congregation told me of her grandmother whose home was the most home she's ever known as an adult. It is her grandmother's mashed potatoes she is most homesick for, now that her grandmother has died. Everytime she went home, her grandmother fixed mashed potatoes. And it's not just the taste of the potatoes she's homesick for, though the taste was wonderful enough, but the going to her home and working alongside her in the kitchen, boiling, slicing, mashing the potatoes, preparing them for the table. When you put them in your mouth, what they tasted like was *home*—love and friendship and comfort and somebody who was there for you when you needed them.

What kind of food are you homesick for?

II

It has occurred to me that the communion table is a kind of Homesick Restaurant. It's a place where we find what we're most homesick for. It's the place homesick people come to. Sometimes we don't even know we're homesick till we get here and suddenly our appetite returns. Funny, when you're homesick, really homesick, you don't ever feel like eating till you get home. And when your legs are finally under that familiar table, you feel like you could eat forever.

The picture we get of the early Church in Acts tells what people found when they met together around Christ's table, things they'd hungered for all their lives.

First, they were fed God's Word. "They devoted themselves to the apostle's teaching." We need some clear word from beyond our own fragile and confused hearts and minds. We need a word from God. The scriptures of the Old and New Testaments provide us with this word, a compass to guide us through stormy and uncharted seas. Jesus said, when tempted by Satan in the wilderness to turn stones into bread, "We human folk do not live by bread alone but by every word that proceeds from the mouth of God." God's Word is what we're homesick for and is what we find as we gather with God's family around the table. "My food is to do the will of the One who sent me," Jesus said. Is that not our deepest hunger, our most poignant homesickness? To sense we are living in God's plan for us? To find that place of peace where what God wants and we want are the same? The Word of God is what you find at the Homesick Restaurant. If you search the menu long enough you'll find what you really need: sturdy guidance, tender mercy, light in the darkness, care for your soul, a song in the night. They devoted themselves to the apostles' teaching.

We're also homesick for *one another,* for communion and community. God did not make us to be alone but to live in deep communion with others. The text says that the early Church also *devoted itself to fellowship (koinonia).* Fellowship, community, is not instant reality. You must devote yourselves to fellowship. It says that they devoted themselves to the breaking of bread and prayers. And it says that they partook of food with glad and generous hearts. Doesn't that sound like a wonderful experience, praising God and having favor with all the people?

What a wonderful picture of the gift of community. They gathered around the Lord's table and prayed together. They ate food together with glad and generous hearts. We're all homesick for that experience—sitting with people we love and who love us, hearts filled with gladness and hearts that want to give and give and give.

They shared everything, the text tells us. Everything was shared in common, even possessions. When you share your possessions, you've shared your very lives.

Leo Bebb, the odd evangelist in Buechner's novel *Love Feast,* threw a Thanksgiving meal and invited anybody in town who would come. When they assembled he said, "The kingdom of heaven is like a great feast . . . a love feast where no one is a stranger." Then he said,

> We all got secrets . . . Hurtful things. Long ago
> things. We're all scared and lonesome, but most of
> the time we keep it hid. It's like everyone of us has
> lost his way so bad we don't even know which way is
> home anymore only we're ashamed to ask. You
> know what would happen if we would own up we're
> lost and ask? Why, what would happen is we'd find
> out home is each other. We'd find out home is Jesus
> loves us lost or found or any whichway.[2]

Home is each other when we are brought together in Christ. It may be the best home or the most home we've ever experienced. In Tyler's novel, Ezra kept trying to get his family together for a meal in his restaurant. They never made it through a meal without getting into a fight, somebody stomping out, everything falling apart. One time they didn't even make it through the appetizer. Jesus says that the best home of all is not the one behind us but the one ahead, the one called the Kingdom of God and the one we can taste, glimpse, touch here and now around the table of the Lord.

What are you homesick for? Justice? Justice you can taste is here, not perfect but more than ever before and more to come. Mercy? Mercy's here, too, like you've never imagined. And peace, well-being in community and with God and inside your own skin: It's here, too. All signs of the kingdom to come but here in part already.

Home is, most of all, meeting Christ: Jesus loving us lost or found or any whichway. That was the startling experience of the disciples after Easter Day. As they gathered around the table and broke bread, they experienced the presence of the Risen Christ.

You meet *Christ* here at the Homesick Restaurant, and he is the one we hunger for most of all.

There's forgiveness here and welcome home. There's a savior here around this table who understands everything because there's nothing human he hasn't experienced. He's felt every human push and pull, every exultation and every desolation, every broken heart and every heart on fire.

And this savior is not sitting arms crossed, just waiting to see if we're smart enough, hungry enough to come. He's the shepherd leaving the ninety-nine safe ones and going after the one that's lost. He's the woman turning the house upside down and looking for her cherished coin. He's a father running, running down the driveway, down the street to greet his son home who he thought was dead. He's the king throwing a banquet and sending his servants to bring in everybody, anybody they can find.

When you come to this table, you meet Jesus Christ, "surprise of Mercy, outgoing Gladness, Rescue, Healing and Life" (George Buttrick). He is the one you are most homesick for because it was through him, for him, and in him you were made. When you come home to him you finally come home to yourself. When you are around him you find yourself saying, So that's who I am!

It has been the experience of the Church for two thousand years, and I've seen it happen over and over again. Christ is the one we meet at the Homesick Restaurant.

He takes an apron and waits on every table. Yours, too.

"What would you like?" he asks.

We stammer and ask for a little time. We're not always sure what we want, what we're homesick for. He is patient.

"Escargot?" we ask, "What is escargot?"

"I don't think that's what you're looking for," he answers. "Have you tried our roast beef and mashed potatoes?"

"That sounds good," we say and smile with sudden recognition.

We're nervous about the price and look over to the right-hand column—the place where the prices are—and, to our consternation, see no prices. You know you're in trouble when the prices aren't even printed!

He sees our anxiety and says, "Don't worry. It's on the house. Welcome home."

NOTES

1. Anne Tyler, *Dinner at the Homesick Restaurant* (New York: Berkley Books, 1983), 124.
2. Frederick Buechner, *Love Feast*, in *The Book of Bebb* (New York: Atheneum, 1979) 306.

4.   The Way Out of a Pigpen

William F. Evans

Luke 15:11–24

Have you ever run away from home? I did once, when I was seven or eight years old. I remember getting angry with my mother one cool, fall day. I don't remember what I was so upset about; maybe she wanted me to do something I didn't want to do. At any rate, I had enough so I left. I ran back into the woods for a while, visited our neighborhood tree house, and them came back out of the woods three houses away and hid in the shrubbery there. I could hear my mother calling me, but her pleas, which at first sounded angry and then progressively more worried, just fell on deaf ears. But then something miraculous happened. It began to turn dark, the air got colder, and I got hungry. Finally I came to my senses and decided things weren't so bad at home after all. Even knowing that I might be facing a scolding or, worse, a spanking, I returned home. To my surprise my mother was thrilled to see me; she hugged and kissed me and had food waiting for me to eat. Boy, it felt good to return home!

You don't have to be a seven- or eight-year-old to run away from home. People do it all the time. Teenagers all over America get frustrated and disillusioned with life at home, and they believe life has to be better elsewhere, so they run away in alarming numbers.

William F. Evans is parish pastor of Trenholm Road United Methodist Church in Columbia, South Carolina. He is the recipient of the Air Force Achievement Medal and the Air Force Commendation Medal for service in the South Carolina Air National Guard, and has served as chaplain for the organization since 1984. A native of South Carolina, Evans attended Wofford College and received his master of divinity degree from Duke University Divinity School.

Not long ago, an article in a national news weekly caught my attention. It was about middle-aged executives and bored housewives who run away from their responsibilities and families. This article estimated that hundreds of thousands of American adults do this each year. The average adult male runaway is usually a successful business executive or professional, forty-four to fifty years old, college educated, making about $50,000 a year. But the pressure finally gets to him and pushes him to the edge. Some turn to alcohol and drugs; some have nervous breakdowns. Many just simply drop out or run away. Some morning, John Doe kisses his wife, hugs his kids, pats the dog, heads out for work, and doesn't return home. Sometimes families track him down, usually finding him in a nearby city living in low-rent, run-down housing, working at a manual-labor job, seeking anonymity and irresponsibility.

This article also said that about as many women as men run away, only the woman is much younger, usually about thirty-five to forty. She marries early, has children, stays at home for fifteen years and feels unappreciated, stifled, locked in. She is looking for what she thinks will be a better life, more peaceful, more satisfying more authentic. One day she just leaves; reaching the breaking point, she runs away.

Do runaways ever find what they are looking for? Usually not. Most discover that the grass on the other side is not as green as they thought it would be.

Our scripture lesson today is about a runaway. This story of Jesus is usually called the parable of the prodigal son. It is one of the most familiar stories in the Bible. "A man had two sons," Jesus said. "And the younger son went to his father, asked for his share of the inheritance he was entitled to, and when he received it, he ran away from home." The Bible says that he went far away from home, and there he lost everything on loose living. Suddenly he was poor and hungry, so he took the only job he could find: feeding pigs. No respectable Jew would have ever taken such a lowly job, for pigs were considered unclean, and pork was not kosher. But this young man was at rock bottom. He had no place to live and no food to eat, so he made his home in the pigpen, and he ate what the pigs ate. Then he realized how foolish he had been and how well off he really was at home. So, he decided to return home, seeking not to be reinstated as a son but as a servant to his father. But his father saw him walking down the road and ran to him and embraced him and welcomed him home again. The father showered expensive gifts upon him and threw a party for him and said to the guests, "Let us rejoice and be happy, for my son was dead, but he is alive again; he was lost, but now he's found."

This story touches us because it speaks of our own rebelliousness and our own desires to run away. It tells how lost we can get when we run away from God and others and responsibility. This young man's rebellion led him to a pigpen. All of us find ourselves in a pigpen of some sort or other whenever we run away from God, when we alienate ourselves from others or when we try to shirk all responsibility. I've been in a pigpen several times in my life, haven't you? It is amazing how big of a mess we can get ourselves into sometimes. But of even greater significance is the ending of this story. It tells of the depth of the Father's love. Jesus says that God is like this loving father, anxiously waiting for us to come to our senses and return home. When we do, he doesn't give us what we deserve, which is punishment; instead, he showers us with love and forgiveness, and he throws a party on our behalf.

It is my hope today that in the midst of our desire to run away from God and to alienate ourselves from others and to hide from our responsibilities we will discover a God who loves us and who calls us to leave our pigpens and to return home. I have titled this sermon "The Way Out of a Pigpen." It could just as easily be "How to Get Out of a Mess" or "What to Do When You Feel Lost in Order to Find Your Way Home Again." The prodigal son went through four distinct stages from the pigpen back to the palace. It just so happens that each stage could start with a word that begins with an *R*, which makes these steps easy to remember.

Recognition

The first stage could be called *recognition*. Jesus said that when the son had reached rock bottom "he came to himself." He realized how foolish he had been to run away from home. He recognized how his own sinfulness and rebellion had led to his downfall. He saw himself for what he was, and he admitted that he had made a mistake. How difficult it is for us to see things clearly, to see things from God's perspective.

It reminds me of a story of a father who frequently took his four-year-old son to the playground at the city park. This park contained a large statue of Gen. Robert E. Lee riding his horse Traveler. The father admired General Lee, and he wanted his son to feel the same way, so each time they passed the statue the father would say to his son, "Say hello to General Lee." The little boy would wave his hand and say, "Hi, General Lee." This went on for months until finally one day the little boy asked his father, "Daddy, who is that man up there riding General Lee?"

How hard it is for us to recognize things clearly and to see from God's perspective. It is also difficult for us to admit we are wrong. It is much easier to blame someone else for our problems.

Two hoboes were sitting under an oak tree talking one day. One of them said to the other, "You know, Jim, this carefree way of life ain't all it's cracked up to be. Think it over. We sleep at night on park benches. We never know where our next meal is coming from. We get run off from one place to another." The other hobo listened and then said, "Well, if that's the way you feel about it, why don't you get yourself a job and settle down?" The first man sat up suddenly with a jerk, exclaiming, "Why, I couldn't do that. Then I'd have to admit I'm a failure."

No one likes to admit they are a failure. No one likes to admit they made a mistake. But the first step out of the pigpen and into the palace is to recognize who we are and what we've done to get us where we are. When we are willing to see ourselves and our situation clearly, and when we are willing to own up to our mistakes, then we are ready to move on to the second stage.

Repentance

The first step is recognition. The second is *repentance*. That is an awfully heavy word, isn't it? But it is an awfully important word in the Bible, and it is an important stage to go through in order to pick yourself up and out of a mess. Repentance simply means a complete change of direction, a complete reorientation of our lives. The prodigal son realized that he was going in completely the wrong direction in his life, and so he turned, made an about-face and headed the other way. He said to himself, "Even my father's servants live better than I'm living in this pigpen. I will get up and return to my father." Returning to the Father is what repentance is all about. Instead of running away from God, we turn around and run to him. Instead of alienating ourselves from other people, we turn around and become open to loving and caring for one another. Instead of running from our problems and responsibilities, we turn around to face them with God's help. This is what repentance is all about. It is what we have to do in order to get ourselves out of a rut.

I once heard a story about a young girl who wanted to take violin lessons. So her parents bought her a violin and arranged for her to take lessons. Learning was a very slow process, but she finally learned one simple little song before she became discouraged and quit. This song had only three notes, and she played it over and over again every day until she drove her parents crazy.

Aren't we very much like this young girl? Don't we easily get in a rut in life, and we find ourselves playing the same song over and over again? We get discouraged, and we give up trying to learn anything new. We play our three little notes over and over, and we refuse to discover that life has more notes and more music to play. Only Christ can show us how to live life fully, abundantly. But we must first recognize that we cannot make it on our own, and then we must be willing to repent, to turn away from living life our way to living life his way. Being willing to change directions is the second step out of a pigpen.

Reconciliation

The third step is called *reconciliation*. At this point, God begins to act on our behalf. In the story of the prodigal son, Jesus says that on his return trip home, his father saw him while he was still at a distance, and the father ran to his side. The son wanted to confess his mistake to his father. He began to speak. "Father," he said, "I have sinned against you. I do not deserve to be your son." But the father cut him short, embraced him, and immediately reinstated him as his son. This tells me that if we are willing to do our part, God will certainly do his. If we will take the first few steps in God's direction, he will help us the rest of the way. The son's desire to return home, coupled with the father's amazing love, brought about reconciliation.

Once, near the end of the Civil War, President Lincoln was asked how he would treat the rebellious Southerners when they were finally defeated and had returned to the Union of the United States. Abraham Lincoln said, "I will treat them as if they had never been away."

Jesus says that is the way God loves us. Even after we have rebelled and run away from him, if we will return he will treat us as though we had never been away. This kind of love is the only kind that can reconcile and restore broken relationships.

Renewal

The fourth and final step from the pigpen to the palace is *renewal*. This experience made the prodigal son a new person, a better person, a more mature person. He learned from his mistakes; he admitted his wrongs; he discovered the depth of his father's love; and this experience renewed his life. Jesus said, "He was dead, but now he is alive again; he was lost but now he is found."

You know, every time I hear the song "Amazing Grace," I listen to those words, "I once was lost, but now I'm found." Sometimes I want to change those words to say, "I constantly get lost and need to be found." That more accurately describes my experience. I have known Christ for years, but it alarms me how easily I take him for granted sometimes, how I so suddenly can begin drifting away from him. Always, when I've been tempted to run away from him, he comes to me with some new sign of his grace and love; he finds me again and again, time after time. And that is amazing grace to me.

Many, many people have known the far country of rebellion like the prodigal son. Many of us have discovered that running away from God can lead us to make a mess of life. But even when we are in the pigpen, we can never seem to get free of our sense of homesickness. The memory of God's love helps us see how lost we are and how much we want to be home with him again. And each time we return, God comes running to us to welcome us home. We can know the joy of the Father's welcome-home party. Jesus tells us that all of heaven celebrates each time a lost child returns home.

Bill Hinson, pastor of First United Methodist Church in Houston, Texas, tells the story of Mr. Sutherland in his book *Solid Living in a Shattered World.* Mr. Sutherland lived in London during World War II. His only family left was his son, Wilfred. Then one day he received news that his son's plane had been shot down over Holland. It was not known whether he bailed out and survived or whether he went down in the wreckage and died. Mr. Sutherland carried the hope in his heart that somehow Wilfred had survived. On Easter morning 1948, Mr. Sutherland thought he saw the familiar face of his son in a crowd of people at a train station. But before he could reach him, he was lost again in the crowd. Mr. Sutherland now knew his son was alive, and he believed he was suffering from some kind of amnesia. He withdrew all of his savings, made up posters with his son's picture on them, and he gave his own address and telephone number, hoping that his son would see one, remember who he was, and return home. Then every Easter Mr. Sutherland stood at the railway station, looking again for his son's familiar face.

Fathers never give up on their lost children, and God never gives up the search for us. He is right now trying to find us, even more diligently than we are trying to find him. As we turn in his direction, we will soon find that he is there to meet us.

5. Follow Your Bliss

David W. Andersen

2 Cor. 3:7–11, 18

A few weeks ago, I was flipping the dial on our television trying to find something to watch, which in itself is interesting because now with cable and over thirty channels, I often find it harder to find something that interests me than when we only had three channels. Anyway, I stopped in the middle of an interview program being conducted by Bill Moyers. I was later to discover the person being interviewed was Joseph Campbell, a leading expert in comparative mythology. But the story he was telling at that moment when I stopped the channel-switching had nothing to do with mythology. It was about a modern-day Babbitt.

I quote from the interview. Dr. Campbell said, "Remember the last line? 'I have never done a thing that I wanted to in all my life.' Well, I actually heard that line when I was teaching at Sarah Lawrence. Before I was married, I used to eat out in the restaurants of town for my lunch and dinners. Thursday night was the maid's night off in Bronxville, so that many of the families were out in restaurants. One fine evening, I was in my favorite restaurant there, and at the next table there was a father, a mother, and a scrawny boy about twelve years old. The father said to the boy, 'Drink your tomato juice.'

David W. Andersen is pastor of the First Baptist Church of Greater Toledo in Holland, Ohio. An American Baptist and graduate of Northern Baptist Theological Seminary and McCormick Theological Seminary, where he received his doctorate of ministry, Andersen is the author of *How to Expand Your Sunday School* as well as numerous articles. Andersen is chairperson of the Commission on Campus Ministry for the Ohio Baptist Convention and is a member of the board of directors of the Samaritan Counseling Center.

"And the boy said, 'I don't want to.'

"Then the father, with a louder voice said, 'Drink your tomato juice.'

"And the mother said, 'Don't make him do what he doesn't want to do.'

"The father looked at her and said, 'He can't go through life doing what he wants to do. If he does only what he wants to do, he'll be dead. Look at me. I've never done a thing I wanted to in all my life.' "

Dr. Campbell said, "And I thought, 'My God, there's Babbitt incarnate!' "[1]

Chills went up and down my arms because in that moment I realized this is often the way we have presented and followed Christ. We have made Christianity more a duty than a choice. We have made it more an obligation than a realization. We have made it more a command than an invitation.

"Drink your tomato juice." In the same way, we have said to the world, "Take Christ." It is good for you. It is a duty; it is an obligation; it is something you should do.

Then we make following Christ an act of conformity. If you are Christian, this is the way you should perform, this is the way you should act. It doesn't matter if we are liberal or conservative. If we are liberal we say, If you are a Christian you should march in a picket line and be concerned about nuclear disarmament and the plight of the peasant in the third world. If we are conservative we say, If you are a Christian you should watch the way you dress, carry your Bible as a witness, and lobby to get prayer in school.

Either way, we are telling people that to be a Christian is an act of conformity to an outside standard. We often do the same in marriage. We marry a person, this unique, wonderful person with whom we fell in love. Then we spend the rest of our years trying to make the person more like ourselves, squeezing out the uniqueness.

When I was in college and preparing for seminary, I came home one day with a new pair of loafers I had bought. My father in all seriousness told me he thought I should have bought a pair of black, lace ups, and his reason was that I was preparing for the ministry. For him the process of becoming a minister was one of being poured into a mold.

For some reason we are scared of what people might become, so we keep trying to put the lid on them. We put the lid on them when we call them sinners in order to make them Christians. We put the lid on them when we say to be followers of Christ, this is how you should act, this is how you should think, this is how you should behave. Always, always, we are seeking to diminish people, seeking to reel them in, seeking to set a law in front of them, seeking to enslave them before offering them grace.

But we are not under the Law. The dispensation of the Law, as given by Moses in the commandments, ended with the coming of Christ. We are under the dispensation of grace. Therefore, how do we present the gospel so its invitation has about it the integrity of grace and lets people know they are under a new dispensation when they come to Christ?

Dr. Campbell said one other thing that struck me. In speaking on the father in the restaurant, Dr. Campbell said, "This is a man who never followed his bliss."[2] I knew right away I was going to preach a sermon on "following your bliss." And here I think is our clue for answering our questions.

What has been absent in so much of Christian proclamation and invitation and discipleship is that we follow Christ and we seek to serve Christ because Christ is the fulfillment of our bliss. As the hymn writer Oswald J. Smith proclaims, "There is joy in serving Jesus . . . Joy that throbs within my heart; Every moment, every hour, As I draw upon his power, There is joy, joy, Joy that never shall depart." We have left out the joy of following Christ.

If you want to lead people to Christ, help them find the place of bliss in their lives. Help them find, no matter how deeply it may be buried, that hidden dream, that joyful thought, that impulse of love. Then tell them that is God speaking to them, that bliss is God.

The word *bliss* means "lightness of heart, gladness, the joy of heaven."

There is no need to begin by putting people down. Your task as Christians is not to damage egos. You may help people see how other things have not satisfied. But your job is to point them to the Master, and you point them to the Master by showing them how God's love is already working in their lives, seeking to persuade them, and helping them see that bliss, that joy, that gladness is a light piercing the darkness. It is the light of life. Help them find their bliss.

Emilie Griffin, in a wonderful spiritual autobiography called *Turning*, which I would recommend to everyone, says,

> converts are plagued by the argument from
> "common sense." It is "common sense"—a sense of
> the ordinary which makes us skeptical of God's
> extraordinary attraction; it is suspect because it is so
> very perfect, so exactly what we wished for; it has
> about it the character of myth and make-believe of
> happy endings. The convert cannot believe in God
> because God is too good to be true.[3]

But your witness is that it is true. We convert to Christ because of the way Christ is the answer to our heart, and we follow Christ because of the joy and the fulfillment and the wonder and the meaning it gives to our lives.

Christians who emphasize remorse as the primary feeling of conversion and who make following Jesus sound like an unhappy duty or a joyless obligation have lost their focus. Their eyes are not on Jesus because when your eyes are on Jesus you are not thinking about what you have to give up but what you have been given; you are not lamenting your sin but rejoicing in your salvation; you are not asking people to look at how much you have done, but you are thanking God that you are in God's army.

Again quoting from Emilie Griffin:

> It may seem off, but I think one of the most striking
> characteristics of the continuing conversion is a
> growth in the ability to find pleasure in ordinary
> experience. As we come to know the Lord better, we
> see how much he has given us in life that is enjoyable
> . . . as we grow in the Christian life, we find that
> pleasure is given to us without our asking.[4]

This is your witness, this is your testimony, there is joy in following Jesus.

St. John of the Cross, a sixteenth-century monk, couldn't contain himself when he sought to write about this joy, so that many of his words sound like the words of a young man passionately in love with a young woman. But John of the Cross is writing about his relationship to God and the passion that comes from this relationship.

He begins one rhapsody with this introductory explanation: "A song of the soul's happiness in having passed through the dark night of faith to union with its Beloved."

Now, listen to these words and hear the passion that informs them and remember these are words about the experience of God's love.

> One dark night,
> Fired with love's urgent warnings
> —Ah, the sheer grace!—
> I went out unseen.
> My house being now all stilled;
> O guiding night!
> O night more lovely than the dawn!
> O night that has united
> The lover with His beloved.[5]

The words might be antiquated, but still we are able to sense in them that there is something different here, more compelling, more reassuring, more inspiring about our relationship to God than what we often hear from the pulpit or are taught in Sunday school. John of the Cross isn't thinking about duty but ecstasy. John of the Cross hasn't reduced Christianity to a conservative or liberal list of Christian do's and don'ts but instead teaches us that maybe, more than our ethical list of do's and don'ts, Christianity has to do with bliss. There is joy in following Jesus.

When C. S. Lewis sat down to write his spiritual autobiography, he titled it *Surprised by Joy*, and I want to end this morning by extending an invitation for you to return to the fountain of that joy in your Christian walk.

You who have lost your enthusiasm, you who upon reflection realize you have made your Christian walk less of a dance than a burdensome journey: Return to the fountain. Drink from the cup. Spend time in prayer. Take a long walk. Reflect on this sermon. Do anything that will begin to put you back in touch with that bliss you first knew in knowing Jesus. Don't let that joy go out, but fan it until once more it becomes the fuel that energizes your Christian service.

And to you who have yet to make a commitment. Don't be put off by negativism either in the Church or in yourself. But listen to those positive messages God is sending you and realize that in those places in your life where you feel the most hopeful and the most joyful, those are places where God is calling to you and saying to you, Come join my parade.

Join the parade this morning. Say your yes to God. Emilie Griffin, speaking of those experiences (of bliss and joy) that eventually led to her conversion, says, "These experiences seemed to me to be God saying, 'Here I am, choose me, it's not nearly so hard as you're making it.' " There is joy in following Jesus.

The Apostle Paul says, "And we all, with unveiled face, beholding the glory of the Lord, are being changed into his likeness from one degree of glory bliss to another . . . " (2 Cor. 3:18).

Follow your bliss. Follow Jesus.

Let us pray: God forgive us when we make being a Christian a drudgery or too boring to follow. We remember today the joy of our salvation and thank you that there is still time to change our tune and sing once more, "There is joy in serving Jesus." Amen.

NOTES

1. Joseph Campbell with Bill Moyers, *The Power of Myth* (New York: Doubleday, 1988), 117, 118.

2. Ibid., 118.

3. Emilie Griffin, *Turning: Reflections on the Experience of Conversion* (New York: Doubleday, 1982), 48, 49.

4. Ibid.

5. Griffin, *Turning*.

6. Celebrating Christ's Mission

Esther Tse

Tonight we are celebrating Christ's mission. To celebrate Christ's mission is to celebrate God's unconditional love in the action, teaching, suffering, life, and death of the historical Jesus. To celebrate Christ's mission is to celebrate Christian discipleship despite the political difficulties in our contexts. To celebrate Christ's mission is to celebrate the Christian's full participation and commitment for the expansion of the Kingdom of God in a critical age.

First, to celebrate Christ's mission is to celebrate the universal and unconditional love of God in the life and death of our Lord Jesus Christ.

I was born in the early 1950s, right after the Communist takeover of China. My parents were trying to stay on the mainland. But finally, when they saw no hope for a better life in Communist China, they put the whole family into a boat, rowed it to Hong Kong, and settled down as refugees. We had no money or nationality, no identity or security, no property or a place to stay, no friends or relatives. Life was really tough. As you know, Hong Kong is a British colony, so my father could not get a job since he had no British educational certificate. My mother tried to earn a living for the whole family of seven, and she ended up being a housemaid in a

---

Esther Lai Fun Cheng Tse is a Th.D. student in systematic theology at the Lutheran School of Theology in Chicago. She was born in mainland China but fled to Hong Kong as a refugee with her family. She has several degrees in theology, philosophy, and religion, and is slated, in 1991, to be assistant professor in systematic theology at Lutheran Theological Seminary in Hong Kong where she will be the first full-time woman faculty member.

middle-class family. During the daytime, she took care of other people's kids, and in the evenings, she had to take care of her own kids. There were five of us. So life went on; life was very tough.

Actually life was too tough for my mother to take. She ran away from us when I was six years old to strive for a better material life and a more secure future. I learned one lesson from this event: to not trust anybody in this world. Even the closest person in my family could betray me. In a conservative and traditional Chinese family, a runaway mother could create a lot of scandalous gossip. I grew up with that scandal and gossip. So did my brothers. One of them attempted suicide. Another tried to escape the scandal by working hard and making money. Still another ran from reality by taking drugs and gambling.

I looked around me, and I saw oppression, poverty, injustice, and suffering in the world. I experienced injustice, unfairness, brokenness, and suffering existentially and subjectively. I asked, Why me? When my friends became prostitutes and gangsters in order to make money for their refugee families, I asked, Why them? We were innocent and nice people. Why do innocent and nice people always suffer from the social and political struggles? I asked whether there is a supreme being in charge of this world. So I turned to religions.

I first took up the traditional job of burning incense to my ancestors every morning and evening. I also tried all kinds of local religions, including animism, and prayed for the prosperity of my family. I went to the Buddhist temples diligently to pray to the Buddhist gods and goddesses. I asked a young Buddhist monk about the sufferings of life. He answered that suffering is a must in our life. If one suffers in this life, it means that one must have done something wrong in one's previous life. To change the present situation of suffering is impossible, and if I did not want to suffer in the next life, I had better try harder in this life. The only thing I could do about the present suffering would be to detach myself from the suffering world. That means that I was destined to suffering. It is a matter of cause and effect; its logic is simple and easy. However, when suffering is so real, how could anyone detach from it? How could anyone ignore and detach from the pain of the broken family, broken nation, and the broken world? How could anyone detach oneself from such suffering and still have compassion for the world and others?

To achieve a better lot for my next life, I would have to try to work harder, to do better, to think and meditate more, and to purify my mind and my feelings. If I saved enough merits *(karma)*, I might have a chance for *nirvana*, though there was no guarantee. Even the wisest monk did not know whether and when one could achieve *nirvana*. This doctrine of reincarnation reappears in a different form in the new religion of the New Age, for which even the famous movie star Shirley MacLaine is one of the advocates.

In response to this, I turned back to my own tradition of Confucianism. But even my own tradition told me that I was born with the wrong sex, in the wrong time, and at the wrong place. Since I was born in the wrong sex, when I was a teenager my family decided not to let me finish my high school education, for if my brothers had no chance to go to high school, why should their little sister have a chance to finish her high school education? I was also born in the wrong time. In the oriental tradition, the older you are, the more respect you get. Unfortunately, I was the youngest at home. Therefore, I have absolutely no place in making a decision for myself. Finally, I was born in the wrong place. There are three obediences required of a woman in the Chinese tradition: obedience to her father while she is at home, obedience to her husband after she gets married, and obedience to her son if she is a widow. There is also a saying that the less education a woman has, the better she is. My father used to say that his little daughter was crazy to pursue so much education, and now that he knows that I am working for my doctorate degree in theology, he does not say anything, because he has just given up. In response to such religion and tradition, I guessed that I just had no hope and was not very good.

So my questions remained. Was there hope and meaning, love and joy in the midst of my existential sufferings and struggles? Was there a breakthrough for the sufferings of my friends and for the brokenness of the world? I went to an evangelical Christian school when I was a little girl, but I never took the gospel seriously. After all, if there was a loving God as the Christians claimed and proclaimed, then why was this God so relaxed and laid back and doing nothing about the suffering world?

During this time, I attempted to end my life twice and ran away from home half a dozen times. I wondered where I could find the unconditional love that would give me the strength, meaning, hope, and purpose to walk through the way of my lifelong struggles. But although I wanted to be embraced by love, I had only hostility. I hated my mother, for she was the one who walked away from me and her family. I hated my father, for he must have done something wrong so to drive even his wife away. And I hated my brothers, for they were jealous of their little sister going to school. I learned to be feisty. I learned to fight for everything—my education, my religion, my career—so that even today I fight to walk against the cultural currents of this world.

When I was seventeen, things started changing. I read the New Testament, as well as other religious scriptures, diligently. I perceived Jesus Christ as one of the greatest teachers in world history, just like Confucius and Lao Tzu, Socrates and Plato, Buddha and Muhammad. Then the good old gospel story became alive to me. I realized that Jesus is more than a great teacher. Jesus died for me. Even though my mother ran away from me, my brothers didn't want me to have a higher education, and the whole world turned against me, this guy named Jesus died for me. Jesus overcomes suffering and death through his very own suffering, Crucifixion, death, and Resurrection.

Yes, all religious leaders and teachers point to some kind of truth, some direction of salvation, and some way toward a better life-style, and they tried hard to achieve their goals themselves. However, we can never achieve the goals ourselves. Instead, Jesus said to you, to me, and to the whole world, "I am the way, the truth, and the life; nobody can go to the Father but through me."

The way of Christ is suffering.

The truth of Christ is sacrificing and crucifixion.

The life of Christ begins with his very own dying.

All religions believe that God is love, but we Christians can point to the Christ event to prove to the world that God is really love in historical reality.

I was finally baptized when I was eighteen. Then I learned a Christian song. I am going to sing you the song, "Jesus Loves Me," in Chinese. Please listen carefully.

One time when I was sharing my story to a very small group of people, we were singing "Jesus Loves Me," and a seventy-year-old gentleman turned to his wife with tears in his eyes and said, "I have not sung this song for sixty years. Now I know how much I have missed. From now on I would like to sing it every day to remind myself that I am a child of God."

Is it not wonderful to be a Christian? Is it not wonderful to be a Lutheran? I became a Lutheran accidentally. I walked into a Lutheran church to participate in Christian fellowship and worship. But I think that it is great to be a Lutheran. We Lutherans know the very heart of the gospel and the very center of the Christian message. We believe strongly in the Reformation principle of "justification by faith alone," the fourth article of the Augsburg Confession, upon which the church stands or falls. According to this article, we believe that our salvation does not come from our better doing, harder working, more thinking or meditating, or our feeling better about ourselves. We are not justified by our skin color or race, our sex or nationality, our social status or position, our physical appearance or health situation. Is is not amazing to know that the love of our God is so inclusive and unconditional? Is it not wonderful to know that the grace of God has always been present since we were born?

And yet, is it not terrible how many times we take the love of God, the gospel of Christ, and the grace in the Holy Spirit for granted? Is it not terrible that we Christians, particularly Lutherans, turn the faith and grace of God into some kind of Christian virtue, human attitude and effort, or self-actualization to achieve a better life, better feeling, or better salvation? Dear brothers and sisters, to celebrate Christ's mission in Hong Kong and around the world is to celebrate the universality and inclusivity of the gospel and the unconditional love of God in Christ Jesus for us. Salvation in Christ includes both sexes, all colors, all races, all walks of life, and the whole Creation of God. The philosophers and theologians are not more saved than you and I, though they may think better. The moralists and the ethicists are not better off than us, though they may make better decisions. The romanticists, the sentimentalists, and even the mystics are not closer to God, though they are richer in feelings and emotions. God's love is so inclusive that even a Chinese woman coming from a poor and broken refugee family could enjoy and experience the freedom and the liberating power of the gospel in Jesus Christ. The psychologists and the sociologists will probably say that Esther Tse's conversion is a social and psychological process of growing. Maybe so, but for me, it is the power of the Holy Spirit. Is it not beautiful that the Holy Spirit of God works in our growing process of human life?

Second, to celebrate Christ's mission is to celebrate our Christian call to discipleship in Christ despite our political future and context.

More than a thousand times, people have asked and will ask me, in various ways, "Are you sure that you are going back to Hong Kong? What about 1997?" Or, "Do you really think that you are making the right decision? Aren't you afraid?" Or, "Everybody is leaving, particularly those people who have money or expertise. Well, you don't have money, but you are already here and pursuing an advanced degree. Why would you and your husband want to go back? Don't you like the United States?" Sometimes when I get a little impatient and annoyed by answering the same question, I reply sarcastically that I am going back to Hong Kong because I know that the United States is neither the Promised Land nor the Kingdom of God.

But, sarcasm aside, a friend of mine in seminary told me that nowadays if one is "male, pale, and frail," and particularly if he is under some kind of quota system, then he has not much of a chance in American Lutheran churches. Well, I am not male, not pale, and not frail. Instead, I have the right sex, right color, right age, and the right beautiful Chinese accent in the United States. I should have no problem in getting a job. Furthermore, the Evangelical Lutheran Church in America has a goal for the inclusivity of membership. By the year 1998, 10 percent of its membership should be minority. It is great. Here my friend said that I should forget the 1997 of Hong Kong and start worrying about the 1998 of ELCA. But let me tell you a different story.

During the 1930s, within the context of Nazi Germany, one of my favorite theological heroes, Dietrich Bonhoeffer, was then a very bright young theologian. He had a great chance to come to the United States to teach theology. His friends were trying to get him a professorship at Union Theological Seminary in New York. Bonhoeffer did come to America. After spending a couple of weeks, he regretted his decision and said to his friends, "If I cannot be with my people during the war, I have no right to share the gospel with them after the war." So he returned to Germany and participated in the resistance movement against Hitler's regime. He was even involved in an unsuccessful plot to assassinate Hitler and was executed in 1945 just a few days before the American army liberated his concentration camp.

What a sad story! Is Dietrich Bonhoeffer's decision foolish, crazy, and unimaginable? Did he give up the great chance to become another great theologian, like Paul Tillich? In his famous book *The Cost of Discipleship,* Bonhoeffer wrote that when Christ calls a person, he calls him to die. Bonhoeffer responded to the calling of Christ with his life. He had no great system of theology like that of Paul Tillich. But neither do Mother Teresa, Bishop Tutu, Martin Luther King, Jr., Dean Farisari of South Africa, Bishop Romero, and Bishop Gomez of El Salvador. Their ways of living, their commitment to Christ and discipleship, and their response to the calling of God become their theology, and they become my paragons. It is true that the friends of my husband and me, particularly our Chinese friends, and our relatives, believe that we made a dumb, foolish, and crazy decision by going back to Hong Kong. We pray that our foolishness and unimaginability of human decision may turn into God's wisdom. We pray that the craziness and the dumbness of the human mind may turn into God's creativity and into God's calling and mission, active and fulfilled on earth and in the world. My husband and I believe that if we cannot be with our people during the transitional time toward 1997, to share the anxiety and fear and struggles of our people, then we have no right to talk about discipleship with our American Christian friends.

God called Sarah and Abraham from the highly developed city of Ur to an unpredictable and insecure future. The Promised Land of Sarah and Abraham turned out to be the wilderness. Despite the desert land, Sarah and Abraham stood upon God's promises that it was the land of milk and honey. Therefore, they are called the parents of our faith.

God called Moses from the politically and economically powerful nation of Egypt into the desert. For forty years, even with the help of Aaron and Miriam, Moses could hardly organize the unruly Israelites, who complained of the simple and meager life and longed for the material goods of Egypt. It is true that Moses did not make it to the Promised Land, though he fulfilled the mission and calling of God. In a sense, Moses was standing on the promises of God's land all along. Later on, God called Deborah, Isaiah, Jeremiah, and Ezekiel from their quiet and peaceful life into the battlefield of critical and unpredictable political contexts. This list of Old Testament heroes could go on and on. In the New Testament, to be a Christian is to take up our cross to follow Jesus and to be a disciple of Christ to meet the social, political, and religious challenges of our time and our contexts. My husband and I have been refugees since we were born. We do not want to be refugees any more, not even in the

United States. Though we may have a better material life here, a more secure and predictable future, we pray that with the help of the Holy Spirit, we may have strength to look beyond our personal needs and respond to the calling of God in our discipleship in Christ Jesus.

Third, to celebrate Christ's mission is to celebrate the Christian's full participation, involvement, and commitment in expanding the Kingdom of God.

Christ's mission is more than sending money and missionaries overseas. Christ's mission is more than sitting back in the pew to enjoy a good sermon. Christ's mission is more than going to Sunday services, serving in church councils and Sunday schools, singing in choirs, involving ourselves in social ministry, and more than going to Global Mission Event or Mission Festival once or twice a year. Do not get me wrong, my dear brothers and sisters. I am not saying that you should not come to Mission Festival next year. I believe that all these church activities are significant for the growth of church life. Nonetheless, the mission of Christ is greater than church activities, greater than sending money and missionaries, and greater than Mission Festival. Christ's mission is our very own participation, dedication, involvement, and commitment in the expansion of God's kingdom through justification and justice, through our words and deeds, through evangelism and social actions and a political awareness of our contexts in the midst of our suffering a broken world.

Money and missionaries can only make us feel a little better and deceive us into thinking that we do care about God's mission and kingdom. Every year we can look at the statistics one more time. Are they increasing or decreasing? Statistics mean nothing to the expansion of the Kingdom of God. But how often do we find ourselves lying back in our rocking chairs, sipping coffee or beer, looking at the statistics, and happily praying to God, "Oh, God, I thank you that I am not like all other people—robbers, evildoers, adulterers—or the people at the IRS, the tax collectors. I go to church every Sunday, and I pay my dues for your mission." Does it not sound all too familiar to all of us? We are familiar with the prayer of the Pharisee since we learned it in Sunday school. But how many times do we say the very same prayer, only in different words? In Hong Kong, the first priority of the Christians is to share the gospel with our relatives, friends, colleagues in schools and factories, and particularly at home with the very members of our families. As forgiven sinners, we are missionaries and ambassadors of Christ in the world. We all remember the story of the prophet Jonah. Yes, even Jonah could not escape his calling and mission to share the good news of the forgiving God to his people, even to his enemies. Jonah's stubbornness and selfishness were embraced by the all-encompassing love of God. And he, the famous escaping prophet, surrendered to the great love of God.

I know that time is running short, but my dear brothers and sisters, as a young Chinese sister from Hong Kong, I come into the Christian church late. I have no money and gold, no silver or jewelry, no name or title, no reputation. I am not even ordained. It is by the grace of God that I can speak with the bishops and the theologians. I have no social status and position, no knowledge or skill, no technique or wisdom. I have only the name of Jesus. I appeal to each one of you, male and female, black and white, brown and yellow, bishop and deaconess, clergy and God's people, old and young, husband and wife, boy and girl, in the name of your Lord and my Lord Jesus Christ, please do not take the gospel for granted. Instead, let us take the grace of God and mission of God seriously. Let us take up the cross and follow Jesus, to share the universality and inclusivity of the unconditional love of God with our neighbors. Let us offer ourselves as living sacrifices to transform the world instead of conforming ourselves to the world. Let us be the disciples of Christ and fully participate in building the Kingdom of God in our prayers, in our decisions, and in our actions. Let us show our support in our thoughts, words, and acts of solidarity with our brothers and sisters in South Africa and El Salvador, with the dying babies and people of Ethiopia, and with those who are suffering in poverty, in economical and political struggles.

> Let us go and tell the good news to the poor,
> tell the prisoners they are prisoners no more,
> tell blind people that they can see,
> And set the downtrodden free,
> And go tell everyone the news that the Kingdom of God has
>   come.
>   Amen.

7. Jesus Christ—Do You Accept?

Laurie Haller

Mark 8:27–38

George Bush and I have something in common: We both attended Yale University. I spent four years at Yale as a graduate student in the school of music and the divinity school; Bush received his undergraduate education there. When I arrived at Yale, I was interested to learn that the university does not have fraternities as other schools do. Rather, they have secret societies, which possess great sums of money given by past members. And of all the secret societies, Skull and Bones is the one to belong to! Cyrus Vance belonged to it; so did George Bush. I'd heard that during Reagan's first campaign for the presidency in 1980, Bush's aides were continually befuddled by those secret coded messages that came from other "Bonesmen."

Rumors around the divinity school had it that members of Skull and Bones were given $10,000 right away to do with as they pleased, and they were guaranteed six-figure incomes for life. But what is of interest to us is how one is reportedly chosen as a member. A senior member of this secret society will approach the unsuspecting prospect, slap him on the shoulders, and thunder, "Skull and Bones—Do you accept?" And the person must respond immediately! He is confronted with a choice, a decision, and he must answer right away.

Laurie Hartzel Haller is pastor of the Hart United Methodist Church in Hart, Michigan. She has degrees from Wittenberg University, the Yale Institute of Sacred Music and School of Music, and Yale Divinity School. She is a contributing editor of *The Michigan Christian Advocate* and has been a pastor of Methodist churches in Traverse City and Ludington, Michigan.

The Christian religion is a little like Skull and Bones, isn't it? For Christianity is a way of life that confronts each one of us with the urgency of making a decision for Jesus Christ. The difference between Skull and Bones and Christianity, though, is that in our case it is *God's* hand upon our shoulders and *God's* voice saying, "Jesus Christ—Do you accept?"

A variation on that question "Jesus Christ—Do you accept?" is found in our Gospel lesson from Mark. "Who do you say that I am?" is the most important question that Jesus ever asked his followers; it's also a question that he asks of us today. And it's because of the urgency of that question that this story is considered to be a turning point in the Gospel of Mark.

Jesus and his disciples were in Caesarea Philippi, which is in the northern part of Palestine at the source of the Jordan River. In ancient history, Caesarea Philippi was a center for the worship of Baal, but it was also the place where the Greeks found one of their most prized gods. According to Greek mythology, the birth of Pan, the god of nature, took place in a cave from which sprang the Jordan River. So you see, Caesarea Philippi was a place associated with many pagan rites and traditions, and it competed for the attention of pilgrims from these two religions. The town used to be called Panias, after Pan's grotto, but because Baal's altar was also there, the name of the town was changed to Banias, which seems to have been a linguistic compromise.

By the time of Jesus, Banias was the site of a magnificent marble temple built in honor of Caesar Augustus. Caesarea Philippi, the Jewish name for Banias, at the headwaters of the Jordan River, was the religious fortress of the pagan world. So why did Jesus and his disciples end up in Caesarea Philippi? Actually, Jesus was on his way to Jerusalem, and Caesarea Philippi was definitely out of the way. It was eighty miles north of Jerusalem and about twenty miles north of the Sea of Galilee.

There is no doubt in my mind that Jesus intentionally led his disciples to this place for a purpose. And I believe his purpose was to confront his followers with the question, "Jesus Christ—Do you accept?" Jesus' disciples had come to a crucial point in their pilgrimage with him. They left everything to follow him, but they had not really made a commitment. In Caesarea Philippi, Jesus decided that it was time for his disciples to choose. Jesus knew where he was headed—he was going to Jerusalem and certain death. He was aware of the trials and troubles and the agony that faced him. He made the choice to follow God's will for him, but he also wanted his disciples to freely choose, to go all the way with him. And what better place to pose the question than Caesarea Philippi, where the lure of false gods was so strong.

On the way to Caesarea Philippi, Jesus asked his disciples, "Who do people say that I am?" Notice he didn't direct the question right at them initially. He asked, "What are folks saying about me? Let's get a perspective on me and my mission." Of course, the disciples were very aware of what the scuttlebutt about Jesus was. They replied, "Some say John the Baptist; others say Elijah; and still others, one of the prophets." All the rumors about Jesus circulated freely among the Jews.

"But," Jesus asked, "what about you? Who do you say that I am?" Peter answered, "You are the Christ." This is the first time in the Gospel of Mark that Jesus has been publicly identified as the Christ. And you need to realize that this was truly a spiritual breakthrough for the disciples. All the pieces about Jesus have finally come together into a surprising discovery—Jesus is the Messiah, the Christ, the Son of God. The disciples may have suspected as much of Jesus, but no one voiced it until Peter did.

Do you sense the urgency of the question? The fun and games were over for the disciples. They'd had a good time with Jesus for the last several years—they lived together as a family; they learned; they laughed; they healed; they witnessed the miracles of Jesus. But now the time had come to make a choice, for no longer were Jesus and his disciples safe from harm; no longer were they going to be accepted and honored wherever they went. So Jesus began to teach them that the way to Jerusalem was not going to be easy. If they were going to back out, now would be the time. But no one left Jesus. They may not have understood why Jesus had to suffer and die or how he was going to fulfill his mission as the Christ, but they made the choice to accept Jesus and follow him to the end.

There are four things to which I would like to draw your attention on this Christian Education Sunday when we honor our church school teachers and consider the importance of education in the church.

First, let's think about the question, "Who do you say that I am?" Isn't that the central question in the Gospels, and isn't that the question that all of us must answer for ourselves?

I am convinced that being a Christian involves a decision, and that decision is whether to accept Jesus Christ as Lord and Savior or not. I believe that every person must struggle with and ultimately answer that question as an individual. You can't get into heaven on anyone else's coattails. Do you remember the gospel hymn we sang in July called "Old-Time Religion"? "It was good enough for my father; it was good enough for my mother; it's good enough for me." Well, we may end up embracing and accepting the same religion as our parents, but we still have to make the choice. No one can ever decide for us that we are Christians.

If we all have to make such a decision, then, how do we do it? I want you to know that there is no one way to become a Christian, and there is no standard age at which one makes that decision. That's where Sunday school comes in. I believe that the purpose of Sunday school for children is to foster an awareness in them of God, to introduce them to the Bible, and to tell them about the love of Jesus Christ. Sunday school should provide an experience that helps youngsters make their own decisions about Jesus Christ.

Of course, we also have confirmation classes in the United Methodist church. These classes are offered to junior high youth in addition to Sunday school in order to teach our youth more about the Bible and about Christianity than a one-hour Sunday school class can do. My husband and I both believe that when our young people are confirmed, they have to make the decision themselves. Apart from parental or peer pressure, we encourage our youth to decide individually if they are ready to publicly profess their own faith in Jesus Christ.

Now I know that other denominations do things differently. Some churches believe that children or youth should not be baptized until they make a decision for Jesus Christ. Some denominations expect that you have to have a spectacular conversion experience in order to be a true Christian. Some believe that even small children can make an informed decision about Jesus Christ.

It doesn't really matter when or how you come to Christ. What matters is the decision: "Jesus Christ—Do you accept? Will you commit your life to Jesus? Is he your Lord and Master? All of us have to say yes or no.

Sunday school provides the place where children can learn enough about Jesus so that they, too, can make that choice. And I believe that parents know that. So often young couples drop out of the church only to return after the birth of their first child. The reason is that they want their children to be informed enough about Christianity so that they can decide for themselves whether to accept or reject the gospel. And who informs our children? Why, it's the Sunday school teachers. Without teachers there would be no learning. I am grateful for all the Sunday school teachers who sacrifice their time and energy to teach our youngsters about God and Jesus. How will they know unless someone teaches them?

The second point about our Scripture is this: After Peter confessed Jesus as the Christ, Jesus began to tell his disciples what it was going to mean to follow him—suffering, rejection, and death. And Peter didn't want to hear it. So Jesus scolded him, "Peter, you're not interested in the things of God but only the things of people." The problem was, Peter's idea of Jesus being the Christ was not the same as Jesus'. He had some incorrect information. Even though Peter correctly identified Jesus as the Christ, that did not suddenly enable him to know everything.

The lesson for us here is this: Once we make a decision for Jesus, the end is not in sight. Once we are baptized, we're not saved for all time. Once we're confirmed, we haven't made it. Once we join the church, that's not all we need. My friends, the Christian life is a journey that does not conclude with our decision to accept Jesus Christ—that's where it all starts. We should be constantly growing, learning, expanding horizons, gaining knowledge, and deepening our relationship with Jesus.

What I'm saying is that church school is just as important for adults as it is for children. Yes, church is important—we worship; we pray; we sing; we listen. But there is nothing like an adult study class for really digging into the gospel, for sharing, for struggling together with faith issues, and for forming bonds with one another. Sunday school isn't just for children—it's for everyone. That's why people like Joanna Ray, Millie Plank, Orville Bailey, Paula Damkoehler, Cathy Olmstead, Marion Johnson, Dudley and Irene Taber, Eva Spence, and many others attend church school every week. It's so easy for the things of this world to seduce us away from God. That's why we come to church and to study groups—to learn more about the things of God and help us to hold on to them in a violent and often meaningless world.

Third, in verse 34 Jesus called the crowd to him and said, "If anyone would come after me, he must deny himself and take up his cross and follow me." Where are your children and your grandchildren going to learn about taking up their crosses, about service and sacrifice? In school? On the soccer field? On the playground? At dance lessons? I'm afraid not. Oh, I don't mean to criticize the secular world. We have an excellent school system, and I think sports are great. But the only place where Jesus is lifted up as the suffering servant is in the church. If you believe in looking out for number one, if you believe in being successful according to the world's standards, if you want your children to think only about themselves, then you don't need the church. But if you believe that whoever wants to save his life will lose it, and whoever loses his life for the gospel will save it, then come to church—and bring your children to Sunday school and to worship.

I hope that you are not thinking about Christmas yet, but those of us involved in programming have been up to our ears in Christmas already. I recently read a story about a husband and wife who went to see their four-year-old son perform in the class Christmas pageant, and it was every bit as bad as those events can be. Finally, near the end, the teacher who was in charge came out and said, "Ladies and gentlemen, we are now getting ready to have the manger scene sponsored by our four-year-old class." About that time the house lights dimmed, everyone looked up, and out from the corridor came three virgin Marys. They marched out onto the stage, spaced themselves around the straw and waved at their parents. Now you may think it strange to have three Marys, but over the years the school had acquired three Mary costumes, and no one could imagine not using *all* of them. Following the Marys came two Josephs. They walked up behind the Marys, wandered around the straw, and found their places. Then twenty little angels came out in white robes and huge gauze wings. They knew exactly where they were going and spaced themselves in seemingly perfect order. They were followed by twenty little shepherd boys who were dressed in burlap sacks and carried an array of objects that were supposed to be crooks.

It was at this point that the problem occurred. During the dress rehearsal the teacher had used chalk to draw circles on the floor to mark where the angels were supposed to stand and crosses to mark the spots of the shepherds. But the children had practiced with their *regular* clothes on. So, on the night of the pageant, the angels came walking out with their beautiful gauze wings and stood on their circles. However, their huge wings covered the crosses of the shepherds as well. So when the time came for the shepherds to find their places, they did not know where to go because the angels took up all their space. There was one little boy who became extremely frustrated and angry over the whole experience. He finally spied his teacher behind the curtains and shouted, "Because of these damn angels, I can't find the *cross!*"

There are so many things in this world that prevent us and our children from finding the cross. There are so many false gods around us like Baal and Pan. But here in this congregation, which believes in the education and nurture of children, we do not hide the cross; we glory in the cross.

Finally, in verse 38 Jesus says, "If anyone is ashamed of me and my words, the Son of man will be ashamed of him." Are you ashamed of the gospel? Are you fearful of making a decision for Jesus? Are you afraid of modeling the love of Jesus to your children? Are you afraid of taking a risk by becoming a Sunday school teacher? Are you afraid of inviting friends and neighbors to church for fear they will think you are strange or weird? If you are, you aren't alone. Many of us have a deep faith but somehow think we mustn't or can't communicate it to others. Many of us are deeply committed to children but do not feel qualified to teach. Many of us have a burden for all those in our community who do not know the love of Jesus Christ, but we don't have the courage to reach out to them. Many of us want others to experience the life-changing power of Jesus, but we don't know how to relate to others. Many of us want to say yes but can't seem to take that leap of faith.

Many of us are timid; many of us lack courage. But that doesn't make it right. When I fail to invite my neighbor to church, God is ashamed of me. When I fail to teach my children the stories of the Bible, God is ashamed of me. When I decide that I know too much to go to Sunday school anymore, God is ashamed of me.

But the *good news* is that God can change even me; God can change even you. God works through us. God challenges us every day with the question, "Jesus Christ—Will you accept?" And if we answer, "Yes, Lord, melt me, mold me, fill me, use me," then the Spirit of the Living God will fall afresh on us and on our children. Amen.

II. EXPOSITORY

8. What We Don't Have Is Time

Walter J. Burghardt

Neh. 8:2–4, 5–6, 8–10; 1 Cor. 12:12–30; Luke 1:1–4; 4:14–21

Several weeks ago I experienced an exhilarating evening. By a for-tunate coincidence, I was privileged to sit entranced at the Kennedy Center's Terrace Theater while a superb songstress thrilled us with her pure soprano timbre. So much that Barbara Cook sang moved me mightily but nothing so profoundly as two lines in a song I be-lieve was composed in part by a long-term AIDS victim:

> Love is all we have for now,
> what we don't have is time.[1]

Such is my song today. It is not simply a plea from the darkening twilight of one preacher's existence. It is not a commercial for one-night love boats. What Barbara Cook sang with such soft anguish to a theater audience, St. Paul wrote with a passionate pen to the Christian community in Corinth. My three movements are three Cs: Corinth, Christianity, and Cook.

My first C: Corinth. You've just heard a reading from "The First Letter (of Paul) to the Corinthians." I'll bet any of you dollars to doughnuts—or bourbon to bagels—that the word Corinthians said absolutely nothing to you. And yet St. Paul was not writing a term paper from a beach at Ephesus, not penning an episcopal pas-

Walter J.Burghardt, a Jesuit priest, currently is theologian-in-residence at Georgetown University and is editor-in-chief of Theological Studies. He has received sixteen honorary degrees from American colleges and universities and is the author of a number of books, including Preaching: The Art and the Craft; Lovely in Eyes Not His; and Grace on Crutches.

toral with a peaceful plume to just anybody and everybody. He was writing to an explosive city called Corinth. Explosive indeed, for Corinth in Paul's time could be a showcase for D.C. and L.A., New York and Las Vegas, Paris and the Riviera all lumped into one.

What do I mean? Corinth was cosmopolitan—folks flocked there from all regions of Rome's empire. Corinth was Washington in miniature—a center of government, a primitive Pentagon. Corinth was commerce writ large, made for merchants. For sports, Corinth could compete with Seoul 1988; its Isthmian games rivaled the Olympics. For lust and license, Corinth would make today's Sin City look like a Trappist monastery. "To live like a Corinthian" meant to wallow in immorality. Corinth's patron saint? Aphrodite, goddess of love—her temple serviced by a thousand prostitutes. Wealth? In Corinth, Donald Trump would have had a field day. Bud Light? In one small area diggers have discovered thirty-three taverns.[2]

This was the city to which Paul had carried Christianity back in 51. Within eighteen months he had an exciting community of converts. Five years later he had to write them a vigorous letter—the letter that was announced in the short selection read to you. Why did he write? In large measure because he was upset. In large measure because Corinth's newborn Christians were torn by cliques, coteries, factions—perhaps as many as four. A better-educated minority was entranced by Apollos: He knew the Old Testament inside out, and he hypnotized his hearers. A second group boasted a particular empathy with Peter, prince of the apostles. A third crowd—the majority, poor freedmen and slaves—rocked and rolled for Paul, apostle of dear old Corinth. A fourth faction seemed to think they were closer to Christ than anyone outside their graced little group.[3]

That situation summons up my second *C:* Christianity. How does Paul react to Corinth's cliques? In two ways. First, he lets them "have it," right from his Christian spleen. Factions founded on favorite ministers of Christ? "I belong to Paul," "I belong to Apollos," "I belong to Peter"? And some Christians "belong to Christ"? "Is Christ divided? Was Paul crucified for you? Or were you baptized in the name of Paul?" (1 Cor. 1:12–13, RSV).

Less angrily, Paul tells the Corinthians what he told you today. You "were all baptized into one body" (1 Cor. 12:13, RSV). And that one body is the body of the one Christ. All of you together are like the human body—the body of a man or a woman—like your own body. Take a look at yourself. Recognize it or not, that body is a work of art. And it's a work of art precisely because it is many-splendored, precisely because you're shaped of so many different parts. Picture yourself as all hands or feet, all heart or liver, all bone or blood, all rib or rump. Not only would you look funny; it just wouldn't work.

What Paul is saying in nonmedical language is that each of you is a single body because all your members, whatever they are, have a role to play in that body. Your blood system, if laid end to end, would circle the equator four times.[4] But even your pinkie, if fractured, would play havoc with your jump shot. Three million sweat glands cool your body. But even the mucus that lines your stomach keeps you from eating yourself alive.[5]

So, Paul tells his Corinthian converts, so is it with the Body of Christ, with the Church. No one of you can say to any other, "I have no need of you" (1 Cor. 12:21, RSV). Of course there are different roles: "Are all apostles? Are all prophets? Are all teachers? Do all work miracles? Do all possess gifts of healing? Do all speak with tongues? Do all interpret?" (vv. 29–30). Obviously not; but, my cherished Corinthians, each of you is an important part of this one Body, this one Christ—"no discord," only "the same care for one another" (v. 25). It reminds me that a century ago some cynic asked Cardinal Newman what good the laity were for. "Well," answered the cardinal with devastating simplicity, "the Church would surely look strange without them."

But at this point—having listed the prominent positions, the center-stage functions, in the Church—Paul rocks Corinth with a masterstroke, utterly unexpected: "I will show you a still more excellent way" (v. 31). More important than any of the offices, any of the gifts he has just listed. More important than being Peter or Paul; more important for the Church than being pope; more important, believe it or not, than being a Jesuit! And what is that?

You're asking for my third *C:* Cook. Paul's "more excellent way" is the couplet that Barbara Cook winged into my heart that Friday evening:

> Love is all we have for now,
> what we don't have is time.

Two pithy, poignant expressions here. First, "love is all we have for now." Now, composers and chanteuse were quite aware that there is more to living than loving. All you need for proof is to lift your eyes to South Africa and Soviet Armenia,[6] to the Middle East and the north of Ireland, to Wall Street and the Bowery. What I find in their song, perhaps read into their words, is a realization that the words are more profound than they sound. Whether it's AIDS or your career, whether it's cancer or Christianity, when the chips are down and you're talking about life-and-death, when it's a question of what it means to be human, then what makes the difference is love. St. Paul put it another way to the Corinthian Christians: "So faith, hope, love abide, these three; but the greatest of these is love" (1 Cor. 13:13, RSV).

It's "the greatest" for your world and for your Church. For your world. You see, love is the one gift that can make any area of this world more human than was Corinth. Other gifts can help: economics and education, health and housing, equal rights and Medicare. But without love—unless deep down we care; unless Wall Street is more than a countinghouse, Georgetown more than a springboard for success; unless love of law is subordinate to the law of love, medicine less for profit than for people; unless competition is less compelling than compassion, technology not simply science but the art of aiding; unless money and power and fame serve not self but the other; and yes, unless we live Christ's command "Love the Lord your God with all your heart . . . love your neighbor as [you love] yourself" (Matt. 22:37, 39, RSV)—the most powerful nation on earth will be little more than a contemporary Corinth.

And love is "the greatest" for your Church, for the Body of Christ. We have our differences, God knows—differences that threaten to tear one Church into more factions than Paul ever imagined. A pulpit is not the place to argue those differences—from contraception to the kiss of peace, from women's ordination to homosexual activity. But a pulpit *is* the place to proclaim this gospel: If our differences destroy our love, we are no longer Christians. I may indeed go to church, receive Christ in hand or on tongue, but without love the rest of it is a charade, playacting. And when the final judgment is passed on me, it will rest on one four-letter word: Did you really *love?*

With that question goes the second line of the couplet: "what we don't have is time." That's true not only of the AIDS-afflicted; it harasses all of us. Not in an obvious sense. After all, I can move from hate to love in an hour, a moment; God's grace is not measured by a clock. And some folk for some reason are given decades to discover love. The point is, I cannot promise myself time. Neither could the fifty thousand plus who perished in Soviet Armenia's earthquake. Neither can you—however young, however strong.

More positively, I lay before you the urgent plea in Psalm 95: "O that today you would hearken to [God's] voice!" (Ps. 95:7, RSV). *Today.* Etch that word on your mind and heart. You can remember yesterday; you can imagine tomorrow; today alone can you live. It's the supreme importance of the present moment. We are tempted to tolerate the routine or rupture of the present with an eye to the rapture of the future, to endure today's travail in hope of tomorrow's ease. Never for a day have I forgotten a framed sign I read decades ago in a convent chapel: "Priest of God, say this Mass as if it were your first Mass, as if it were your last Mass, as if it were your only Mass." Something similar can be said to each of you each day: "Child of God, live this day as if it were your first day, as if it were your last day, as if it were your only day."

So, too, for your loving. Not a tension-packed day into which you crowd all your caring; that way madness lies. To be aware that "what we don't have is time" is rather to realize that each dawn ushers in a new creation; each moment is a fresh chance to be Christlike; each human you touch, an invitation to be better than you are. It makes so much more sense than two blood sisters refusing to speak to each other for half a century. It alone makes impossible another Auschwitz, another *Mississippi Burning.*[7] It alone makes the difference between a jungle and a city, between people and educated animals, between marriage and an armistice, between a Catholic collegiate community and a campus clogged with six thousand intellectuals hell-bent on self-satisfaction.

Good friends: A well-known singer and bandleader, now eighty-one, wrote in his autobiography: "Women, horses, cars, clothes. I did it all. And do you know what that's called, ladies and gentlemen? It's called living."[8] Wouldn't it be more satisfying if someday you could say about yourself: People—those I liked and those I didn't— all people, but especially the homeless and the hopeless, the naked and the hungry, the lonely and the unloved, the brown and the black, the drug-addicted and the AIDS-afflicted. I did *not* do it all, but I did what I could. And do you know what that's called, ladies and gentlemen? It's called . . . loving."

> Love is all we have for now,
> what we don't have is time.

NOTES

1. The title is "Love Don't Need a Reason"; words and music by Peter Allen, Michael Callen, and Marsha Malamet.
2. See Richard Kugelman, C.P., "The First Letter to the Corinthians," in Raymond E. Brown, S.S., Joseph A. Fitzmyer, S.J., and Roland E. Murphy, O.Carm., eds., *The Jerome Biblical Commentary* (Englewood Cliffs, NJ: Prentice-Hall, 1968), 2:254.
3. For problems associated with this "Christ faction," see Kugelman, "The First Letter to the Corinthians," 256.
4. *World Book Encyclopedia*, 1975 ed., s.v. "blood."
5. See the delightfully informative book by Richard Selzer, *Mortal Lessons: Notes on the Art of Surgery* (New York: Simon and Schuster, 1976), 106, 118.
6. A reference to a horrible December 1988 earthquake that killed over fifty thousand and left more than half a million homeless.
7. A reference to a powerful film on racism in the 1960s, described by critic Richard Corliss as "a big, bold bolt of rabble-rousin', rebel-razin' movie journalism" in "Fire This Time" *Time*, (January 9, 1989), 57.
8. The autobiographer is Cab Calloway; the quotation is excerpted from *Time* (January 9, 1989), 69.

9. King on the Mountain
David W. Crocker

1 Kings 18:20–29, 36–39

When I was growing up, the boys in my neighborhood would play a game called "king on the mountain." It was the kind of game that developed young boys' macho image. Standing on a little hill that was sometimes no more than a small rise in the ground, we would see who was strong enough and crafty enough to keep the others off the hill. If one of us was successful at throwing the others down the hill, he would stand at the top, beat his skinny chest, and boast, "King on the mountain!" (Obviously, this was before the days of Nintendo video games and skateboards, but it was our way of entertaining ourselves and building ego along the way.)

Now I see that my friends and I were not the originators of this game. In fact, it was played almost three thousand years ago . . . in Israel. The place was Mount Carmel, and the conbatants were Elijah and Ahab and a host of pagan prophets. Ahab was king of Israel at the time, but Elijah challenged him and his huge staff of state owned and operated preachers. There was one king already on the mountain that day, but Elijah would see to it that that would change.

But, of course, the contest between Elijah and Ahab's prophets was no game. It was a confrontation of epic proportions. And there was much more at stake than which man would be left standing on the mountain. It would decide who was God—Baal or Yahweh. It would decide who was the real king on the mountain.

David Crocker is pastor of Central Baptist Church in Johnson City, Tennessee. He received his doctorate of ministry from Southern Baptist Theological Seminary in Louisville, Kentucky. Dr. Crocker was a contributor to the fourth volume of *Award Winning Sermons*.

I

When we pick up the story, Israel has been in the throes of a killing drought that would make the drought of 1988 in this country look like an extended high-pressure system. Some time earlier Elijah had said that it would not rain until he said so. Sure enough, it didn't. The crops died. Pastures withered. Streams dried up.

Elijah was not a popular guy. But he was no fool either. He hid himself for the duration, first by the brook at Cherith, then with a widow at Zarephath. At long last it was time for the drought to end. Elijah came out of hiding. He went to Ahab to tell him that rain was on the way.

You'd have thought that would be welcome news and that Elijah might be given a hero's welcome home. But, no, Ahab resented Elijah's power, and he accused the prophet of turning against his own country. He called him the "troubler of Israel."

Well, Elijah wasn't about to take the rap for Israel's problems. Ahab was the problem. He'd married the Canaanite princess Jezebel, who introduced the worship of Baal in Israel. Baal was the pagan fertility god of that region of the world. The non-Hebrew people held to their worship of Baal in spite of the fact that he was little more than a figment of their imagination. Now Jezebel was evangelistic in promoting Baalism, even in Israel. This is why the writer of Kings says of Ahab, "Ahab did more to provoke the Lord . . . to anger than all the kings of Israel who were before him" (1 Kings 16:33, RSV)

The people vere expected to participate in the worship of Baal. They were expected to bow down before a statue and pray as they had done before God. It was a matter of royal decree. And in those days when the queen said, "Do it," you did it. Unless, of course, you were Elijah. Here was a man who was accustomed to standing alone, whose commitment to God could not be shaken, who could not be intimidated into compromise. So when Jezebel led the weak Israelites away from God, Elijah spoke out. He denounced Ahab and Jezebel, his wife, and Baal, her god.

Being henpecked, Ahab sided with his wife. He lashed out against Elijah. Even when the prophet came with the news that rain was on the way, Ahab accused Elijah of bringing unfair suffering to Israel. That's when Elijah decided to play king on the mountain with Ahab.

II

Elijah said to Ahab, "Round up the prophets of Baal, come to Mount Carmel, and we will see who is the trouble for Israel." And so they came . . . 850 of them—450 prophets of Baal and 400 of Asherah, the Canaanite mother-goddess who figured prominently in the fertility cult of the people of Canaan. And there was Elijah—one single prophet of Yahweh, the living, faceless, imageless, omnipotent God.

I want you to get the picture of this scene on Mount Carmel: 850 to 1. If you thought the Los Angeles Dodgers were overmatched against the Oakland A's, what must you think of this contest? You thought the Alamo was bad odds; this battle on Mount Carmel was infinitely worse!

This is one of the many places in the Bible where the majority is wrong. They were wrong when as the children of Israel they became disenchanted with the hardships of their new freedom from Egypt and told Moses they wanted to go back. They were wrong when they ignored the warnings of Jeremiah that the Babylonian army would win. They were wrong when they clamored for Jesus to be crucified. They were wrong when they charged Paul with violations of their laws of exclusion. You see, the majority is not always right. Even if they win, they may still be wrong.

You and I need to hear this. We have been so heavily influenced by democracy that we have begun to believe that the majority is the way to decide everything. Find where the largest numbers are and go with them. Give everyone a vote, then go with the majority. This is a good way to conduct government. It is better than monarchy, better than dictatorship. It is the best way for a society to choose its leaders and enact laws to govern itself. But it is not necessarily the best way to decide morality.

The democratic process is a good way for the church to make decisions. It is better than having the pastor and staff do it, better than having denominational leaders do it. But this is not the way we decide what we believe. As Baptists we are committed to the congregational form of church government in which everyone has equal voice and vote, but we do not let the majority tell us how we must interpret the Bible . . . or pray. These are individual rights and responsibilities.

The majority can seduce us into believing it is always right. If the majority does it, it must be okay. This is particularly appealing to teenagers, but we old folks aren't immune to it. We are like the fly in the old fable. Once a spider built a beautiful web in an old house. He kept it clean and shiny so that flies would patronize it. The minute he got a customer he would clean up on him so the other flies would not get suspicious.

Then one day this fairly intelligent fly came buzzing by the clean web. The spider called out, "Come on in and sit." But the smart fly said, "No sir. I don't see other flies in your house, and I'm not going in alone."

But presently he saw on the floor below a large crowd of flies dancing around on a piece of brown paper. He was delighted. He wasn't afraid if lots of flies were doing it, so he came in for a landing.

Just before he landed, a bee zoomed by, saying, "Don't land there, stupid! That's flypaper!" But the fairly intelligent fly shouted back, "Don't be silly. There's a big crowd there. Everybody's doing it. That many flies can't be wrong!" And with that he became one stuck-up fly.

You see, the majority is not always right. If they had taken a vote on Mount Carmel, Elijah would have found himself on the first bus out of town. He would have been written off as a demented, religious fanatic, a man who was sadly tied to the old ways and unrealistically resistant to modern ways, especially modern religious thought. He would have missed the chance to show who was the real king on the mountain.

III

When everyone had gathered on Mount Carmel, Elijah threw down the gauntlet. He said, The time has come to decide once and for all who is God. If Yahweh is God, then serve him; if Baal is God, then serve him. You cannot go on vacillating between the two. Not only is it indecisive, it is an insult to God. He won't share your commitment. He will have no part in a divided loyalty. With God, it's all or nothing.

Now the Hebrews knew that. They had recited the Shema for generations: "Hear, O Israel: The Lord our God, the Lord is one; and you shall love the Lord your God with all your heart, and with all your soul, and with all your mind, and with all your strength." But that was old hat. You can't expect yesterday's religion to be good today. Things change. Baal is in now.

We, too, have a hard time accepting Elijah's word on Mount Carmel. Even with our advantage of history, we have trouble seeing the total commitment demanded by God. Even with the help of Jesus who repeated the Shema and added, "No one can serve two masters; for either he will hate the one and love the other, or he will be devoted to the one and despise the other. You cannot serve God and mammon" (Matt. 6:24, RSV), still we just can't get there. Oh, we're committed all right; just not totally committed. There is always something we hold back—some of our love, a little of our availability, a pinch of our loyalty.

A former missionary to Brazil reports of an encounter with the operator of a magazine stand who was a committed Communist. Said the Communist: "The Communists are changing the world. I am fighting for a course that nature has predestined to succeed. No matter what it costs, I intend to carry out my mission of making the world Communist. You Christians profess that your beliefs will change the world. I have read several of your books. Your writers talk about sacrifice. I dare you to show me a dozen Christians who would be willing to give their lives for what they claim to believe. I could show you a hundred Communists tonight who would. That is why we will win and you will fail."[1]

IV

That is the kind of commitment Elijah showed on Mount Carmel. He ordered that two altars be built and prepared for sacrifice—one for Baal and one for God. The prophets for each would implore their God to bring down the fire to ignite the sacrifice. The God who answered would be the real God.

The prophets of Baal prayed all morning long. They cut themselves to convince their God of their sincerity, but there was no answer. No fire came, and no sacrifice was offered to Baal.

Then Elijah took his turn. With a flare for the dramatic, he ordered that his sacrifice be thoroughly doused with water, then a second time, and a third. Then the courageous, singular prophet called to God, "O Lord, God of Abraham, Isaac, and Israel, let it be known this day that thou art God in Israel . . . " And fire came down, ignited the wood on the altar, and "licked up the water in the trench" around the altar. And when the people saw it, they fell on their faces and said, "The Lord is God; the Lord, he is God!"

At last Elijah was king on the mountain. He'd won. He'd stood alone against Jezebel and her spineless husband, Ahab, and beaten them. He'd stood alone against 850 pagan prophets and beaten them. He'd beaten them all! The writer of 1 Kings doesn't say so, but I can just see Elijah standing atop Mount Carmel and thinking to himself, if not shouting, "King on the mountain! King on the mountain!"

But Elijah was not the king on Mount Carmel . . . and Ahab was not king that day. God was king! The God who answers prayer and brings fire. The God of Abraham, Isaac, and Jacob. The God who is a majority by himself.

V

There was another sacrifice on another hill on another day. It, too, served as a climax in the confrontation between God's sole servant and an overwhelming majority. It, too, exposed the weakness of the officials and the fickleness of the masses. Like the one in the ninth century before Christ, this sacrifice proved who was God.

But unlike the sacrifice on Mount Carmel, this one was not on a crude altar made of twelve stones surrounded by a trench. It was on a Roman cross flanked by two convicted thieves and surrounded by the most vile prejudice and vicious hostility any so-called religious people can offer. And, unlike the one on Mount Carmel, this sacrifice was the last one ever needed to cover men's sins. Finally, unlike the sacrifice on Mount Carmel, this one cost more than a bull; it cost God's only Son.

E. V. Hill is a well-known black preacher in Los Angeles. He tells of a personal crisis he and his family faced during the Watts riots years ago. Another pastor had already been killed, and word was that Hill would be next. He received a threatening phone call. When his wife asked who had called, he said, "Some things you don't need to know." Sensing danger, she pressed Dr. Hill to know. Finally, he relented, saying, "The caller said, 'Don't be surprised if you discover a bomb in your car.' "

The next morning he awoke to discover his car was gone from his driveway. In a few minutes he saw the car pull around the corner and into the driveway. His wife got out of the car and went into the house. Hill asked his wife, "Where have you been?" She said, "I decided that if somebody was going to be killed, I'd rather it be me." He says he never again asked his wife if she loved him.[2]

And that's why God is God and why he is King on Mount Carmel and Mount Zion and *every* mountain.

NOTES

1. Richard Douglass, "True Believers," *Proclaim* (July 1979): 33.
2. Told by Dr. John Sullivan at the Conference on Biblical Preaching, Southern Baptist Theological Seminary, March 8, 1988.

10. The Transforming Power of a Holy Curiosity

Roy Honeycutt

Exod. 3:1–12

The proverb "curiosity killed the cat" describes the efforts of some people to discourage questioning. While curiosity may not "kill the cat," the lack of it most certainly will kill a maturing Christian discipleship.

Fortunately, many know that proverb, but few follow its counsel. We should be grateful for this inattention. For the inquisitive, questioning mind always open to new truth remains the clay from which our LORD shapes disciples. It is also our hope for the twenty-first century as we Christians confirm the relevance of our spiritual convictions.

Imagine the vacuum in our religious experience should we eliminate from the Bible all questions and answers. How impoverished faith would be without the curiosity of Moses watching a burning bush, Job demanding God's justice, or Jeremiah interrogating God.

Unwilling to walk old paths merely because they are ancient, curiosity asks, Why? Standing before a bush that burns without being consumed, inquisitive faith asks, How?

Some people assume faithful Christians blindly accept every biblical interpretation or circle tradition. To the contrary, authentic faith lives with the conviction that God never stifles a sincere questioner.

Roy Honeycutt is president of Southern Baptist Theological Seminary. An Old Testament scholar, Dr. Honeycutt has written numerous books, commentaries, and articles in his field.

Biblical personalities experienced faith as a creative, imaginative experience with the LORD. At times people argued with God, as did Jeremiah. On other occasions they questioned like Habakkuk. Or they remonstrated as Job.

Human curiosity and inspired understanding led to divine revelation. For Jeremiah this happened in the chance sighting of a bush budding (Jer. 1:11), a pot boiling (1:13), or a potter working on the clay (18:3). A workman with a plumb line in his hand prompted God's revelation for Amos (Amos 7:7–8). Later, the prophet experienced God's Word while reflecting on a basket of summer fruit (8:1–8).

Common places, sights, and experiences all activated God's revelation. Through holy curiosity, individuals discovered God in the common places and were uncommonly transformed.

What does God do in response to our "holy curiosity"?

God Transforms the Years We Waste (v. 1)

For Moses, curiosity transformed the years he seemed to have wasted. Confronted by the burning presence of God, Moses turned his past into an avenue to the future. Someone once said that the greatest achievement of the human spirit is to live up to one's opportunities and to make the most of one's resources. Reluctantly, many of us confess we seldom achieve such noble objectives. Often we recognize our opportunities too late. We fail to make effective use of our resources.

Moses' call is an illuminating parallel not only of our failures but the certainty of God's providence, which can transform our negligence. Moses was the adopted son of Pharaoh's daughter and widely accepted as an Egyptian. He had both opportunities and resources denied other Hebrews. Above all other privileges, Moses enjoyed freedom.

Despite his opportunities and resources, you also recall Moses' rapid collapse from Egyptian favor. Seeing an Egyptian beating a Hebrew relative, Moses killed the oppressor. Later, the Egyptians accused him of murder, and he fled to the land of Midian. Escaping Egyptian justice, Moses lived as a seminomadic sheepherder. Midianites adopted him, and he married a Midianite woman.

Considering Moses' potential, we might conclude he wasted

those years. After all, there are few more remote and insignificant places than the region of Moses' banishment.

Notwithstanding our negative circumstances, God does not waste our years. Certainly, he does not waste people nor their potential. Regardless of the seeming waste of Moses' life, it was during his perplexing banishment that he experienced the LORD's presence. Unknown to Moses during his exile from Egypt, God was preparing him for unique leadership.

Few could have believed that such heroic responsibilities lay ahead for Moses. Godly revelation transformed a fugitive from justice hiding as a sheepherder into an agent of divine mission.

Looking at our lives we also discover what one might call "the wasted years." Like Moses, we often squander our opportunities and waste our resources. Yet, in Christ we can discover a place of "beginning again." My personal experience confirms this assumption.

In my midteens I began work at a serious level and at seventeen I volunteered for military service. By the age of eighteen I was in an infantry division in the Philippines. While in military service, I earned university credits at Auburn and the University of Alabama. Following my discharge from the army I enrolled at the University of Mississippi but remained in the school of business for only a semester. Then I transferred to Mississippi College.

By the time I graduated from college I had attended four universities: the University of Alabama, Auburn, Ole Miss, and Mississippi College. My transcript was a composite of four universities, three vocational commitments, and a scrambled academic record to match that ambiguity.

Enrolling at Southern Seminary gave me the opportunity to redeem those years. There I discovered new motivation and the inspiration of faculty who integrated faith with life. This became the occasion for recommitting my life to the excellence synonymous with Christ's call to authentic discipleship.

In retrospect, the years I once thought insignificant have acquired new purpose. Without cataloging those experiences, I can say that most of them make a positive contribution to my function as president of Southern Baptist Theological Seminary. I remain more convinced than ever that God can transform our wasted years.

Some of you may have had comparable experiences. If this is so, we can redirect our lives. We can recommit ourselves to excellence consistent with God's call to every Christian. The grace Moses experienced can become ours, and we can reclaim years we believe we have squandered.

The reason this is possible rests not in ourselves but in God. He is the inventive environmentalist who never loses anything he creates. In loving grace he redeems our lives. He gives us opportunities to begin again.

God Rewards the Curiosity We Demonstrate (vv. 2–5)

Curiosity provoked Moses to experience God's fuller revelation. According to the biblical text, "the bush was burning, yet it was not consumed." And Moses said, "I will turn aside and see this great sight, *why* the bush is not burnt" (Exod. 3:3, RSV).

God Encourages a Holy Curiosity

A friend of Mackintosh McKay traveling with Bonar Law "took out of his bag a book which he had just been reading. It was Henry Jones's Gifford Lectures on *A Faith that Inquires*. He handed it to Bonar Law, remarking that it was worth reading. Bonar Law took it up and then said, *'But is its title not a bit of a contradiction?'* "[1]

There is no contradiction between faith and honest inquiry. To the contrary, there is something essential missing with a faith that is unwilling or afraid to turn aside to the impartial weighing of any fresh evidence. The LORD never stifles a sincere inquiry. To the contrary, God rewards the spirit of the fearless and painstaking investigator.

God Transforms Our Common Places

God met Moses in a burning bush and made the common place holy. Other persons had seen the bush and beheld nothing. Moses had seen its like and had seen nothing. Then, one day God filled the commonplace. That was the light. That was his presence. That was the difference in meeting God or not—this God who alone can lead us out of our wilderness.

Frankly, we often miss our burning bush because we do not associate God with the commonplace. He comes through a deed of kindness, an understanding spirit, a sympathetic word, a child's inquisitive, upturned face, the New Testament's cup of cold water "given in my name." Even the crises, problems, and burdens of life mirror his reflected presence. For God has the strangest ways of turning up in the most unexpected places.

God Rewards Our Curiosity

God rewards the curiosity of a sincere questioner. St. Augustine once said that a free curiosity has more efficacy in learning than a frightful enforcement.[2]

At this moment in our educational pilgrimage we need to carry out Augustine's wisdom for at least two resons. *First,* we cherish both the voluntary exercise of religion and the liberty of conscience. *Second,* people by nature are more responsive to self-generated curiosity than to artificial attempts to coerce conformity.

God rewarded Moses' curiosity by revealing himself to a curious sheepherder who met the LORD in one of life's common places: tending sheep on the back side of the wilderness, wondering why a bush seemed to be burning but was not consumed. The LORD's response is clear: *"When the LORD saw* that he turned aside to see, God called to him out of the bush, 'Moses, Moses!' "* In response to Moses' inquisitive curiosity, the LORD revealed himself to Moses.

God still rewards a holy curiosity that has enough faith to "turn aside to see" and to ask, Why? The same God who implants curiosity in our personalities responds positively to the spirit of conscientious research and honest investigation.

Lacking that curiosity, we miss God's presence through laziness or indifference or unwillingness to examine and understand, as through secret sin or open wrongdoing.[3]

God Preserves the Continuity of Our Faith (vv. 6)

Frequently, individuals caution others about allowing intellectual inquiry to destroy their faith. We need have no such fear. Faith endures because of the object of our faith, not its intensity. Let us be certain that our relationship with Christ remains personally dynamic. Then what we believe will care for itself within the framework of the biblical revelation and the life of the Church. Experiencing the LORD'S presence as Moses did at the burning bush, we will discover a theological continuity in our faith.

Faith described as "once for all delivered to the saints" (Jude 3) affirms the central Christian proclamation. We join other believers in affirming the fundamental nature of that proclamation. Contending for that faith, however, does not deny the necessity for each generation to reinterpret the faith for itself.

Years ago, Wheeler Robinson sharpened my understanding of the need for each generation to reinterpret faith: "Scientific knowledge can never invalidate religious faith, however much it may lead to the restatement of the ways and means of God."[4]

Each generation bears the responsibility of restating "the ways and means of God." That obligation is both imperative and hazardous. It is *imperative* because we cannot live spiritually on the memory of another generation's interpretation of faith. The task is *hazardous* for may reasons. For example, some Christians become disturbed about people tampering (as they would describe theological reflection) with "the faith which was once for all delivered to the saints." Yet, such a responsibility is ours if we are to minister effectively in the third millennium of the Christian era. Else, we will find ourselves providing answers for questions no one else asks. Perhaps more disastrous, we will be unprepared to provide answers for questions that a new generation *will ask.*

Within all changes that we face, it is God who assures continuity. It is the God of Abraham, Isaac, and Jacob who is also the God of Moses and who now reveals himself in a new manner to Moses. The term *God of your fathers* refers to a distinct phase of religious life characteristic of patriarchal times. The God of your fathers was unique in that this God was not identified with a shrine but was associated with persons—Abraham, Isaac, Jacob. He was not a local deity but the God of the clan. He was the God of history in that he entered into covenant with those in the clan.[5]

The phrase underscored the distinction between patriarchal religion and the revelation mediated through Moses. At the same time it affirms the essential continuity between the religion of the patriarchs and the worship of Yahweh during later Israelite generations.

When Moses asked God to share his name, the LORD said, "Say to this people of Israel, 'I AM has sent me to you.' " Earlier when God had defined himself he said, "I AM WHO I AM" (Exod. 3:14, RSV).

Those who had experienced God as God of the fathers are now to understand the same God from a different perspective. From this point forward his name is I AM. Commonly we translate that name Yahweh, or in the Revised Standard Version, LORD.[6]

The new does not eradicate the old understanding of God but builds on it and goes beyond that discernment. For example, notice these important emphases in the name I AM or Yahweh. First, self-affirmation or self-definition is fundamental to understanding who God is. The phrase *I will be whoever I will be* is like those phrases in which deities affirm their nature out of their own being.

Second, the name *'ehyeh* (I AM) is not nominal or adjectival but verbal. The dynamism of the verbal mode of expression is characteristic of God's action. When one describes the LORD, he or she does so with a verb. This is no grammatical whimsy. It is a profound theological insight into the nature of God. Theology is a verb, and God is verbal.

Third, there is both revelation and concealment in the name of God. While disclosing himself, God also withholds himself from total apprehension. *I will be whoever I will be* affirms that God is present. *Will be* implies continuing presence with the people of God. But who or what God will be, he alone determines. He will be whoever (whatever) he will be. He will be to Moses as the circumstances and times imply. He will be to Isaiah as to Isaiah living in the eighth century B.C. He will be to the apostles, the church fathers, the Reformers, and us today *whatever (whoever) he chooses to be.*

Early in our faith experience we knew only the God of the fathers, the God of Abraham and Isaac and Jacob. This conveyed a profoundly meaningful relationship with God, but it did not exhaust God's self-revelation. Like Moses and Israel of the Exodus period, there was more to God than the God of the patriarchs. The God of redemption and covenant, Yahweh, called on both Moses and the people to stretch their commitment to embrace a larger understanding of God. Creatively open to the unfolding presence of God, we share the exciting responsibility of building on the foundational understandings with which we begin and proceeding to the fuller revelation of God.

Let us approach our responsibility with quiet confidence in God. May we trust his Word, both written and living. As we restate the faith, we will pray for the guidance of the Holy Spirit. By so doing we will "rightly divine the word of truth," as Holy Scripture encourages believers. In the full scope of this challenging task we will bring to sharpest focus the gifts that we bring to our vocation as both students and faculty.

God Suffers with Us through the Adversities We Experience (vv. 7–9)

How does God respond to your crises? Frankly, I have identified and then discarded several ways of characterizing God's response to our suffering. From one perspective, God redeems our suffering. Or, he transforms our suffering. Knowing the power of transformation operative in the cross, we are better able to confront our crises. Yet, God does more.

God Suffers with Us through Our Crises

There are times when we best describe God's response to our suffering with the word *share:* God shares our suffering. He does not exempt us from trouble nor does he eliminate our trauma. Sometimes it remains day after day, year after year.

How does God respond to our suffering? Four verbs express with simple yet majestic force God's personal participation with our burdens. God *remembers*, God *hears*, God *sees*, and God *knows:* "The LORD said, I have *seen* the affliction of my people who are in Egypt, and have *heard* their cry because of their taskmasters; I *know* their sufferings . . . " (Exod. 3:7, RSV).

Sculptors and artists have portrayed the loving care of Jesus following his death primarily through the role of Mary. Most famous of those depictions is Michelangelo's sculpture *The Pieta* at St. Peter's in Rome.[7] Nothing approximates as does the Vatican *Pieta* such lifelike beauty coupled with human suffering chiseled into the purest of Italian marble. One gazes upon the work of art with the wondrous feeling that the marble figures could easily come to life and move off the pedestal.

Other artists and sculptors have sought to copy Michelangelo and failed. The sculptor himself executed other *Pietas*. One in Florence, for example, is muscular and so unlike the *Pieta* in Rome as to be repulsive. None can compare with the Vatican *Pieta* in beauty of expression and depth of compassion.

There is another graphic portrayal of the loving care and suffering following the death of Christ. In some respects its message is more striking than that of Michelangelo's *Pieta*.

The artist's painting of the tender care of the dead Christ now hangs in the Fraumuenster in Zurich. Not Mary but God the Father holds the limp form of the dead Christ. it is the suffering God who forms the centerpiece of this "Pieta." Jürgen Moltmann, author of *The Crucified God,* is reported by a friend of mine in Zurich to have commented when he first saw the painting that he had never witnessed so striking an illustration of the suffering Father.

As the suffering Father bears the dead body of the crucified Son, so our Father shares our suffering. Given both our freedom and our sinful rebellion, there are times when God can only suffer with us, his broken children. In such circumstances God does not cut out our troubles. Nor does he erase our crises. Facing the ambiguity of such circumstances, we wait patiently with the suffering God as he holds us in his arms. If you have failed to discover such solace in the arms of God, either you have not lived very long or you have not yet suffered deeply.

God Does More Than Suffer: He Sends Someone to Deliver His People

In response to his participation with suffering humanity, the LORD said to Moses, "Come, I will send you to Pharaoh that you may bring forth my people, the sons of Israel, out of Egypt" (Exod. 3:10, RSV). The God who boldly announced, "I have seen . . . and . . . heard . . . I know their sufferings, *and I have come down"* (3:7), now shifts the focus. "Come, I will send *you* to Pharaoh that *you* may bring forth my people, the sons of Israel, out of Egypt" (3:10, RSV).

Is not this a contradiction? And, if so, how does one resolve that inconsistency? Shall one appeal to literary criticism and conclude that two sources, one from the south (J) and the other from the north (E) have brought their separate witnesses into a single passage? Or, shall one attempt other maneuvers to avoid the contradiction?

The answer emerges from another direction. This is no contradiction. It is a commentary on the ways of God with humanity. What God does he does through human personality dedicated to his will. No better illustration of this exists than the Incarnation: "The word became flesh and dwelt among us, full of grace and truth; we have beheld his glory, glory as of the only Son from the Father" (John 1:14, RSV).

God Confirms the Future We Question (vv. 10–12)

Responding to Moses' reluctance to accept his calling, God promised to give him a sign.

> "Come, I will send you to Pharaoh that you may bring forth my people, the sons of Israel, out of Egypt." But Moses said to God, "Who am I that I should go to Pharaoh, and bring the sons of Israel out of Egypt?" He said, "But I will be with you and this shall be the sign for you, that I have sent you: when you have brought forth the people out of Egypt, you shall serve God upon this mountain." (Exod. 3:10–12, RSV)

The sight is more than Israel's presence at the mountain, more even than her worship. The sign centers in God's presence in Israel at the mountain. The future would confirm Moses' present call.

Like every person, in the nightmare of crises we echo Moses' plaintive appeal, "Who am I that I should go?" (Exod. 3:11); "Why did you ever send me . . . ?" (Exod. 5:22). When such questions challenge the validity of your course of action, remember three guideposts to point the way in your ambiguity. No person rightly judges you, nor can we properly judge ourselves, apart from these qualities. Neither can we appropriately judge someone else until we know these driving forces. What is our *objective,* our *strategy,* and our *motivation?*

When the future seems most questionable, we desperately seek God's endorsement. In return there is only the ominous refrain: After the long course of your task is complete; when the plagues are over, the shadow of the death angel gone, and the sea of chaos crossed; when the murmuring is over and the thirst is quenched and hunger filled; when you stand upon your mountain wherever it may be, and God shares his presence in worship—then you will know that he has sent you. You cannot be certain until then—not absolutely certain!

Conclusion

Meeting God at some quiet place where the flame of his presence burns with beckoning power, can we today respond with a "holy curiosity" dedicated to the LORD? If so, you may be sure that in your burning-bush experience God will redeem your wasted years, reward your curiosity, maintain the continuity of faith, suffer with you through crises, and guarantee the future you question.

All of this began with a sheepherder on the back side of the wilderness who saw a bush glowing without being consumed and said, "I think I'll go over and see why the fire isn't consuming that bush."

Yes, curiosity may not kill cats, but the lack of it will certainly kill the authentic witness of the Church and the dynamism of a zealous faith.

NOTES

1. James Hastings, ed., "The Book of Exodus," in *The Speaker's Bible* (Speaker's Bible Office, 1943), 25.
2. Rudolph Flesch, ed., *The Book of Unusual Quotations* (New York: Harper & Brothers, 1957), 54.
3. Hastings, "The Book of Exodus."
4. H. Wheeler Robinson, *Inspiration and Revelation in the Old Testament* (London: Oxford University Press, 1946), 184.
5. Albrecht Alt, "The God of the Fathers," in *Essays on Old Testament History and Religion*, trans. R. A. Wilson (Oxford: Basil Blackwell, 1960), 1–77.
6. LORD, in upper case, always refers to the Hebrew *yhwh*, translated by some (incorrectly, I believe) as "Jehovah." He is the God of covenant who redeems Israel.
7. *Pieta:* literally, from the Italian, meaning "pity" (compare Latin *pietas:* "pity"). In fine arts *The Pieta* is a representation of the Virgin Mary mourning the body of the dead Christ, usually shown held on her lap.

11. What We Are Awaiting
Jacques Ellul

Isa. 40:1–8; Mark 1:1–4; 2 Pet. 3:8–10

We shall attempt today to consider all three texts that are given to us, for they complement one another in a remarkable way. But this sermon will be centered on the text from Isaiah. This announces God's promise of his coming among the people. Mark takes up again the same text in order to proclaim that the promise is going to be fulfilled now and that John will be the precursor, precisely the one of whom Isaiah speaks. Finally, in the letter attributed to Peter, comes a new proclamation. Peter echoes the promise: After the first fulfilling of the prophecy of Isaiah, in the humility of Christmas, we await the second fulfillment, the coming of the incarnate Word of God in glory. And this step from one text to the other, which ought to characterize Advent, places us in another time of waiting, as it was for Israel before the birth of the Messiah, waiting that is characterized by vigilance and patience. Vigilance—because as long as unanswered expectation lasts, it is necessary to remain awake, not sleeping in our religious practices, not overlooking the signs that God sends to us; and it is necessary to keep faith alive, ready to welcome the Christ who is coming. Patience also—for Peter warns us that this waiting can continue for a long time. God is in no way bound by delays and by the seeming permanence of things. Waiting is a test of faithfulness, as Jesus declares in several parables. Be-

Jacques Ellul recently retired from a distinguished career as professor of Law and professor of the Sociology and History of Institutions at the University of Bordeaux in France. He has written more than forty books, including *The Politics of God and the Politics of Man, The Theological Foundation of Law,* and *The Technological Society.* This sermon was translated from the French by James W. Cox.

tween the last prophecies of the Old Testament and the coming of Jesus, it has already been perhaps three hundred years, during which time the people of Israel have waited with fidelity. And we may even speak of Israel's present fidelity, which is millenary and an example for us, awaiting the Messiah's coming, while this Jewish people has not had the joy of a first fulfillment as we have experienced it. Peter is more than right to tell us that, in spite of our impatience and weariness, there is no "slowness" in the return and the new creation, the coming of the Kingdom of God, for it is a reality that we ought to be aware of constantly: "With the Lord one day is as a thousand years." Let us not be more impatient than God who is patient toward us.

How, then, is the prophecy of Isaiah presented? It seems to me to include three proclamations: The first has two aspects. From the very outset, Isaiah issues this order from God: "Comfort, comfort my people." Thus the first decisive act of God is always consolation, and not, as we have too often heard in sermons, the threat of condemnation! "Comfort" for all human misery in history! But today that is very much more assured than in Isaiah's time, precisely because in Jesus Christ we *have* the consolation assured. He—the Good Shepherd —has come to take charge of a helpless flock. This flock is not only Israel; it is all humanity, for the Father is universal and has sent the Son to save all people. The people of God is now the whole of humanity. It is to her that the affirmation is addressed: Comfort my people because her "time of service" is ended. For Isaiah this means concrete historical servitude, but in Jesus Christ it has to do with all constraint, with all servitude. Jesus Christ is the one who liberates from everything, as his Father has liberated his people Israel from Egypt.[1] Your slavery is ended! In Jesus Christ this is the slavery of sin, of fear, of anguish, and, at last, of death. All this slavery is abolished in Christ for the one who believes. And it causes us to enter, already, into "the glorious liberty of the children of God." Putting it a bit more philosophically, we will say that Jesus Christ causes us to leave the world of necessity, of determinism, etc., in order to cause us to enter the world of freedom. But again we must have—we ourselves—the faith to receive this consolation and this freedom. Also, we must have the courage to live this freedom. The freedom that comes from God is never easy to live. The Hebrews with their forty years in the wilderness knew what it was like! They were liberated, but afterward they had to learn a hard freedom—of uncertainty, of privations, and the like. So, freedom is not automatically "happiness" nor facility in doing whatever one chooses to do! To put into practice this freedom that comes from Jesus Christ will put us into conflict almost certainly with the rules of society, or our profession; it will foster new political exigencies; it will transgress economic laws! But, in addition, this freedom ought to come to expression with regard to ourselves, our passions, our ambitions, our egoisms, our concern for comfort and getting more money! Freedom from all that. Most certainly, and this ought to be comforting to us.

Now we come to the other aspect of this first proclamation: "Tell them that their iniquity is pardoned—that God has paid double." How can we fail to see here a prophecy of the plan of God fulfilled in Jesus Christ? Israel has committed "crimes." It is necessary to pay penalties or the price of peace: And here it is precisely God himself, the one first and foremost offended by these crimes, who is going to pay the price, who is going to take upon himself the weight of pain and vengeance, and who not only pays the price but pays double. Beyond all that we can imagine! This indeed is precisely what happens in Jesus Christ: Not only at the moment of his Crucifixion, in the death that cleanses us from sin, but again (and, I may say, even more) in the terrible adventure of the Incarnation. One never thinks of that sacrifice, when the Father has to be separated from his Son, and when the Father is willing to give himself in his Son in order that absolute justice might be accomplished. Jesus is truly the price to pay in order that absolute justice might be accomplished, that is to say, that all the sins of all humanity might be expiated and that no one might anymore be able to be remembered as a criminal in the presence of God (Hebrews 9). But this is not only the sacrifice of Jesus, the man, the Son of man; it is still more the sacrifice of Christ, the Son of God (Philippians 2). And that sacrifice is made at the moment of Christmas. We are accustomed to live Christmas as a joyous festival, and doubtless for humanity it is joyous news, that which the angels sing—the coming of God himself on earth and the full revelation of his love. But is it not fitting to ponder this tragedy of the separation of the Father and the Son, of the Father absolutely Father, who is willing to give up his Son, absolutely *the* Son, the Unique One—this tragedy of God who takes upon himself all the heinousness that humanity is capable of accumulating in the course of its history, the crimes from the very beginning and those of our present time . . . all that taken in charge by God himself? What other price could cover, compensate for the totality of the evil and the hate that humanity has contrived over the last fifty thousand years?

Isaiah's second proclamation places us before *our* responsibility, before our share in God's work. And the prophet moves in three-part time in order that all this that he is placing before us be indisputable. "In the wilderness prepare the way of the Lord." There is our responsibility! The main thing—that which far surpasses all other deeds, all enterprises for doing good, all acts of solidarity and the like—the main thing is that God is going to come! Prepare a way for him! But why? Isn't God powerful enough to make his own way? Of course! Read, then, once more all this history of God with humanity. God makes a place for our action while, to be sure, he has no need of it; God brings us into his plan. Do you recall Jesus and the Samaritan woman? It is Jesus who *first* makes a request—"Give me some water." To prepare a way by which God will pass? What is this saying? We see, of course, John the Baptist who has prepared the way of Jesus by proclaiming repentance and the announcement of his coming! And Mark has not hesitated to apply the prophecy to him. But is this fulfilled, exhausted by its coming to expression in John the Baptist? Not at all! It has to do with us; it puts the meaning of our life in question. What shall we do when we are "Christian"? It does not have to do *first of all* with good works or political engagement or mystical rapture: It is precisely a matter of preparing a way for God in our wilderness. For our world has become a desert for God. It is not only Jesus who has not a stone on which to rest his head. And how does the poet put it: "Is there a place where the angel of the Lord would be able to place his foot?" Desert for God! Desert of unbelief, desert of hardness of heart, desert of ambitions, desert of false loves! Any way we look we see but a wilderness encumbered with things, with objects, with machines, and at the same time with the poor, the starving, and the struggling. There is where we have to lay out a road by which God may pass; a road in unjust institutions, in foolish philosophies, in parched hearts, in the arrogances of science; a road among the desperate and those thirsting for riches or glory. It is necessary that *we* prepare the way, that is to say, that we become capable of getting a human heart, become capable of welcoming God when he comes. And if each of us would get this, should this be only one person attentive to the Word, to the promise, and no longer obsessed with self, then this would be the only work needed to transform the world. Preparing the way, like John the Baptist, for Jesus Christ at the time of his return will also need to be welcomed. And there is no evidence that such will happen. Did Jesus not say, "When the Son of man returns, will he still find faith on the earth?" This is a terrible word, a word that Jesus must have uttered with profound sadness. But to open this way requires not only the preaching of the gospel, it requires combat against falsehood, against dishonesty, against injustice, against extravagance, against slavery. We *are obliged* to do it because God requires it of us, and we *are able* to do it because Jesus has conquered the powers of the world.

The *second* time of this prophecy seems still more difficult for us! But it is still our work that God awaits: to bring down the mountains, that is to say, empires, money, political power, the arrogance of technology, dominions of all kinds—those are our mountains —and to raise up the valleys; to smooth away human conflicts, separations, but also to raise up the weak, the downtrodden; and to deliver the oppressed—all of which ought not to be done by instigating revolts and by fostering in the the poor a spirit of hatred, *but by placing the powers again under the power of God.* Then the work of Jesus Christ, who came as a pauper, is accomplished. As one who did not preach revolt, he manifested the power of God far beyond that of the mighty ones. It is necessary that what was done once for all in Jesus Christ find its fulfillment, its realization in our own conduct.

Then, if this was, in fact, the action, the work, the being of the Church, the third time of this prophecy would be fulfilled: The glory of the Lord would be revealed; everyone would know who Jesus is! John the Baptist was faithful in opening the way, in leveling the path, for the one who was supposed to come. Would it not be the same for the one who is to return? For what has happened at Christmas has caused the glory of God to appear not in his power but in his love. It is true that all flesh would be able to see it, as we see it in faith. Because at this moment the Word of God has been truly spoken, incarnated in every respect, declared on earth. "The Word has been made flesh, and it has dwelt among us," as John says, in line with our text from Isaiah: "And all flesh shall see it at the same moment: *for the mouth of the Lord has spoken!*" Thus we have an immense responsibility in this work of God: The Word of God has come, the glory of the Lord has been revealed. But notice—all flesh did not see it at that time and does not see it now! But that is our fault. If we were genuine bearers of this Word, then there would be a radical change in the world and not only in our heart. Then the world would receive consolation, liberation, and be ready for adoration. But this work that is required of us is difficult, even disagreeable, and this leads to the third message of our text.

The prophet, that is to say *we,* as the Church and as Christians, individuals, ought to proclaim in this world, first of all, that it is fragile, passing, that it has no real power. It can be rich, powerful, and as beautiful as a flower garden, yet it takes only a gust of wind from the desert to turn it all to dust. Put another way, in this present world one tiny mistake is all that is needed to blow up everything or to make the worldwide economy collapse. And the comfort, the progress, the development, the knowledge—all that will wither where it stands; it would count for *nothing.* So here is where we have to be these *prophets* still, right here in this world. For now, it is no longer as in the time of John the Baptist with the proclamation of the Messiah's coming in humility, in poverty and human weakness, that God has willed to share with humanity. What we wait for, what we have to announce, is the coming of the Messiah in his glory, which implies at the same time the fading of human glory and the dazzling appearing of the *Word* that no one can any longer debate: "Then all flesh will recognize it and hear it." Today this Word is silent, and we often with discouragement experience the silence of God. Nevertheless, we ought unceasingly to believe and proclaim that it is the only solid, durable, eternal reality that generation after generation consoles, delivers, reveals, reconciles. This same Word was the creative Word at the beginning of the world. It was the Word incarnated at our very humble level at Christmas. It was the Word that resurrected Jesus Christ. And now it remains the only rock on which we can build our lives, our families, and a lasting future for the world. And, finally, this Word is that which, because it endures forever, will come in order to establish this world that we await with the whole Creation—"the new heaven and the new earth where justice will dwell." At that time, the prophecy of Isaiah will be brought to complete fulfillment, and we cannot doubt that it will be accomplished, because, already, whatever be the errors of the churches and the dangers of the world and the omissions of Christians, the two first stages of prophecy have been fulfilled, and we are

able to contemplate the love of God, in his humility at Christmas, which assures us that we shall also receive this love in Glory!
Amen. Hallelujah.

NOTE

1. We should perhaps recall that Egypt was called in Hebrew *mitstrain,* which means "double distress."

12. Hearing for Eternity
Charles R. Gresham

Luke 8:9–18; Mark 4:23–25

Thoreau, the great American naturalist, was right when he said, "It takes two to speak the truth—one to speak and another to hear." This is why so much preaching fails! It is not always the fault of the preacher, for some great preachers have failed. Paul failed at Athens as he spoke on Mars Hill (the Aeropagus). Why? Because his audience disbelieved; they scoffed at his message concerning bodily resurrection (Acts 17:16–32).

This same preacher failed twice at Caesarea. On one occasion when he preached on "righteousness, self-control, and judgment to come," his hearer, Felix, the governor, was deeply moved, but his hearing did not eventuate in obedience. "When I have a convenient season," Felix said trembling, "I will call on you" (Acts 24:24, 25, KJV). Then again when he proclaimed passionately before King Agrippa the reality of Messiah's coming (and his verification in Resurrection), there was that somewhat flippant reply: "In a short time you will persuade me to become a Christian" (Acts 26:28, NASB).

The fault in all these instances was not in the speaker nor his message, but it was the failure of his hearers. The texts in Luke 8 and Mark 4 speak to such failure. "Take heed how you hear," reports Luke (Luke 8:18). "He that hath ears, let him hear . . . but

---

Charles R. Gresham is professor of Bible and Christian Education at Kentucky Christian College and is dean of the master's program there. He is affiliated with the Christian Churches and Churches of Christ and has been minister of First Christian Church, Elizabethton, Tennessee. Dr. Gresham has degrees from several schools, including Southwestern Baptist Theological Seminary, and he has taught at Dallas Christian College, Midwest Christian College, Manhattan Bible College, and Emmanuel School of Religion.

take care what you hear" (Mark 4:23, 24) is from Mark's account of this same episode in Jesus' ministry. Both emphases are true and, undoubtedly, reflect accurate reporting. *Matter* and *manner* of hearing are always related. The *what* and *how* can never be separated. *What* we hear depends upon *how* we hear; and *how* we hear, the kind of hearers we are, and the mental attitudes that we adopt, depend upon *what* we have heard and welcomed and used.

That unknown poet graphically points out this interrelatedness in his prayer poem:

> And Warden of my soul's stained house, where
>   love and hate are born,
> Oh, make it clean, if swept must be with
>   pain's rough broom of thorn!
> And quiet impose, so straining ears with
>   world-din racked and torn
> May catch what God doth say.

So let us look at these two texts together, analyzing their major significance. To do so we use those three interrogative words— What? How? Why?—as the pegs upon which to hang the fabric of our thinking about our subject, "Hearing for Eternity."

What?

"Take heed what you hear" follows that preliminary statement, "He that hath ears to hear, let him hear." We all hear, but *what* do we hear? John Bunyan, in his allegory *Holy War*, very rightly makes "Eargate" the busiest place in the city of "Mansoul." Here comes Diabolus with his false but seductive speech, and here come the messengers of the great king. The transactions of Eargate decide the fate of Mansoul.

This is still true. What we hear determines our destiny. How prodigal we are with that gift of hearing. "Let him who hath ears to hear," hear . . . but, oh, let him take heed what he hears. Do we listen to that filthy story without a twinge of conscience? Do we listen to that piece of gossip and pass it on whether there is any truth or not in the rumor? Have our minds grown dull of hearing the precious Word? Have we so heard the Word that it has become "old hat," so familiar that it breeds contempt? *Take heed what you hear!*

Sometimes we think with pity of the heathen who have not heard the Word, but we may be far more to be pitied because we have heard so often. Mrs. Cecil-Smith of the China Island Mission tells of an incident that occurred as she and the native workers associated with her were leaving a place where the Word had been preached for a short time. "As we hurried away," she said, "the cry came after us, and it has been ringing in my ears very often since that night, 'Can I be saved with hearing only once?' " The answer of course is yes, because of what was heard. But what of us who have heard more often than we can remember—what of us?

In the Greek New Testament, "obedience" is expressed by the Greek verb "to hear" followed by the genitive case. And this is why so much importance is attached to *what* we hear. We tend to believe *and* obey what we hear, to what we have given careful attention. The question is, Is it the Word of God we hear and obey, or is it the devil's siren call? Take heed of *what* you hear, for we are all *hearing for eternity!*

How?

Jesus also said, "Take heed *how* you hear." The parable of the soils lies behind this injunction. Some hear *carelessly,* and hearing does not issue in obedience—the birds of the air swoop down and eat the seed. Some hear *heedlessly,* and such hearing produces some results- —but the ground is rocky and the heat of the day causes the growth to wither. Some hear *double-mindedly*—the good seed grows, but so also do the weeds that choke out the good grain's growth.

How do we hear? Hearing is perhaps more important than preaching. Shakespeare notes:

> A jest's prosperity lies in the ear
> Of him that hears it, never in the tongue
> Of him that makes it.[1]

And Lord Macaulay, the great English statesman, remarked when explaining the failure of one of his speeches: "Demosthenes was right when he said that the power of oratory is as much in the ear as in the tongue."

Have we genuinely considered the "awesome power of the listening ear" (the title of one of John Drakeford's books on counseling)? We have often dwelt upon the awful responsibility of the preacher, the pulpit; but the responsibility of the hearer is just as terrible. As J. Russell Lowell has noted:

> God is not dumb, that He should speak no more,
> If thou has wanderings in the wilderness
> And find'st not Sinai, 'tis thy soul is poor;
> There towers the Mountain of the Voice no less,
> Which whoso seeks shall find, but he who bends,
> Intent on manna still and mortal ends,
> Sees it not, neither hears its thundered lore.

Take heed *how* you hear. The hearer must be active, not passive, in his hearing. J. H. Morrison suggests that he must hear the Word with *attention*. It is not easy to give attention to spiritual matters, but we must. Our very life is at stake, and what ultimately concerns us captures our attention. We can't expect every teacher or preacher to be scintillating and sensational, breaking down the barriers we have erected. (Sometimes we act as if we are daring the preacher to interest us.) We need to move with the preacher, giving attention to the Word. If we give careful attention, a mighty poor preacher can aid us in our spiritual growth.

We need to hear the Word with *humility*. So often our pride is impenetrable. We must be more teachable. Pride-filled minds must be converted, as Jesus notes, and become as little children. When we listen to the preacher or teacher, with childlike humility and hopeful expectation, no matter how poor or ill-prepared the teacher or preacher, we will come from the experience enriched.

We need to hear the Word with *sympathy*. Hostility or even indifference creates a climate where no preaching or hearing can occur. The word *sympathy* means "to suffer along with another." Sometimes we have to do that literally. But let us be concerned enough, sympathetic enough, that our hearts and minds are open to the passion of the preacher, his concerns. But more, let us be open to the Christ who is central in every faithful preacher's message. If we must have bias, let it be on the side of the angels, goodness and truth, self-sacrifice and holy love.

Above all, we must hear the Word with *obedience*. The climax and crown of hearing is obedience. "He that heareth these words of mine and doeth them is like a wise man who built his house upon the rock" (Matt. 7:24), said Jesus. His half-brother James speaks with the same language: "Be ye doers of the Word and not hearers only, deceiving yourselves. For if anyone is a hearer of the Word and not a doer, he is like a man who looks at this face in the mirror and goes away, and immediately forgets what manner of man he is. But the one who looks intently at the perfect law of liberty and abides by it, not becoming a forgetful hearer but an effectual doer, will be blessed in all that he does" (James 1:22–25).

Take heed *how* you hear! You are *hearing for eternity!*

Why?

Why? Because Jesus says, "For whoever has, to him shall more be given; and whoever does not have, even what he thinks he has shall be taken away from him" (Luke 8:18). We are tempted to cry out, "Can this be our Lord speaking? That is unjust! Are we to give to those who least need the gift? Are we to take away from those who can ill afford the loss? Can anything be more unlike all we know about the character of Jesus than that he should approve the principle of stripping the poor in order to add unnecessary luxury to the rich?"

Yet, this is what he said. And when we give careful consideration to the principle, we will see that it is a general truism by which the world is governed. "Much will have more" is a proverb that is seen in human experience. "The rich get richer and the poor get poorer" is too true of human life. "You have to have money to make money," we say *and* correctly. Whatever this may say about economics and social ethics, the principle is too often seen.

But Jesus is not talking about economics of wealth or expressing some kind of materialism. He is speaking about the principle of intellectual growth and spiritual formation. Here, too, the principle is correct. *The more a man knows, the easier it is to add to his knowledge. The more spiritually aware we are, the more that spiritual awareness and apprehension build up Christian growth.*

But the negative is also true—"What one thinks he has will be taken away." No better illustration of this can be seen than that in Charles Darwin's *Memoirs* where he gives an account of the growth and decay of the various faculties of his mind. He wrote, "My mind seems to have become a kind of machine, grinding general laws out of large collections of facts. I have tried lately to read Shakespeare, but found it so dull it nauseated me. I have lost my taste for pictures and music."

And that man, who began earlier in his life to study for the ministry, not only rejected those things related to the higher intellectual and aesthetic pursuits, but, ultimately, God and faith. "What he had, had been taken away."

In contrast, James Stalker refers to what Dr. Whyte, the great preacher at St. George's in Edinburgh, had said at the funeral of one of his elders. This elder (Whyte affirmed) had the kind of mind that enriched everything it heard out of its own inner resources. Stalker also adds,

> There are such minds which magnify and glorify
> what the preacher has said, as, in a belfry, if you
> strike one of the bells, the others will begin to
> vibrate so that a chime instead of a single note is
> heard by an attentive ear. It is not unusual for a
> preacher, even in his study, to be aware of one
> hearer in the congregation beneath whose
> intelligence he must not fall on Sunday; but there
> are whole congregations so intelligent that the mind
> of the preacher almost unconsciously sways to their
> intellectual level; and there are congregations, too,
> through which there is diffused such a spiritual
> strain that a secular tone in one who is preaching to
> them is an outrage.

So, our Lord justifies his conduct in making known the mysteries of the kingdom (see vv. 9, 10), not to the mixed crowd of careless, heedless hearers, interested only in food for the stomach and spectacle and entertainment for the ear and eye, but to select disciples who "have ears to hear."

But to them, the warnings are presented: "Take heed *what* and *how* you hear!" Their hearts may not be hardened by roadside indifference, but the noxious weeds could grow and the scorching sun could wither. One of their number would not take this warning to heart, and the weeds of greed or disappointed ambition would cause him to betray his Lord in the blackness of the night in that lovely yet tragic garden. Why? Why should we take heed what and how we hear?

> Unto Him that hath Thou givest
> Ever more abundantly.

Lord, I live because thou livest,
Therefore, give new life to me;
Therefore, speed me in the race:
Therefore, let me grow in grace.

We are all *hearing for eternity!*

There was an official of the Ethiopian government riding in his chariot on the way home from a pilgrimage to Jerusalem, where he had worshiped. He knew *what* to hear. He was reading aloud from the scroll of Isaiah. He came to that passage,

As a sheep led to the slaughter,
or a lamb before its shearers is dumb,
So he opens not his mouth.
In his humiliation justice was denied him.
Who can describe his generation
For his life is taken from the earth. (Isa. 53:7)

He repeated it again and again. The whole context was read. It baffled him. He knew what to hear, but he did not know *how* to hear with understanding.

A lonely figure ran up. "Do you understand what you are reading aloud?" The Ethiopian official replied, "How can I; it is too mysterious. Is Isaiah speaking of himself or someone else?" That one who had suddenly appeared (Philip) was asked to join the Ethiopian, and he began from that Scripture and "preached unto him Jesus" (Acts 8:35).

Now the Ethiopian hears clearly. Now he hears obediently. "Here is water, what hinders me from being immersed?" "If you believe, you may." "I believe that Jesus is the Christ, the Son of God" (8:37, KJV). The chariot stopped; the two went down into the water; the Ethiopian officer was immersed.

This preacher had not failed, for his audience, who knew *what* to hear, now knew *how* to hear. He went on his way rejoicing. He had heard for eternity! Take heed what and how you hear!

NOTE

1. *Love's Labour's Lost*, act 5, sc. 2, line 869.

13. Found Faithful: A Daily Commitment

Brian L. Harbour

1 Cor. 4:1–2

Let me begin this morning by asking the basic questions of life: Who are you? And what is expected of you?

We are given many different answers to those questions.

Science tells us that we are simply a blob of protoplasm that exists for a brief period of time; here today and gone tomorrow.

Secular society pictures us as pleasure machines whose continuous passion must be satisfied.

Psychology likens us to a rat running through a maze. Life in this case is simply a response to outward stimuli.

Philosophy tries to give us reasons for running through that maze.

History tries to tell us how we have done as we have run through that maze.

Who are we? And what is expected of us? Somewhere on our lonely journey between two hospitals—the hospital in which we were born and the hospital in which we will die—we need to find an answer to those basic questions of life.

Brian L. Harbour is pastor of Immanuel Baptist Church in Little Rock, Arkansas. A graduate of Baylor University, from which he received a Ph.D., Harbour has also pastored Baptist churches in Texas, Mississippi, and Florida. He is the author of many books, including *Famous Couples of the Bible,* and is a frequent contributor to *The Ministers Manual* and to religious periodicals. Harbour is a previous winner of the Best Sermons competition.

Our text for today provides an answer to those questions, a simple answer that in different forms and different shapes is declared through all the pages of this book.

Who are we? Listen to what the Bible says in verse 1: "Let a man regard us in this manner, as servants of Christ, and stewards of the mysteries of God."

There are two key words here: *servants* and *stewards*.

The word for *servant* is *huperetas*, which means "under-rowers." Picture a group of men on a boat, each with an oar in his hand, and the captain of the group standing at the end of the boat, giving orders to row.

Here is the picture the word *servant* paints for us. Christ is the captain of the boat. We are the ones who have the oars. We are under-rowers, men and women working under the command of Christ, to move the boat of his kingdom forward.

The word for *steward* is *oikonomous*, which means "house servant." This is the person who managed the household under the supervision of the owner of the house. He had a great deal of power, a great deal of authority, and all of the owner's resources at this disposal. But he had to wield that power and use that authority and manage those resources under the supervision of the owner.

Here is the picture the word *steward* paints for us. Christ is the owner of the house. He puts us in charge of certain parts of the house and provides the resources we need to do our job. But we are accountable to him, and we must work under his supervision.

That's who we are as Christians: men and women to whom God has given a responsibility and to whom God has also given the resources to carry out that responsibility.

But there is this second question. What does God expect of us, his servants and stewards?

We have an answer to that question in verse 2. Listen to what Paul said: "In this case, moreover, it is required of stewards that one be found trustworthy." The Greek word here, *pistos*, is more accurately translated with our word *faithful*.

That's what God requires of us as his servants and stewards. He requires that we be faithful. What a tremendous thought!

God doesn't require that we be *successful*. Isn't that great?

We are living in a world that is enamored with success. So much have we come to worship success that when we are not on the top of the heap, when we are not number one, we convince ourselves that we are not worth anything at all.

But the Bible does not say that God requires us to be successful. He only requires that we be faithful.

God doesn't require that we be *rich*. Isn't that good?

Because of the power inherent in money we have become convinced in our day that the accumulation of money is to be life's primary venture. So much have we come to worship money that when we do not have as much money as others, we feel as if they are better than we are.

But the Bible does not say that God requires us to be rich. He only requires that we be faithful.

God doesn't require that we be *talented*. Isn't that wonderful?

How envious we become of those super-talented people who seem to be able to do everything. They can teach. They can sing. They are able to lead a group. They are quick-witted and personable. How many times do we draw back in the presence of these multitalented people and say to ourselves, "There's really not much I can do for God."

But the Bible does not say that God requires us to be talented. He only requires that we be faithful.

God doesn't require that we be *intelligent*. Isn't that encouraging?

All around us today are people who seem to be Einstein reincarnated. Mention a subject, and they know about it. Mention a problem, and they have a solution for it. These high-IQ people sometimes so intimidate us that we refuse to say anything for fear of showing our ignorance.

But the Bible does not say that God requires us to be intelligent. He only requires that we be faithful.

This verse (1 Cor. 4:2) is one of the most encouraging, uplifting, thrilling verses in all the Bible, because it reminds us that the thing God requires of us is something that all of us can do.

Not all of us are successful. Not all of us are rich. Not all of us are talented. Not all of us are intelligent. But all of us can be faithful.

"It is required of stewards that one be found faithful." What marvelous news that is!

But what does it mean to be faithful? Let me make some simple suggestions.

Being You

First of all, being faithful means being you.

In one of his stories, Jesus focused on this aspect of faithfulness. The story is found in Matthew 25. It is the well-known parable of the talents.

Jesus told of a man who was going on a journey, so he entrusted his possessions to three of his servants. To one servant he gave five talents; to another, two talents; and to another, one talent. And then he went on his journey.

When the master returned from his journey, it was time for the servants to give an accounting of their lives.

The one to whom five talents were given invested his five talents and brought back to the master five talents more, ten in all.

The one to whom two talents were given invested his two talents and brought back to the master two talents more, four in all.

The one to whom one talent was given was afraid to do anything, so he did not invest it at all. Consequently, he returned to the master only the one talent he had been given.

You remember the response of the master to the servant who did not invest his talent. The master said,

> You wicked, lazy slave, you knew that I reap where
> I did not sow, and gather where I scattered no seed.
> Then you ought to have put my money in the bank,
> and on my arrival I would have received my money
> back with interest. Therefore take away the talent
> from him, and give it to the one who has the ten
> talents . . . . And cast out the worthless slave into
> the outer darkness; in that place there shall be
> weeping and gnashing of teeth. (Matt. 25:26–28,
> 30, NASB)

Do you remember the response the master made to the other two servants?

The response to the five-talent servant who brought back ten is found in verse 21: "Well done, good and faithful slave; you were faithful with a few things, I will put you in charge of many things; enter into the joy of your master."

The response to the two-talent servant who brought back four is found in verse 23: "Well done, good and faithful slave; you were faithful with a few things, I will put you in charge of many things; enter into the joy of your master."

Did you notice something about those two messages of praise? They were identical. They were exactly the same. To the slave who brought back ten talents and to the slave who brought back four talents, Jesus gave the same words of praise. Why? Because God does not require that we be *the* best, only that we be *our* best. He only requires that we be faithful with that we have.

Faithfulness does not mean accomplishing as much as other Christians. It means accomplishing as much as you can with the talents you have been given.

Faithfulness does not mean being like other Christians. It means being true to the person God has made you to be.

Faithfulness does not mean giving as much as other Christians. It means giving what you are able to give.

Doing the job that God has gifted you to do—that's faithfulness.

Giving to God's work what you can afford to give— that's faithfulness.

Filling the places of responsibility that you are able to fill—that's faithfulness.

Faithfulness means being you.

Staying True

But there is more. Faithfulness not only means being you. It also means staying true. That is, faithfulness not only involves what you do. Faithfulness also involves what you are.

Daniel illustrated in his life this kind of faithfulness. What a man Daniel was. We don't have time to review all the details of his life. Let me simply remind you that he was one of the young men of Israel who was taken away into Babylonian captivity. Very quickly, however, he emerged from the crowd and distinguished himself as a person of unique character. So much was the limelight on Daniel that all of the other young princes in the court became jealous of him. In a desire to undermine his power, they sought to find some flaw in his character, some skeleton in his closet.

But listen to what the Bible says: "Then the commissioners and satraps began trying to find a ground of accusation against Daniel in regard to government affairs; but they could find no ground of accusation or evidence of corruption, inasmuch as he was faithful" (Dan. 6:4, NASB).

Faithfulness means that what you are on the outside is the same as what you are on the inside. Faithfulness means that the inner commitment to God is reflected in outer service for God.

I remember what an old country lady once said. She said, "Be what you is, because if you be what you ain't then you ain't what you be!"

Faithfulness means being you and staying true.

Seeing It Through

Notice this third thought. Faithfulness not only means being you and staying true. It also means seeing it through.

Faithfulness is synonymous with persistence or perseverance.

It means that you will be you at all times, that you will start out being you and that you will end being you.

It means that you will be true at all times, that you will be true when it is easy and that you will be true when it is difficult.

Faithfulness means that you will keep on serving and keep on giving and keep on loving and keep on working and keep on sharing to the very end.

Faithfulness is not just a one-time commitment. It is a daily commitment.

Clarence Jordan was a man of unusual abilities and commitment. He had two Ph.D.'s, one in agriculture and one in Greek and Hebrew. He was so gifted that he could have done just about anything he chose to do. What he chose to do was to serve the poor in Christ's name.

In the 1940s he founded a farm in Americus, Georgia, and called it Koinonia Farm. It was a community for poor whites and poor blacks where they could farm the land and live together.

There was, as you might imagine, strong resistance from the citizens of the area. They tried everything they could to stop Clarence Jordan. They boycotted him. They slashed his workers' tires when they came to town. For fourteen years, they relentlessly opposed and harassed him.

Finally in 1954, the Ku Klux Klan decided to make one more push and get rid of Clarence Jordan and his Koinonia Farm. They came in the middle of the night with guns and torches. They set fire to every building on Koinonia Farm except for Clarence's home, which they practically destroyed with bullets. They chased off all the families except one black family that refused to leave.

Clarence recognized the voice of one of the Klansmen to be that of the local newspaper reporter. The next day, the reporter came out to see what remained of the farm. The rubble still smoldered, and the land was scorched. The reporter found Clarence in the field, hoeing and planting.

The newspaper reporter said, "I heard the awful news of your tragedy last night, and I came out to do a story on the closing of your farm."

Clarence just kept on hoeing and planting. The reporter kept prodding, kept poking, trying to get a rise from this quietly determined man who seemed to be planting instead of packing.

Finally, with a haughty voice, the reporter said, "Well, Dr. Jordan, you got two of them Ph.D.'s, and you've put fourteen years into this farm, and there's nothing left of it at all. Just how successful do you think you've been?"

Clarence stopped hoeing, turned toward the reporter with his penetrating eyes, and said quietly but firmly: "Sir, I don't think you understand us Christians. What we are about is not success. What we are about is faithfulness."

That's what I want to say to you about the Church. That's what I want to say to you about the Christian life. We're not about success. We're about faithfulness. Always remember that.

14. That We May Receive Our Sight

William Hethcock

Mark 10:46–52

Everyone here at one time or another has tried to imagine what it would be like to be blind. Maybe it was when you were a child. You closed your eyes or you put on a blindfold, and you groped around the house running into things and perhaps laughing. Or maybe you were at a birthday party, and you were playing pin-the-tail-on-the-donkey. Everyone was blindfolded, and the one who pinned the tail of the donkey nearest to where the tail is supposed to be won the prize. Everyone has experimented, even if only for a few minutes at a time, with what it would be like to be blind, to have no sight at all, to live in darkness all the time.

That's not quite what we need to imagine to understand this reading this morning. The situation of blind Bartimaeus is a little different from those games we played. Bartimaeus has *never been able to see.* What happens for blind Bartimaeus is that through the work of Jesus, Bartimaeus comes to be able to see *for the very first time* in his whole life! That's entirely different from practicing blindness for a few minutes and then opening our eyes. Bartimaeus had never been able to see. There is probably no one here who has any idea what that would be like!

William Hethcock is associate professor of Homiletics at the School of Theology, University of the South, Sewanee, Tennessee. An Episcopalian, Hethcock has been rector of St. Luke's Church in Durham, N.C., director of program for the diocese of North Carolina, and director of field education for the School of Theology, University of the South.

Jesus and his disciples are traveling along, and their journey is suddenly interrupted by the shouting of blind Bartimaeus, who is sitting by the roadside. He begins to make quite a disturbance when he hears that the passing crowd is being led by this Jesus of Nazareth, about whom he has heard. "Jesus, son of David, have mercy on me!" he cries. He makes so much noise that he embarrasses his friends.

But Jesus finally hears him. And after Bartimaeus has gone out into the road where Jesus is passing, pointing his face to the sky and tapping his cane, Jesus asks him a funny sort of question. The question comes as a surprise. You would think Jesus would already know the answer. Jesus asks Bartimaeus, standing there, poor and disheveled, confusion on his face, his stick in his trembling hand: "Bartimaeus," says Jesus, "*What do you want me to do for you?*"

What a strange question! "What do you want me to do for you?" asks Jesus. We can imagine what Bartimaeus felt. "This guy must be kidding. I know my blindness is obvious to everyone. And surely no one *wants* to be blind. My life is a mess," thinks Bartimaeus, "because *I can't see the way everyone else can.* This guy Jesus must not be so smart after all.

"But I know better than to be angry or sarcastic," thinks Bartimaeus. "I'm helpless, because I can't see. I'm used to this kind of sarcasm. When you're down and out; when you have to beg in order to eat; when you get around Jericho with a white cane; when you wonder what your wife and children, your neighbors, really look like; when you've never seen a tree or the sky or the people you love; you take all the sarcasm and degradation and punishment you have to take to get what you need to live in the world."

"What do you want me to do for you?" asks Jesus. And Bartimaeus responds, "Master, let me receive my sight." Bartimaeus answers the question as if he really believes that Jesus doesn't know what he wants.

"Go your way; your faith has made you well," says Jesus. And immediately Bartimaeus receives his sight and follows Jesus on the way!

That's the end of the story. That's all Mark tells us about Bartimaeus in his Gospel. So this is where we have to do some thinking on our own. What would it be like, if we were blind and always had been, to receive our sight for the very first time? How can we imagine what happened to Bartimaeus after that?

I read an article by an eye specialist telling what it would be like to receive your sight for the very first time. You would assume there would be overwhelming joy. Wow! Look over there. Is that a tree? No kidding! And what is that thing? A house? I can scarcely believe it! And what is that? A human being. Wow. You're not what I had in mind, but you're not so bad. Seeing is fun! I'm going to like it!

No. That's not what it would be like, says the specialist. Seeing for the very first time is a very *unpleasant* experience. The first thing that happens is complete disorientation, a disorientation more severe, we are told, than losing our sight and becoming blind would be. The subject who sees for the first time suffers dizziness and falls to the ground. It's all he can do to open his eyes and look around. And do you know what happens next? The guy gets sick to his stomach. He is likely to lose his lunch. A person who suddenly receives his sight for the first time is compelled to conclude at first that seeing is not all it's cracked up to be.

And so here is Bartimaeus, struggling along with the crowd following Jesus. He can't bear to look at where he is going. Seeing is confusing for him. And he doesn't feel so well. So he makes his way along with the cane in one hand and the other hand over his eyes.

And when late afternoon comes, he realizes that he has to get on home and face his family with this new and wonderful thing that has happened. His wildest dream has come true. He can see. But Bartimaeus doesn't know *how* to *see* his way home, and his friends and helpers have abandoned him because they assume that, since Bartimaeus can see, he doesn't need them. Bartimaeus wouldn't recognize his own house, so he covers his eyes and uses his cane to get home. It's the only way he can handle this new thing, this seeing.

What do you suppose is happening a week later? Bartimaeus is into *new* problems. His family is not so willing as they used to be to wait on him, to tote and fetch, to take care of him the way they were when he was blind. And Bartimaeus used to beg for a living, but no one gives money to a sighted beggar who has had a miracle healing. "Well," say Bartimaeus's friends, "old Bart will be going to work now. He'll be getting a job, now that he can see. Or at least he had better, unless he wants to starve to death." And no one stops by to lead him to the marketplace or the highway every morning, as they once did.

Bartimaeus is now well. He can see! The world calls on him to be responsible, to take care of himself, to move out aggressively and end his dependency. "Oh, my," says formerly blind Bart. "This seeing business is not all it's cracked up to be. I thought it would be great, but now I'm not so sure. I knew how to handle things when I was blind. Now I'm not so sure of myself anymore. *How do you handle things when you can see?"*

Do you wonder why this little story is tucked into Mark's Gospel about Jesus and his disciples? It's a funny little story, sort of a *non sequitur,* as it were. Jesus and his disciples are on their way to Jerusalem, where all hell is going to break loose for Jesus. He is going to get into big trouble with the authorities. He's going to be arrested, given a mock trial, beaten, and brought to a humiliating and torturous execution.

And suddenly here is this little story about a blind man who receives his sight. "What do you want me to do for you?" asks Jesus. And Bartimaeus says, "Master, let me receive my sight." And so Jesus does it. Jesus heals Bart, and Bart discovers that this seeing is not all it's cracked up to be. Weird!

Do you know what Mark is really telling us in this story? Mark, who is writing this story about Jesus and Bartimaeus, is telling you and me something important about ourselves. The important truth from the Lord Jesus to you and to me by way of Mark is that *you and I are blind.* That's it. In the Lord Jesus' terms, you and I can't see for sour apples. We're blind and that's the truth.

Are you surprised? Don't be. Blind is probably the way we want ourselves to be. You know, being blind isn't so bad, because when you are *blind* you don't have to *see* things as they are.

There is a civil war in the Sudan, East Africa, and it has religious overtones, Christians versus fundamentalist Muslims. The primary *weapon* in the war is *food.* Those who have food will defeat those who do not. A reporter tells of encountering a young boy whose arms are the size his fingers should be. He is starving. The boy endeavored to stand to speak to the reporter, and he could not because of his weakness. Millions are in a similar state. They will die, because those *with* the food will win the war by starving their foes to death. When we are healed of our blindness, we see things like that.

Hurricane Joan has ripped through Central America with winds of up to 125 miles per hour. Mudslides have engulfed wooden huts, people have died in their homes, and tens of thousands of homes have been destroyed. Whole villages in Nicaragua have been destroyed. The death toll has yet to be calculated. The pain of the disaster and the rebuilding will continue years after we finish reading about it here. When we are healed of our blindness, things like that can't be easily dismissed. When our blindness is healed, we see things we don't want to see.

An elderly woman appeared on television recently, bewildered, lonely, frightened. She lives in fear of leaving her tiny apartment in one of our major cities. It isn't because she has no money, not really. She is afraid of the gangs of violent people who will do her harm when she walks on the city streets to visit her friends and to buy her groceries. She is a prisoner in her own home. When we are healed of our blindness, we will see things like that.

And here in this quiet and lovely community, where everyone seems so happy, is a beautiful school with a bright student body and a talented and informed faculty. Men and women who come here are proud and happy, and they learn and excel. Our community is lovely, but in spite of that loveliness we enjoy, there is much here that makes life painful and difficult for some. There is unhappiness here, deep and agonizing unhappiness, and it is possible that that unhappiness is right behind the faces of our very good friends. Disappointment and hopelessness are not far from us even in this wonderful place. There is pain and unhappiness and confusion right here in this beautiful chapel where we worship this morning. When we are healed of our blindness, we will see things like that, even though we don't want to see them. *And those things will interfere with the peacefulness of our former sightlessness.*

Jesus is asking us, "What do you want me to do for you?" It's *not* such a strange question after all. But it is tough to answer. We don't want to be disoriented and dizzy. We don't want to fall to the ground and become ill. We don't want to see the world as it is. Our answer is, "Nothing, thanks, Lord. Everything is OK the way it is. We don't see so well sometimes, but, as you know, Lord, your world isn't perfect." Well, that's one answer.

But the question does not come only once. Jesus is asking us, "What do you want me to do for you?" All right. We hear you, Lord. OK, Lord. We'll go for the other answer. *Master, let us receive our sight.* We think we're not going to like it. We only know how to handle things when we are blind. We know that seeing is not all it's cracked up to be. But in spite of that, let us receive our sight. After all, we have to have our sight, Lord, for it is only with seeing, really *seeing,* that we may be your people in the world and make the difference here you want us to make!

15. Keep the Faith—Anyhow!
Frank Pollard

2 Tim. 4:7–18

Are you disillusioned with church? or disappointed? or disgusted? Do you see flaws in the Church of our Lord Christ? Have you been jolted by the startling news that Christian leaders, some of the most visible ones, those who preach the most, actually practice the least? In our nation, "born again" has become a comedian's funniest line. Our Lord's Church and its servants are caricatured on comic pages and in the editorial sheets. There may be more than a few church members who are dropping out because Christianity is losing its social respectability. It may be embarrassing to some to be called Christians.

I once met a young lady who worked as a receptionist. She was a beautiful person: caring, friendly, warm, witty, real. But she didn't consider herself to be an attractive person. On the inside of the closet door just beyond her desk was a small mirror. Occasionally she would feel it necessary to use that mirror to check makeup or the arrangement of her hair. On top of the mirror was taped a one-line message of encouragement: "Praise the Lord anyhow!"

Do you have what it takes to look at the reflection of who we are as God's representatives—not just our flaws individually but collectively—and say, "Lord, I'm still here. I will keep the faith anyhow."

Frank Pollard is pastor of First Baptist Church in Jackson, Mississippi. A Southern Baptist and former president of Golden Gate Baptist Theological Seminary, Pollard has hosted the television program "At Home With the Bible." In 1979, *Time* magazine named him one of the "seven most outstanding Protestant preachers in America." He is the author of several books, including *How to Know When You're a Success* and *Keeping Free.* Pollard is a previous winner in the Best Sermons competition.

Our pattern for how to do this with open honesty and integrity comes from a section of Holy Writ penned by a servant of Jesus Christ who is writing his last letter. He has been tried and imprisoned for preaching the gospel. He knows he is soon to die. In every other letter he talks of journeys he plans to make, things he plans to do, but not in this one. Here he says,

> The time has come for my departure. I have fought the good fight, I have finished the race, I have kept the faith. Now there is in store for me the crown of righteousness, which the Lord, the righteous Judge will award me on that day; and not only to me, but to all who have longed for his appearing. (2 Tim. 4:6–8, NIV)

"I have kept the faith," he says. In the lines that follow, he notes the despairing failure of his coworkers. One has left the faith, loving the world more than the Lord. Another brother has done him great personal harm. All the church of Rome has neglected, "deserted" him, he says, in his hour of need. And he writes to a friend, a coworker, a partner of two missionary journeys, a son in the faith for some fifteen years. His name is Timothy. Let's read about it in 2 Tim. 4:9ff, (NIV):

> Do your best to come to me quickly. For Demas, because he loved this world, has deserted me and has gone to Galatia and Titus to Dalmatia. Only Luke is with me. Get Mark and bring him with you because he is helpful to me in my ministry. I have sent Tychicus to Ephesus. When you come bring the cloak that I left with Carpus at Troas, and my scrolls, especially the parchments. Alexander the metalworker did me a great deal of harm. The Lord will repay him for what he has done. You too should be on your guard against him because he strongly opposed our message. At my first defense no one came to my support, but everyone deserted me. May it not be held against them. But the Lord stood at my side and gave me strength so that through me the message might be fully proclaimed and all the Gentiles might hear it. And I was delivered from the lion's mouth. The Lord will rescue me from every

evil attack, and will bring me safely to His heavenly
kingdom; to Him be glory forever and ever. Amen.

He is imprisoned in the cold, damp dungeon with winter coming on and no cloak to keep him warm, no reading material to satisfy his large need for intellectual stimulus, openly offended and hurt
by the actions of two fellow workers, neglected by the local church.
Yet he can say, "I have kept the faith." There are large lessons here
for you and me.

First, *we can keep the faith in spite of life's disappointments.*

Disappointing things had happened to him. Paul did not finish
his ministry as a big-shot preacher with a TV network and millions
of admirers. In his last days, we see him huddled in the cold of yet
another dungeon, another prison cave. There had been several of
those in his experience. In Acts 16, we read of how he and Silas
were beaten, locked in stocks in the dungeon of a prison in Philippi.
They could have reacted in several ways, but they kept the faith.
They sang songs and praised God at midnight, and God used them
to turn a raw deal into a revival.

Because he spoke of Christ, he had felt the sting of whips, the
brutal impact of stones. His body was covered with scars. He had
come to be proud of those scars; he wore them like medals of honor.
He called his scars the marks of the Lord Jesus Christ. He kept the
faith.

Not only did he suffer the disappointments of events but maybe
the hardest thing of all—the disappointment of people. Friends
turned foe, turned their backs, walked away, did him harm.

"Demas," he says, "has deserted me because he loves this
world." Two times in other scriptures Paul sends greetings from
Demas, once calling him a fellow worker. But now this one who has
stood by his side, one thought to be faithful, has turned his back and
walked away.

Alexander is mentioned in 1 Tim. 1:20 as one who is a member
of the Church but a blasphemer. Here he is identified as having
done Paul a great deal of harm.

In verse 16, Paul tells Timothy that the whole group of Christians in Rome has deserted him. Paul had written the Roman
church. Remember the Letter to the Romans? He shared with them
the love and convictions of his life. In Romans 16, he had written a
whole page of personal greetings to them, naming almost thirty

people individually and telling them to greet their families. These were his friends in that Roman church. Yet when he is brought to Rome for the second time, on trial for sharing the same thing they believed, he didn't hear from any of them. "Everyone has deserted me," he says.

Would you notice how he handles those personal disappointments? He does not do anything to get even. About Alexander who had hurt him badly, he says, "The Lord will repay him." But he warns Timothy to watch out for him. About the church that neglected him, he prays, "May it not be held against them." He is practicing what he had preached.

To the same church in Rome he had written in chapter 12, verses 17–19, (NIV):

> Do not repay anyone evil for evil. Be careful to do
> what is right in the eyes of everybody. If it is
> possible, as far as it depends on you, live at peace
> with everyone. Do not take revenge, my friend, but
> leave room for God's wrath, for it is written, "It is
> mine to avenge. I will repay," says the Lord.

Well, you can keep the faith in spite of disappointments. And *you can keep the faith in the fellowship of those who did not disappoint you.*

"Luke is with me." Ah, Luke, what a man! He was a physician, the first medical missionary. Luke, like Paul, was an intellectual giant. He wrote both the Gospel of Luke and the Book of Acts. His writings show him to be a highly educated and intellectually sophisticated man.

In this day when media seem to caricature Christians as those whose elevators don't go all the way to the top, we need to remember who is really with us. "Luke is with me," says Paul.

A recent edition of *The Baptist Record* told of four Mississippi Baptists being appointed to foreign missions. One of those was Dr. Earl Hewitt, a modern-day Dr. Luke. Dr. Luke was the first medical missionary. Dr. Earl Hewitt may be the latest one to be appointed. This young man, from our church, has been pursuing medical training for many years because he felt God's call to medical missions. I am thankful that, along with the rest of us, God often calls the brightest and the best to his service. This young doctor will be paid less than your mail carrier and receive more reward than a corporate chief executive officer.

It is time to remember that among the Christian ranks are some of the world's most brilliant. C. S. Lewis became a Christian in his adulthood, as did T. S. Eliot and Malcolm Muggeridge. The late Dag Hammarskjöld, former secretary-general of the United Nations, was a committed Christian. In his diary one New Year's Day, he recorded this prayer: "For all that has been, thanks; for all that will be, yes."

Some of the brightest intellectuals of history have lived in the confidence of the sovereignty of God. "For all that has been, thanks; for all that will be, yes."

"Luke is with me," and there is Timothy. "Timothy, I need you," says Paul. "Come to me quickly. Pick up Mark and bring him. Go by Troas and get the cloak I left there." It's comforting to know that Paul left his overcoat somewhere also. "And bring my books, especially the parchments." In verse 21, he says, "Do your best to get here before winter."

Paul probably didn't last through that winter. But I'm almost certain, aren't you, that before winter hit Rome, Timothy and Mark and the overcoat and the reading material were with him in that dungeon? You can keep the faith in fellowship with those who do not disappoint you.

Here's the ultimate truth, the third thing in this passage. *You can keep the faith because of Christ.* Verse 17: "But the Lord stood by my side and gave me strength." "He took his stand by my side. He *strengthened* me." The word *strengthened* literally means "he poured power into me."

Tell me, where is your power? In whom or what do you believe and trust in your quest to keep the faith?

Is your trust in yourself? That's not enough. "Too many fall from grace and good for us to doubt the likelihood." I think most of us know that.

Is your trust in someone, maybe a leader in the church? That, my friend, is dangerous and ill-placed faith. Don't hang all your hopes on that peg. It may come loose. Someone said there is so much good in the worst of us and so much bad in the best of us that it hardly behooves any of us to talk about the rest of us.

Put your trust, all of it, in the Lord. Paul told the Philippian Christians, "I can do all things. I can face anything I have to face because it is Christ who strengthens me." He stands by our side and pours power into us.

I come to our worship center often, when no one else is here, and sit in one of those chairs where you sit. I think what it must be like to be a member of this church. I think about the people you see around you, the people you know who are a part of this fellowship. There are some disappointing people. We have those. There are some Demases, those who embarrass the church and destroy the faith of others because they love this world and its ways.

There may be an Alexander or so. You know, Alexander was so sure that what he thought was right and what Paul preached was wrong he became destructive and mean. I really don't know any of those here.

You may be thinking, "If all these people knew the burden I'm bearing, the hurt I feel, they would minister to me." And I think you're right. If all of us knew how many hurts are in the lives of people around us, we would act much differently toward one another. But maybe it's because they don't know, not that they don't care.

You may see Demases and uncaring Christians. You may even see an Alexander in our fellowship, but, please, would you also notice the *Lukes?* They're here. And the *Marks.* Remember, Mark let Paul down once; he quit on a missionary journey. But he came back, and Paul wanted him at his side during his last days. *Timothy* was apparently not a strong, assertive, forceful, and visible leader—like Paul. But he was totally dependable, was always there, always willing to help. There are a lot of Timothys here. Please see them, too.

But most of all, would you see our blessed Lord? He wants to be your Savior, your brother, your friend. He will never let you down. He will never leave you or desert you. He will always be there standing by your side. He will always be there pouring power into you. In this service, we've tried to point you to him. We've sung "Glorious Is Thy Name, O Lord," "Blessed Saviour We Adore Thee," "Jesus, Name Above All Names."

In just a moment you'll be reminded in a song that it is not we who are calling you, it is he. "Softly and Tenderly Jesus Is Calling."

III. DOCTRINAL/ THEOLOGICAL

16. The Churchless Kingdom of God

David G. Buttrick

I saw a new heaven and a new earth, for the first heaven and the first earth were gone away. . . . And I saw the holy city, New Jerusalem, coming down out of heaven from God, prepared like a bride decked out for her husband. And I heard a great voice from the throne, saying, "Look, the dwelling of God is with people. God will dwell with them, and they with God. . . ."

And the one on the throne said, "Look, I make all things new! . . . I am Alpha and Omega, the beginning and the end. . . ."

I looked and saw no religious buildings in the city, for the [only] temple is the Lord God Almighty, and the Lamb. . . .

And God's servants shall serve, and they will see God's face, and God's name will be on their foreheads. There will be no night there anymore . . . or light of the sun, for the Lord God will shine on them, and they will reign for ever and ever. . . .

Amen, Come Lord Jesus!

——Revelation 21–22 (selections)

There was a wonderful exhibition a few years ago—"An American Village." In it were little houses, stores, farmyards, even little people, all reproduced to scale. What made the exhibit exciting was that the village moved through time: There was the village in pioneer days, then the same village at the time of the Civil War, and finally the village in the twentieth century. Though the village didn't grow much, there was one noticeable difference: churches! In pioneer days, there was one little log church, but by the twentieth century there were

David G. Buttrick is an ordained Presbyterian minister currently serving as professor of Homiletics and Liturgics at the Divinity School at Vanderbilt University in Nashville, Tennessee. His extensive writings include the text *Homiletics* and *Preaching Jesus Christ.*

rival steeples sticking up everywhere. Well, multiply the model village a quarter of a million times and you can begin to see the American scene. There may be one God and one faith and one Lord Jesus Christ, but the people of God are subdivided!

I

So let's take a look at America today. *What's going on with the churches?* What is the mood of the American churches in 1989? Will the single word *survival* do for starters? Nowadays most churches are into survival. In a troubled, changing, frightening world we seem to be trying to hold onto ourselves. Maybe it's the membership rolls that keep on shrinking in mainline churches; American Christianity is dropping off at an alarming rate. Or maybe it's that we sense down deep the world of the future is going to be different; American power is on the wane while once sleepy continents are stretching awake. Whatever the reason, American churches are into self-preservation. There was a famous abbé in Europe. They asked him what he did during the French Revolution. He shuddered. "Survived," he said. "I survived." Well, in the past decade, our churches seem to have been pushed into a corner, trying to survive. So Southern Baptists are rapidly backing into the past, clutching their inerrant Bible. And Presbyterians are talking endlessly about "the Reformed tradition," though no one seems to know what that is! Methodists are pasting "Catch the Spirit" bumper stickers on their cars. And Catholics, Catholics are drawing themselves up and repeating that wonderful Catholic phrase, "But the Church has always and everywhere taught . . . " We are desperately trying to preserve who we are and what we've got: These days, survival is the name of the game.

Meanwhile, *meanwhile, the gospel suffers.* The good news of God is trapped in competitive Christianity. Yes, we know we are supposed to reach out with the gospel. And surely we are meant to spread Christ's love throughout the earth. But, there are too many steeples to keep painted. Too many church lawns to be mowed. We spend ourselves in maintenance! Let's take a case in point. A few years ago there was a town in West Virginia—a little more than five thousand people. Yet they had twenty-seven churches there lined up in a row. So when the Presbyterian church bought a new mimeograph, every church wanted a new mimeograph. And when the Methodists picked up an opaque projector for their education program—a kind of opaque projector lust spread through the community. But, that same year, you could take a plane to New York City and drop in on a tiny church down near the Brooklyn Bridge. In four city blocks near the church there were ninety thousand unchurched people living in housing projects. Yet a denomination closed down the tiny church because it didn't seem to be self-supporting. Why? Because we had to keep twenty-seven churches competing for the American soul somewhere in West Virginia! Free enterprise may be a swell idea when you're selling hamburgers—fast-food stores cluster—but when it comes to serving Jesus Christ, ecclesial free-enterprise simply scuttles the gospel. So we cling to our separate steeples, and the work of God suffers.

Now mark this: *We don't seem to be able to change.* We can't seem to break out of the pattern, can we? Somehow we are locked into denominational loyalties. Maybe it's because we have to belong. Or maybe, deeper still, our own identities are at stake. Look, we know it's wrong. Did not Jesus Christ throw back his head on the night before the cross and pray that all his disciples be one? And old St. Paul, remember how he insisted that there is neither slave nor free, Jew nor Gentile—Methodist nor Baptist nor Presbyterian—male nor female, for we are all one in Christ? And, yet, we aren't. There are buildings involved and cash down and jobs at stake (every denomination has a power structure) and —well, what can you do? Some years ago a statue was on display in a Pittsburgh art gallery. It was a Crucifixion: Jesus Christ stretched on the cross. The only trouble was that he was disconnected; his arms didn't join his shoulders or his head on his neck, and his legs were not hooked onto his torso. Jesus Christ was broken into pieces. The title of the sculpture? "Denominationalism"! Can the dividing up of Jesus Christ be anything but sin? No. Yet, we seem to be helpless. Somehow we can't seem to let go of ourselves.

II

Now turn around and *take a long look into the future of God.* Take a look at what God will bring to earth. "And I, John, saw the Holy City, new Jerusalem, descending from God. . . . And I heard a great voice from heaven crying, 'The dwelling of God is with people.' " The Bible may begin with the chaos of Creation, but it ends with a vision of God's new order, a city of God reconciled. God who has created all things is working through time and space, generation on generation, to bring about unity. Some day all God's children will be gathered together in peace. Someday! And someday all the labels—Lutheran and African Methodist and Churches of God—will be utterly forgotten. If anyone shows up in the kingdom with a label, the air will be filled with unseen laughter like the tingling of a billion bells. God's people shall be one. And "God's servants shall serve, and they shall see God's face, and they shall reign for ever and ever." At the end of the Broadway show *West Side Story*, the divided street gang kids stand in a blasted city street and sing, "Somewhere there'll be a place for us—someday, somewhere, somehow." That same song fills the last chapters of the Bible with glory. Someday, somehow God will gather the whole wide world into unity. God's Word is as good as gold; as gold as golden streets and bright pearl gates. "I saw the Holy City, new Jerusalem descending from God."

But guess what? Take a second look at the vision. *There will be no more churches in God's kingdom, not a one.* "I saw no temple in the city for the temple is the Lord God Almighty and the Lamb." Think of it: no steeples, no pulpits, no preachers, no folding chairs in fellowship halls, no straight-backed Bible study circles. The dream gets better all the time, doesn't it? Oh, we still build churches as thick as bank buildings as if we had forever, but in God's good purpose, we're headed for a phaseout. For listen, who will need churches when everyone will know the Lord? The church is not an ultimate. The Church is not the end of God's purpose, only a beginning. Who was it who suggested that church buildings ought to be as insubstantial as folding tents? Why? Because the Church is meant to move around the human world telling God's story until, in God's purpose, everyone does know the Lord and the whole wide earth is filled with praise of the Lamb. So, in God's future, guess what, there will be no more churches at all.

III

So, time to ask a question. *How will church unity happen?* What will it take to draw us together? Answer: Jesus Christ. We must be willing to follow Jesus Christ, yes, to the cross. For our first loyalty is not to John Wesley or Martin Luther, Roger Williams or John Calvin— not even to St. Peter. And certainly our loyalty is not to creeds (they must be continually rewritten) or to hymns or steeples. They are not our lords or saviors. Our only loyalty is to Jesus Christ, who died so that something new might happen in the world. We are called to follow him all the way to the cross, willing to die as denominations for God's future. For in God's strange ways, new life can only come by death and resurrection. There's a great story about the artist Rodin, who one day saw a huge, carved crucifix beside a road. He arranged to have the crucifix carted back to his house. But, unfortunately, it was too big for the building. So, of all things, he knocked out the walls, raised the roof, and rebuilt his home around the cross. The calling of the American church! How can we let go of ourselves and, renewed by Jesus Christ, rebuild ourselves into the larger Church, the one Church that dares follow Jesus Christ? Bluntly, we must be willing to die as denominations so that a new, freer, braver, united Christian word may be spoken

Look, we need not be frightened. After all, we celebrate God's future in most churches on a regular basis. In the midst of our brokenness, at table, we form a living sign of the kingdom. By being here we are saying that we will live beyond ourselves, beyond our separate labels. For all we are pledged to follow Jesus Christ until the day when God will be all in all and every steeple falls. Down in Arizona there's a little slum church that meets in a discarded school building around a borrowed kitchen table. Every week folks crowd together—black and Indian and Chicano and Anglo. If you're there in the circle, you've got someone's baby in one arm, and you're steadying an old man on a cane with your other arm, and you join in the singing. For every week the people sing, "My eyes have seen the glory of the coming of the Lord, who is bringing in the kingdom according to God's word." So here we are in the present tense, but in breaking bread together we are forming a sign of God's future perfect when the work of the Church will be done and, listen, all will be one.

You wonder how church unity survives, particularly nowadays when denominations are digging in. Do you know the secret? Because church unity is clearly a part of God's future, that's why. And you who are here, you must be brave enough to sit loose in your traditions, not holding onto yourselves too much. For in Spirit you know we are meant to be one—one in faith, with one Lord, under one holy God. Amen.

17. Resurrection Life Now and Hereafter
Ernest Nicholson

1 Kings17:17–24; John 11:17–27, 38–44

Martha said to Jesus, "Lord, if you had been here my brother would not have died. Even now I know that whatever you ask of God, God will grant you." Jesus said, "I am the resurrection and I am the life."

The story of the raising of Lazarus from the dead is unique to St. John's Gospel. Mary and Martha, his sisters, are mentioned in Luke but not their brother or the story of the miracle of which he was the beneficiary. All that we know about him is told us by John, and he supplies us with only the barest information. We know nothing of Lazarus before his sickness and death, and after his restoration to life we are told only that some Jews sought to kill him and that people came from the region round about to see this man who had been raised from the dead. And that's all; and it was evidently all that St. John needed for his purpose. This minimal amount of information he records about Lazarus already makes it clear that he was not concerned merely with recording a certain incident in the life of Jesus and of this individual Lazarus and his family. It is more to the point to understand what the Evangelist has written as *proclamation* rather than the mere recording of biographical reminiscences.

Natural curiosity throughout the ages has wished that he had said more about Lazarus's experiences during those few days when

Ernest Nicholson is Oriel Professor of the Interpretation of Holy Scripture at Oxford University. Among his authored works is the recent book *God and His People: Covenant and Theology in the Old Testament.*

he was dead: What was it like to die? What did he feel or see or hear? Was he able to know anything about his loved ones who remained alive on earth? Or did he get a glimpse of loved ones who had already died, perhaps his mother and father or other old friends? Did he understand things more clearly and more quickly, that is, does being in the afterlife improve intellectual capacity? Did he get a glimpse of heaven or, indeed, of hell? The fascination with Lazarus as one who had been dead and buried, then restored to life again, was such that medieval theologians used him as a mouthpiece for presenting their ideas about life beyond death. And the curiosity about his experiences as one who traversed death's portals and returned has continued into more modern times. The poet Tennyson, for example, in a few well-known stanzas in his poem *In Memoriam,* asks why it is that the Evangelist has not told us of Lazarus's experiences during the days of his death and entombment:

> Where wert thou, brother, those four days?
> There lives no record of reply,
> Which telling what it is to die
> Had surely added praise to praise.

> From every house the neighbours met,
> The streets were filled with joyful sound,
> A solemn gladness even crowned
> The purple brows of Olivet.

> Behold the man raised up by Christ!
> The rest remaineth unrevealed;
> He told it not, or something sealed
> The lips of that Evangelist.

Legend has tried to fill out what St. John left unsaid. One such legend, for example, records that some hostile Jews put him and his sisters and some other disciples to sea in a leaking boat, which miraculously did not sink, however, but carried them as far as Marseilles in France, where Lazarus became a bishop. According to another story Lazarus was thirty years old when he died and lived a further thirty years after his restoration to life by Jesus.

But such preoccupation with the historical Lazarus and the curiosity about his experiences during the days of death, as well as the speculation about what became of him after his restoration to life by

Jesus, have had the effect of drawing attention away from the deeper dimensions of what St. John seeks to say, or rather proclaim, in this narrative. And the same is true of all those "rationalistic" explanations so characteristic of the new spirit of skepticism of the nineteenth century of what really happened on this occasion described by St. John. One such explanation, for example, claimed that Lazarus was not, in fact, dead but merely in a trance or coma, so that when Jesus came to the tomb, Lazarus was, by a happy coincidence, just reviving. Jesus was thus able simply to summon him, "Lazarus, come forth." Another and even more fantastic explanation was that the entire episode was an intrigue, a ruse plotted and carried out by some disciples at Bethany who arranged for Lazarus to pretend to be dead so that Jesus could be seen by his enemies to have the power to raise a dead person. Jesus, we are expected to believe, willingly took part in the deception. Once again, it's not just that such ideas are far-fetched and unworthy; they entirely miss the point of what the Evangelist is here concerned with. Their mere curiosity with the surface level of what is narrated has blinded them to the deeper dimension of the meaning and significance of this story. So let us see what this is.

The story falls at a strategic place in the Gospel. It is the final and most notable of the miracles or, to use St. John's own description of them, "signs" wrought by Jesus, beginning, you recall, with the sign at Cana of Galilee where Jesus turned water into wine at the wedding feast. And it comes immediately before St. John's lengthy preparation for and lead-up to our Lord's Passion and Resurrection. But what it most striking, if you know St. John's Gospel, is that what is narrated at this stage about Lazarus's death and restoration to life is clearly intended to be read and understood in the light of Jesus' own Resurrection. Already a hint in this direction is given by the details so carefully supplied by the Evangelist of Lazarus's grave clothes, including the "napkin" or "cloth" wrapped round his face. For why bother drawing attention to such details unless it is that they remind us of what is later described in John 20:6–7 about the Risen Lord's grave clothes? It seems that the raising of Lazarus from the dead here narrated is a sort of "dress rehearsal" for Jesus' own Resurrection. (Incidentally, this explains those paintings depicting the Risen Lord with a small inset of Lazarus.)

But what makes it abundantly clear that this raising of Lazarus is to be seen in the light of the Resurrection of Jesus is, of course, what

Jesus here declares to Martha: "I am the resurrection and I am the life." It is after this saying that Lazarus is raised, and we miss entirely the point of the story if we do not understand this raising in the light of what Jesus declares in this great saying. This raising is no mere restoration to mortal life, though it includes this; it is not at all like the resuscitation of the boy by Elijah in the Old Testament reading we heard this morning. This raising of Lazarus is nothing less than a raising to eternal life so that in this way Lazarus becomes the prototype, so to speak, of all those who are in fellowship with Christ and as such have entered into a new life, eternal life, now already during their mortal life. What Jesus declares is in response to Martha's words, "Lord, if you had been here my brother would not have died." This Jesus is one who can raise the dead to life. But "life" here, though it includes this physical life, Lazarus's present mortal existence, is to be understood as qualitatively much greater: "Whoever believes in me, though they die, yet shall they live, and whoever lives and believes in me shall never die."

Resurrection, therefore, means not only the resurrection "at the last day," as Martha said of her brother, but the resurrection life that begins here and now and is fulfilled after death. And this is what St. John is proclaiming here, just as he already has done earlier in the Gospel, for example, in the saying, "Truly I say to you. Whoever hears my word and believes him who sent me, has eternal life, and does not come to judgment, but has passed out of death into life" (5:24). This is the theme that is so central to St. John and in it one comes to the heart of the gospel he proclaims. Those who receive Christ and are incorporated into him have been "raised" to life with him, and this new life renders our mortal life qualitatively different and transcends our mortal death.

That our life in Christ, now begun, is fulfilled beyond our death— that is our faith and hope, not only the message of Eastertide but the Christian's perennial joy. There's something of a reluctance today to talk much about life beyond the span of our earthly existence. There are various reasons, I think, for this. There is perhaps an understandable reaction against that "pie in the sky when you die" tradition, especially against that unworthy and cruel employment of this teaching in the Church's history when men and women were expected to live out lives of abject misery during this present life and were offered only the distant comfort and consolation of a better life in the "next world." Thus was human life, and the conditions in which it should be lived by all, cheapened and degraded. We think, for example, of the slaves whose life here was such a misery, so filled with a sense of worthlessness that they could only yearn in those moving Negro spirituals for a true life beyond death, "across Jordan" where they would be released from their inhuman bondage and degradation. There is also, of course, that view, perhaps more prominent today than in the past, that this life is all we have and that when we make our final exit, that's it. Such a view is not without a sort of stoic virtue, and it has rightly been pointed out that it is not necessarily an irreligious view. The mother of the boy in our Old Testament reading this morning had only such a belief, or at least little better. And such a view has the virtue of focusing, our attention and our energies upon our life here and now as something of sacred value in and for itself and to be lived to the full. Such a belief can also have the desirable ethical effect of reminding us of the dignity of human life, of human rights of which our world today is in as great a need as ever.

But though it is not without virtue, such a belief falls far short of Christian conviction, not only in a strictly religious or theological sense, but in the sense of the infinite value we place upon humanity, the deep mystery we find in life, and the element of transcendence we sense in our being. It surely never is the case that anyone can say, "My life is complete, full, perfected." We, each one of us, sense that incompleteness and, indeed, incompletability of our lives. There's always room for regret, always room for improvement, no matter how well we may have lived or think we have lived. There is that awareness, which increases with the passing of our years, that we are always just beginning, just *now* learning for the first time, just *now* unlearning mistakes, just *now* being led to see things differently, making a fresh start just *now*.

We know of continuities through our life from our earliest childhood recollections, and we form a sort of picture of ourselves. We give ourselves an identity like a still picture or photograph. We get ourselves into a sort of mold. And yet, in spite of all this, in spite of this sense of being the same individual as we were in years gone by, we know that we are, in fact, different people today from what we were yesterday and that we shall be different again in the future. There seems to be a continuous unfolding of our being and of those whom we know and love. Yet always there remains something of a continuing mystery about our being. But what strikes us most is that we sense that all that really matters in life remains steadily deficient in us. At a level familiar to us all, think of those most intimate relationships between husband and wife, parent and child, or the deep friendship we have with one another. William Cowper wrote of these seventy years or so as being insufficient time for such relationships to come to full fruition and so ended a letter to a friend with these words:

> For you must know that I should not love you half so well, if I did not believe that you would be my friend to eternity. There is not room enough for friendship to unfold itself in full flower in such a nook of a life as this. Therefore I am, and must and will be, yours forever

But more especially, think of our relationship with God. We cannot possibly think that this is ever full, complete, satisfying. We perceive in this "nook of a life" only the outskirts of the vision of God. We see through a glass darkly. We have only the hope of transformation and of full fellowship with God, begun now but to be completed in the fullness of God's time. And it has been said that if these fleeting years of our mortal life are all we have, then such glimpses of the glory of God and of his perfect love that we may attain now would be like a springtime without a summer to follow.

Into what would otherwise be despair—not a despair motivated by a gut fear of death and oblivion, as though anyone has anything to fear of that, or by a childish desire for "pie in the sky when we die," but a despair about that incompletableness of all that is true and good and lovely and loving in our lives—into what would otherwise be this deepest of all despairs are addressed those words: "I am the resurrection and I am the life. Whoever believes in me, though they die, yet shall they live, and whoever lives and believes in me shall never die." It comes, of course, not only as a hope and assurance but also as a summons, a call to fellowship with Christ here and now, to the life of those who *are* risen with Christ. There is nothing complacent about this, no resigned acceptance of life as mere fate, but a summons to enter into life in the joy of Christ's Resurrection and so into the new, the eternal life he imparts now and which he will bring to fulfillment in us in the fullness of time.

"Do you believe this?" Jesus asked Martha, as he still asks us today. "Do you believe this?" She answered bravely that she did. Yet her understanding of it all was no doubt rather fumbling and stumbling, not at all fully grasped and understood, a sort of twilight faith at best. And so at best is ours, yours and mine. Yet what an incalculable difference it makes to hold this faith, however rudimentarily—to place our trust in God's strange love for us and the salvation he has wrought for us in Christ and to hold the faith that in him our hopes are not just dreams or wishful thinking but rather audacious prophecies of what one day will really be—that transformation of ourselves into his divine likeness, who is the resurrection and the life.

And so, blessed be the God and Father of our Lord Jesus Christ, who according to his abundant mercy has begotten us again unto a living hope by the Resurrection of Jesus Christ from the dead, to an inheritance incorruptible and undefiled, and that fadeth not away, reserved in heaven for all who believe in him; to whom with thee, O Father, in the unity of the Holy Spirit, be given all honor and glory, dominion and power, now and forever.

O God, who through the mighty Resurrection of thy Son Jesus Christ hast delivered us from the power of darkness and brought us into the kingdom of thy love: Grant that as he was raised from the dead by the glory of the Father, so we also may walk in newness of life and seek those things that are above, where with thee, O Father, and the Holy Spirit, he lives and reigns forever. Amen.

18. Disbelief for Joy
Penelope Duckworth

Luke 24:36b–48

Come Holy Spirit. Come as the wind and cleanse us. Come as the fire and purify us. Convict, convert, consecrate us that we may know the joy of resurrection. Amen.

When asked if he believed in an afterlife, Woody Allen replied, "Yes, but I'm afraid no one will tell me where it's being held." All of us wonder just what will happen to us when we die. What has happened to our loved ones who have already died? Like Woody Allen, we have a vague fear of being left without all the necessary information.

Several years ago, when I was a parish priest, the retired former rector of the parish, who had remained in the church and worshiped there for many years, died. Shortly after he died, I had a dream in which he visited me. He had a book with him, and he gave me the book and asked me to take it to his wife, Helen, and tell her that everything would be all right. I awakened and decided that I would call on his widow. I did, and I told Helen of my dream. Of course, I did not have the actual book to give her, but I did have the comforting words, and I did feel that I had been honored to be commissioned with such a message. Helen was deeply moved and thankful that I had come. I felt that we shared a special intimacy in the years that followed, and this last Good Friday at about noon, Helen died. I know that she, too, is all right. I did not know the title of the

Penelope Duckworth is Episcopal chaplain at Stanford University. A graduate of the University of California at Berkeley, Duckworth was awarded her master of divinity degree from the Church Divinity School of the Pacific. Her poetry has been published in several periodicals, and she has won an award for her poetry from the Montalvo Center for the Arts.

book I was given in the dream, but I suspect it was the Bible, which tells us of the good news of Christ overcoming death.

Just what it our Christian understanding of death? A common response to the question of what happens when we die is an assured belief in the immortality of the soul. Such a belief is comforting and seems to be validated by modern out-of-the-body accounts of those who have had near-death experiences. However, this is not our Christian understanding. It is actually a Greek philosophical idea that found its way into our culture and our churches and so has remained. This idea holds that when the body dies, the soul is at last released and goes on to eternal life. Our Christian faith teaches us, from Genesis, that body and soul are one. The Spirit of God breathes into a body, and that body becomes a living soul.

If we assume that when the body dies, the soul does not, as the ancient Greeks believed, the body is viewed as a prison house, excess baggage, something even gross and embarrassing. We see the effects of the separation of body and soul in many aspects of contemporary culture. The body is seen as imperfect baggage holding back the perfect soul. Consequences—from face-lifts and body tucks to surgical sculpting—result from an attempt to curb the body and make it conform to the ideal of the soul. The Swiss scholar Oscar Cullman contrasted the death of Socrates with the death of Jesus. In the *Phaedo,* Plato described the serene death of Socrates, willingly drinking the hemlock, as if he simply shed his outer garment and peacefully flowed into eternity. Jesus, on the other hand, was agitated and fearful, asked his disciples to stay with him, and then died in agony and despair. He died this way because he truly died; all that he was went into death because it was only by dying that he could enter death's domain and then overcome it.

In Christian doctrine we believe in the resurrection of the body. It is stated in all of the major creeds. It began with the Resurrection of Jesus, but such life is the Christian hope for us all. We don't just have a body; we are a body, and when we die, all of us goes. Our Jewish heritage praises and nearly sings, in the Song of Songs, of the glory of the body. Jesus enjoyed the life of his body so much that he was accused of being a glutton and a drunk. When his friend Lazarus died, Jesus did not speak of the soul's happy escape. Rather, he wept. Death was real. The whole person, the sum of his parts, was gone. And death came into the world because of sin; the wages of sin is death. This equation began in Genesis. It is to this scheme of events that Jesus came. To alter it was why he set his face toward Jerusalem. And from his self-giving love a new divine act of creation emerged, and the man who was dead became the man who lives.

In today's Gospel from Luke, we hear of one of the Resurrection appearances of Jesus. He suddenly appears in the room as the disciples have been discussing him. They are frightened and afraid that they are seeing a ghost. Jesus addresses their fears and invites them to touch his body and to look carefully at him. They doubted out of being overjoyed, and then Jesus asked them if they had anything to eat. It is such a casual and comfortable request, such as we would ask family or our closest friends. And they gave him a piece of fish, which he ate before them. This is an interesting detail and one that emphasizes the corporeal, just as his sudden appearance in the room, his moving through walls and doors, emphasizes the spiritual dimension of his resurrected body. Then Jesus spoke to them and taught them. He opened their minds so they would at last understand what he had tried to tell them before. Then he commissioned them to preach to all nations in his name.

The Gospel accounts of Jesus after the Resurrection are stories full of wonder and contradiction. From them we can find some common threads. For example, in several instances Jesus was not recognized, then became known through the breaking of bread or through showing his wounds. He also appeared suddenly among the disciples, as in our Gospel reading today, and then he would do something very physical, such as eat or prepare a meal. From these accounts it is clear that the disciples were confused, overwhelmed, and so overjoyed that they doubted what was happening. It is also clear that the resurrection body of Jesus had new properties as well as some very familiar ones. The resurrection body is a new creation of the divine will, but it bears the imprints of the suffering and sacrifice that we have done for love while we have lived on earth. Someone once said that the things we take with us when we die are the things we have given to the poor. It may also be that we will be recognized when we die by the scars of our moments of self-giving love.

There is wide divergence among biblical scholars and people of a faith concerning the Resurrection of Jesus. There are those more orthodox who believe in the objective evidence as presented in the Gospel accounts, and there are also, within the household of faith, those who believe that something happened of tremendous significance, but they can only place that event within the disciples' subjective experience. All agree, and even agnostics and atheists must concur, that something so extraordinary happened that the measuring of time since has been dated from the life of Jesus.

Despite differing opinions on the actual Resurrection of our Lord, Christian doctrine still maintains the resurrection of the body as the hope for us all after we die. The statement of belief in the creeds refers to us: "The forgiveness of sins, the resurrection of the body, and the life everlasting," as we say in the Apostles' Creed. The appearance of Jesus to his disciples showed them the "firstfruits" of what was to come. No doubt they disbelieved for joy. After dreading and yet realistically expecting death all of your life, would you not disbelieve such a joyous reversal? G. K. Chesterton once wrote, "Joy, which was the small publicity of the pagan, is the gigantic secret of the Christian." Unfortunately, in many cases it has remained secret. Our missionary zeal has often done more to propound belief than to convey joy. But joy is there. This body, at least some recognizable facsimile thereof, is bound for glory, and the same can be said for each of us. That is cause for joy.

However, we are aware that bodies that die seem to remain in the grave. This seems problematic in the light of Christian hope. It is here that we come to understand why the Greek idea of the immortality of the soul offered a solution to the dilemma and so crept into Christian thinking. Christian understanding of what happens when we die is basically a hope of resurrection, but again there is a divergence of understanding within the household of faith. To be clear, we speak of eschatology, or the last things. The New Testament, taken as a whole, was dominated by the thought that a new age was at hand. This new age would be ushered in by a final judgment in which the dead would be raised.

In the intervening centuries, the immediacy of that expectation has had to change. We have come to see the new age, the Second Coming of Christ, as always at hand, as both here and coming. Consequently, our understanding of the resurrection of the dead has changed to accommodate our eschatology.

In the last century, Emily Dickinson wrote:

> Safe in their Alabaster Chambers,
> Untouched by Morning
> And untouched by Noon,
> Lie the meek members of the Resurrection,

Rafter of satin,
And roof of stone.[1]

Orthodoxy holds that there is an intermediate state, that the members of the resurrection are in a state of waiting, whether that be a state of simple anticipation or purgation. The more evangelical attitude is that the faithful departed are immediately in joy and felicity. As for our bodies, whether immediately or later, all agree that we will be clothed with a new creation, a resurrection body that differs from this one in that it is imperishable.

In any event, the death of those who follow Christ is ultimately cause for joy. But wait a minute. In all of this focus on future bliss, we might smell a rat. Haven't we heard something before about pie-in-the-sky? Hasn't this been used to justify the misuse and drudgery of many, many lives? We live in a culture and a world obsessed with death, capable of global death while constantly denying its reality. Isn't this more justification of our greed and privilege with the assumption that equity and justice will come about later on when there will be no material or social limitations? Isn't this just more of the same? To this, Jesus responds that he came that we might all have life and have it abundantly, beginning now.

Jesus did not die on the cross so that our lives on earth would be simply a preamble to our joy in heaven. Rather, Jesus came to teach us how to live on the earth so that we might realize its wonder, so that we might learn to love now.

In Thornton Wilder's play *Our Town*, Emily Webb has an opportunity to return from the dead, to return to earth for just one day. She chooses her twelfth birthday. She goes back with the knowledge of what will happen and of her death. She begins the day with the poignant awareness that we the living have no idea how beautiful and precious and fleeting this life is. "Oh, Mama," she says under her breath, "just look at me one minute as though you really saw me. Mama! Fourteen years have gone by!—I'm dead—You're a grandmother, Mama.—I married George Gibbs, Mama!—Wally's dead too.—Mama! His appendix burst on a camping trip to Crawford Notch. We felt just terrible about it, don't you remember? But, just for a moment let's be happy. Let's look at one another!"

But they don't, and Emily cannot stay the whole day. She says she cannot do it: "It goes so fast. We don't have time to look at one another." She returns to the dead, looking back, exclaiming, "Oh, earth, you're too wonderful for anyone to realize you!"[2]

In the Gospel of John, Jesus says, "These things I have spoken to you that my joy may be in you, and that your joy may be full." The possibilities of awakening to full consciousness and self-awareness and to full human responsibility happen within our biological life span. It is here that we do or do not achieve the image of God for which we were created. And as liberation theology has helped to point out, our salvation begins here and now.

The medieval rabbis used to say that, if we could only see, each person is preceded by legions of angels singing, "Make way for the image of God." And so each of us is meant to be the image of God, the Christ, and our destiny is to permeate the mysteries that have challenged us this morning. Now we are a bit like chickens trying to comprehend Einstein's theory of relativity. So, we approach the mystery of love at the heart of eternity with the tools on which we've come to rely: our data banks and computers, our firm belief in facts and rationality. And we see as through a glass darkly. Someday we shall see face-to-face. But this we know now: There is joy in the final denouement. It is a divine comedy and not a tragedy in the end. "O death, where is your victory? O grave where is your sting?" There is celebration, abundant life, and great joy at the heart of the universe. As Chesterton observed, "We sit in a starry chamber of silence, while the laughter of the heavens is too loud for us to hear."

Let us pray. O God, whose blessed Son made himself known to his disciples in the breaking of the bread: Open the eyes of our faith, that we may behold him in all his redeeming work, who lives and reigns with you, in the unity of the Holy Spirit, one God, now and forever. Amen.[3]

NOTES

1. Emily Dickinson, *The Complete Poems of Emily Dickinson* (Boston: Little, Brown and Co., 1960), 100.

2. Thornton Wilder, *Our Town* (New York: Coward-McCann, Inc., 1938, 1939), 82–83.

3. Collect for the third Sunday of Easter, *The Book of Common Prayer*, modified.

19. *Arrivederci* . . . I Will See You Again

Matthew V. Labriola

Easter is a time of remembrance. For the friends of Jesus it would become the heart of their memory. So it is for me.

For me it brings immediately to mind my Italian grand-mother.

My grandmother came to these shores from her native Italy at the turn of the century, a young mother, several children in tow. When her husband inappropriately died, like many of the pioneer women before her she plunged into the American wilderness and carved out a life for herself and family in the forbidding frontier of Passaic, New Jersey. What was unique about her was that in the for-ty-eight years that she lived in her adopted country she never felt it necessary to learn a word of English. If Italian was good enough for the pope, it was good enough for her was the way she put it. There was no doubt in her mind that God conversed in Italian, Neopolitan dialect.

It did not hinder her a bit. I can remember as a boy of eight being taken by the hand and led downtown to a dry goods store to purchase a pair of trousers. In good European tradition, and to my utter embarrassment, she proceeded to bargain with a Jewish mer-

Matthew V. Labriola is pastor of the Memorial United Methodist Church in Modena, New York. Labriola received his bachelor of divinity degree from Drew Theological School and is the author of *The Prophet Meets Madison Avenue,* a collection of chancel plays. Labriola's Gospel in Art program, a worship service in art, music, and word, has been presented in over four hundred churches on the East Coast.

chant, himself newly arrived to these shores. At my advanced age of eight, I knew more English than the two of them combined. And so with the proper waving of hands, the moaning of sighs in all their nuances, the upward rolling of the eyes, all wonderfully choreographed, they both struck a happy bargain. And young Matthew received a pair of corduroy knickers. To this day I have a hard time buying trousers.

The phrase that I will always associate with my grandmother is *arrivederci*. It expresses the essence of her personality. Recently immortalized in song by American crooners, it means "until we meet again." However, my grandmother gave her own inflection to this melodic word, and it usually came out, *"We will meet again!"* For my grandmother there were no good-byes, no finality of farewells. And although in Italian there are many such words, they simply were not in her lexicon. For her, there might be the illusion of space or time but never separation from the circle of her love; this would always remain unbroken. So every leave-taking was an occasion for arriving. It is appropriate that the stem of *arrivederci* in both English and Italian is "arrive."

So it was that when time began to do to her body that which the American frontier could not, when she was well into her eighties, she took sick and took to her bed for the first time in her life. Since she had lived with us all my life, I saw her often. On the final day as I prepared to leave, not knowing that she too was preparing to leave, she smiled wanly and said *"Arrivederci! Arrivederci!"* It was Eastertide. It was her style. "We will meet again." I do not doubt it.

Two thousand years ago, on a fateful Thursday evening, a Jewish teacher named Jesus gathered his friends around him in the quietness of an upper room, there to prepare them for his leave-taking the next day. His accent was Aramaic, but his word was *"Arrivederci!* . . . I will see you again." In what we now call the "farewell discourses," John records it in this fashion:

> A little while, and you will see me no more; again a
> little while, and you will see me . . . because I go to
> the Father. . . . Truly, truly I say to you, you will
> weep and lament . . . you will be sorrowful, but your
> sorrow will turn into joy. . . . You have sorrow now,
> *but I will see you again* and your hearts will rejoice,
> and no one will take your joy from you. (John 16:16,
> 17, 20, 22, RSV)

"I will see you again." *"Arrivederci."*

And so Jesus speaks of that strange mixture of leaving . . . arriving; sadness . . . joy! If there must be an ending, then it leads to a new beginning.

Now, we must understand that Jesus knew full well the depths of their sadness. He was not saying that there would not be any pain. He was the supreme realist. What makes the life of Jesus meaningful to me and to you was that in him God shared every experience of our humanity. He knew our joy; he knew our pain. He knew our laughter; he knew our tears. Make no mistake about it. Remember when he heard the news about the death of his dear friend Lazarus? John writes simply, "Jesus wept." (Another memory: that church school teacher who taught us this was the shortest sentence in the Bible. But how much is wrapped up in those two words.) Jesus shares all that we are called to share. Even our dying!

But with a difference. For Jesus knew that the pain that we feel today grows out of love that we knew yesterday . . . and that it will go full circle and evolve into love once again. For we are never out of the circle of God's love. If we know pain, it is because we have known joy; if we know separation, it is because we have known love. And we cannot separate them. They are two sides of the same experience called "the magnificence of being human." For God has made us a little lower than the angels and has bestowed upon us the gift of love, the joy of human companionship, all that are hints of the greater love that we shall receive from him. But with this there is also the gift of freedom, of choice, of will, that leads us into the valley of decision, of tension, of pain. But who would have it any other way? For the only other way is to be created like shiny porcelain dolls: pretty, unstained, but without feeling, only good to be placed upon a shelf. But to be granted the divine spark is to be given life with all its possibilities . . . to be godlike.

But hear Jesus again:

> When a woman is in travail [labor] she has sorrow,
> because her hour has come; but when she is
> delivered of the child, she no longer remembers the
> anguish, for joy that a child is born into the world.
> So you have sorrow now, but *I will see you again* and
> your hearts will rejoice, and no one will take your joy
> from you. (John 16:21, 22, RSV)

Ah, the strange mixture of pain . . . joy, of death . . . of life. Having experienced fatherhood, which I am quick to point out is not the same as motherhood, I have seen firsthand that paradox of joy coming out of pain. The great miracle is that the pain is soon forgotten in the joy of new life—or what mother in her right mind would go through the ordeal of labor again . . . and again? Being the father of five children, I must confess that I am in awe of the event. But this I do know. I have seen the glow that surrounds a new mother when the baby is placed into her hands for the first time. And there is no word to describe it.

I remember officiating at a wedding in my church. As the organ erupted into those magnificent chords that proclaim the wedding march, I looked over at the mother of the bride, standing nearly in front of me and toward my right. Tears were streaming down her cheeks, as she contemplated this little girl who overnight had become a woman. Then I looked up the center aisle, and there was the bride, resplendent in white, beaming in her own radiance, a smile of sheer happiness singing from every part of her face.

Is it any wonder that, when John in his Revelation attempted to describe the Kingdom of God and the new Jerusalem, he cried out, "prepared as a bride adorned for her husband"?

The paradox of it. Sadness . . . joy! Leaving . . . arriving! Endings . . . new beginnings! *Arrivederci!*

On that Thursday evening, in the quietness of the upper room, Jesus could speak with confidence that "I will see you again," because for Jesus death was not the end. Rather for Jesus, death was a doorway into a new realm of experience with the Father. And so on that night he would describe our pilgrimage with God as a house with many rooms.

> Let not your heart be troubled; believe in God,
> believe also in me. In my Father's house are many
> rooms. . . . I go and prepare a place for you, I will
> come again and will take you to myself, that where I
> am you may be also. . . . I will not leave you desolate;
> I will come to you. . . . Because I live, you will live
> also. . . . Peace I leave with you; my peace I give to
> you. . . . Let not your hearts be troubled, neither let
> them be afraid. (John 14:1–3, 18, 19, 27, 28, RSV)

Life with God, a life in many rooms.

Perhaps Jesus with his great love of Scripture was bringing his own personal dimension to the psalmist who said, "And I will dwell in the house of the Lord forever."

For we dwell in many rooms. Today we inhabit our earthly rooms, our own mortal tabernacles. Created out of the dust of the earth, in our reflective moments we are only too aware that they are subject to the ravages of time, the wear and tear of living, the frailty of our humanity. In the fullness of time, each in his own way must give up this earthly tent and pass through the doorway of death into that other room. What the room is like we do not know. But we do know that the Father is there to meet us, that Jesus Christ has gone on before us to prepare a place for each of us. And if we do not know what the room is like, we do know that it is not a room of darkness but of light, not of hate but of love, not of pain but of peace, not of death but of life. And it marks not an end but a new beginning.

Sometimes we who are so rooted to this earthly room can see no other. We trust only what our experience has taught us to see and to touch. Yet deep within the soul of man there cries out a need for "something more." As though a part of us, designed to live in this terrestrial vale, also points toward celestial worlds. "For heaven is our home," proclaims the poet, and the poet in each of us cries out, "Amen!"

Yet as faith often begins as we look to the world around us and there view the hand of the Creator pointing, teaching, inspiring, and often merely nudging, so the Father allows the scales to fall from our eyes through his human parables.

We have heard many times the nature parable of the lowly caterpillar who spins his cocoon and seems to die to that life, only in time to break forth in the brilliance of the butterfly. Perhaps this is God's way of causing us to say *perhaps.*

However, it is Jesus's moving description of the mother in labor that speaks to me. For having shared in that experience in my own stumbling, masculine way, it proclaims a new and vibrant life as nothing else does. Dr. Peter Marshall has taken this another step and illuminates our *perhaps* with an *of course.* In describing the miracle of conception and growth of the child in the womb of the mother, Dr. Marshall exults that all this points to a life beyond. For within the womb, the child is developing qualities and characteristics that are useless at the moment but point to possibilities to come:

eyes that do not see; ears that do not ear; lips that cannot speak; fingers that do not grasp. All designed for the life beyond the womb. And then the child seemingly dies to the womb-life and enters a new room of experience where all the same qualities are now developed to their fullness, and more . . .

For now in this new "life" the child develops qualities that set him apart from any other creature in the Creation—the qualities of love, gentleness, sacrifice, loyalty, service. They say he is meant for more. These qualities are godlike, to be used in this earthly room, yet they seem to take us a lifetime to nurture. It is as though God were training us for more—for that "more" where all these gifts would come to their glorious fruition.

I need to merely think of my mother, and it all makes sense. For here is one who had a Christian nature marked by what I would call "sweetness" and gentleness. Yet she lived a life filled with pain, suffering, and heartbreak, life experiences that seemed to mock all that she believed and held dear. One cannot imagine her life snuffed out without meaning at the peak of her spiritual journey. Her life for me points to that door that leads into the "other room."

Now, the key to these words of Jesus, that put music and muscle in our own shout of *arrivederci*, are found in his assertion, "I go to be with the Father." *The Father. Abba, Father.*

All through his ministry Jesus was concerned about the Father. Jesus said very little about what eternal life is like. But he spoke again and again about what the Father was like. It is because we know the Father that we know about eternal life. We do not believe in eternal life merely to believe in eternal life. That in itself is hollow. It is because we believe in a God who is eternal, and grants to each of us the gift of life with him, that we are the inheritors of a life that is eternal. For it is God the Father who gives meaning to our present life, who gives meaning to eternal life.

Sometimes we put the cart before the horse. Reinhold Niebuhr warns us that we spend too much time describing the furniture of heaven and the temperature of hell, both of which are irrelevant.

Actually it is the "unknown" that makes us anxious. We who feel we are in control of our lives are suddenly uneasy at the thought of the unknown. Just as when we were children we imagined the darkness to be filled with goblins, so we populate the unknown part of our existence with fearsome creatures. It has always been thus. In the early years of maritime exploration, when mapmaking was still a primitive art, whenever a mapmaker would try to describe a part of the world that was unknown, he would often draw great sea monsters, all imaginary.

The world beyond the other room is not illuminated because we have a secret map. It is because we have the Father and in Jesus Christ all that is unknown is now made known. While we need knowledge, it is not knowledge itself that dispels the darkness. Rather, it is a presence. It is the knowing that we are not alone, that we are known, that we are loved. This is why at Christian funerals we recite, not from our theological texts, but rather, "The Lord is my shepherd. . . . Yea, though I walk through the valley of the shadow of death, I fear no evil; *for thou art with me. . . .*" And this is why we proclaim with the Apostle Paul, "For I am persuaded that neither death, nor life, nor anything in all Creation, will be able to separate us from the love of God in Christ Jesus our Lord."

Many years ago when I was in the service, the army sent me on a free, all-expense-paid train trip from Newark, New Jersey, to Seattle, Washington. As we passed through the Midwest, the train stopped at a station in a farm community. I watched with some interest when an elderly couple placed in the care of the conductor a young boy of about eleven or twelve years of age. It seemed that the boy was visiting with his grandparents and was now returning home to a distant city in one of the western states. The boy seemed quite happy and at ease. I asked the boy if he were afraid to make this long trip on the train all by himself. He replied, "No, because I know that my father will be there to meet me."

And this, too, is the Easter proclamation. "I know that my father will be there to meet me." In Christ Jesus you know the Father. You know that he loves you. In him you are known. In him you are never alone. And it is because you are in the circle of his love and his eternal presence that all our leave-takings echo with *arrivederci.* For they are always arrivals and mark new beginnings in the household of God.

"Let not your heart be troubled. . . . In my Father's house are many rooms."

"You will weep and lament. . . . but I will see you again."

"Your sorrow will turn into joy . . . for you will know that I have gone to be with the Father . . . and no one will take your joy from you."

Arrivederci!

20. Old Age, New Age
Dale Rosenberger

Mark 13:24–27, 32–37

Christmas is the season when most of us get "malled." That is, we descend into the shopping malls, the Eastlands and the Northlands, only to emerge frantically as though chased by a pack of wild animals.

If you are like me, any bookstore along the way is a favorite haven from the crush of Christmas shopping. Why, I can hide out in a bookstore, scanning books and magazines, pretending to shop for an hour at a crack. But my latest attempt at literary refuge from shopping malls left me assaulted in a different way.

Do you remember how in recent years most chain bookstores would have an aisle marked "mystery and occult"? In many stores those same aisles of books are now marked "New Age." I plunged into this new and unfamiliar designation. Hmmm, New Age, I wondered. Sounds like it has something to do with my own line of work. At least our Gospel lesson today would indicate so.

But these book titles spoke a different message. How about a handsome book for your grandson entitled *Confessions of a Kamikaze Cowboy?* Or a paperback for a distraught and searching friend by the name *The Secret Is in the Rainbow: Aura Interrelationships?* Maybe this for the man who has everything: *The Oracle of Geomancy: Techniques of Earth Divination.*

Dale Rosenberger is senior minister of the First Congregational Church (United Church of Christ) in Columbus, Ohio. He is a graduate of Thomas Jefferson College and Yale Divinity School, where he received the master of divinity degree. Rosenberger has also been a pastor in Illinois and a research assistant at the Connecticut Mental Health Center.

Books like these no longer come from arcane publishers selling a few thousand copies to an obscure audience. Instead, sales range from a couple hundred thousand into the millions. This is no mere publishing ripple but a tidal wave.

You know, time was when the spiritually seeking could enter most any bookstore and find titles like *The Shaking of the Foundations* by Paul Tillich or *The Confessions of St. Augustine* or Reinhold Niebuhr's *Nature and Destiny of Man.* Those days are gone. Today bookstores might offer pop inspirational books or deluxe editions of the Bible for the broad evangelical market. But serious Christian reading is not to be found unless you locate the titles in a seminary bookstore.

These are the signs of the times. We live in an apocalyptic age. Out west, some ambitious engineers attempted to neutralize nuclear waste and spray it on the crops as fertilizer. The program was underway at several farms and was hailed as a trend. Then a farmer in Nebraska found a frog with nine legs in his pond. New Age theology has seemingly sprung from the same waters.

Did you know that for merely $275 you can chat with some highly evolved being channeled across space and time into the present? Shirley MacLaine consults with Ramtha, once a barbarian warrior, now a 35,000-year-old ascended master, considered beyond deity. These disembodied personalities often accept individual consultations for roughly $100 per hour. Half an hour on the telephone goes for just over $50. And, by the way, they do accept VISA and MasterCard, no kidding.

It is our anxiety that marks us as an apocalyptic age. Today we have the ability to destroy ourselves outwardly several times over by nuclear annihilation. This has received so much worldwide attention that nations are finally seriously addressing the issue. But no less insidious is our ability to destroy ourselves inwardly by our leisure self-absorption, our material success, or most frightening, our self-deification. Should it surprise people of faith that in many respects the outward threat is less serious than the inward?

Why is this so? All parties clearly recognize the threat of multiple-warhead, nuclear attack missiles as the mark of the beast. Even intractable enemies like the United States and the Soviet Union now willingly collaborate to reduce them.

I remember the sermon of a grizzled, retired Marine on Laity Sunday. Ernie was military issue from shirttail to socks, a rough-

and-tumble veteran. But having witnessed an experimental hydrogen blast in New Mexico years before, Ernie flat out told our mainline church not only that hell exists, but that he had been there. The perspiration on his forehead and the whimper in his voice told us that we didn't want to get near. Yes, the outward threat gets lots of air time.

The inward threat is more subtle and hidden and, therefore, more dangerous. It is more sophisticated and genteel and clever. It is never even perceived as a threat in many circles. Increasingly it is highly exalted.

Admittedly, my first reaction to the New Age phenomenon was bemusement. Here the 1960s Age of Aquarius children and 1970s Werner Erhard graduates trudge on to the latest efflorescence of pop religion, I tell myself. How quaint, really: responsible adults with crystals under their pillows to erase negativity and recharge energy stores; wide-eyed talk of out-of-body experiences, polarity therapy, lost cities, rhythmetiques, goddesses, and spirit guides.

It reminded me of camping out in my backyard, someone bringing a ouija board, and breathless talk about spirits roaming our subdivision. New Age religion will eventually go the way of those delirious backyard talks with my friends. But there will be much confusion along the way.

Initially I respond to the Shirley MacLaines of this world as does Gary Larson in his absurdly funny cartoon "The Far Side." There he depicts one fretful Gila monster atop a large rock talking to another. It is a desert landscape. "There it is again," says the reptile, agog with excitement, "a feeling that in a past life I was someone named Shirley MacLaine."

Eventually, however, one cannot help but look beneath the glitzy surface at the substance. And this is more disturbing given its wide popularity. On a television special, MacLaine and her spiritual adviser faced the Pacific on Malibu Beach with arms outstretched to the cosmos. "I am God! I am God! I am God!" they shouted in unison.

And when MacLaine's beloved Ramtha channeled into the "Merv Griffin Show," he declared, "What is termed God is within your being. . . . And that which is called Christ is within your being. . . . And when you know you are God, you will find joy." I do not mean to pick on Shirley MacLaine. I have nothing against her personally. But I view her theological reflections like most VFW posts view the foreign policy of Jane Fonda.

For me, bemusement ends where blasphemy begins. Those who have not yet learned the difference between becoming *godly* and becoming *godlike* have also failed to grasp that good has a malevolent twin named evil. And those who manipulate gods into serving them, instead of serving the one true God, do not channel to any ascended master but to the oldest descended master of them all.

To paraphrase G. K. Chesterton, when people stop believing in God, the problem is not that they believe in nothing but that they believe in everything. Let all of my yuppie generation who abandon the seemingly outdated and irrelevant faith of our mothers and fathers be advised. Nature cannot tolerate a vacuum. And where one spirit once dwelt then departed, seven evil spirits now enter and dwell. And the last state of such a society is worse than the first. So it is with this generation.

Looking at the shelves of our bookstores and such bizarre television specials and weekend workshops, I cannot help but ask, What is happening to the soul of our country? Now, I can understand our people succumbing to gods like money, military might, status, and accomplishment. These gods almost look good compared to these new waves of crass paganism. After all, though false, they do offer some small, temporal satisfactions amid this earthly order. But Ramtha? What does he deliver but a bloated VISA bill?

We live in an apocalyptic age. This means that we are to expect religious ferment, as most contemporary institutions uneasily bubble and churn. This also means that we dare not judge too hastily or too harshly those who struggle after meaning in this utterly mad world. For our search is the same, even if we look in different places.

Still, our Gospel lesson urges us to say something more. We live in a day when the search for meaning and belonging has become desperate. In our contemporary age, the searchers are more vulnerable and exploitable. And because we live life only once, there is urgency to our decisions about the true and the false, the authentic and the fraudulent. Human life is easily misguided and ruined. The stakes are higher than any quick glance at our workaday routines might suggest.

So remember this. If a faith speaks only of endless possibilities to be enjoyed, never of limits to be faced, it is a sham. If religion seeks to remove all tension from this highly conflicted world in which we live, it is slack-spined.

Notice especially what a faith does with evil, suffering, and death. To brush these aside as irrelevant with harmonic convergences or higher life forms is whistling in the dark. Remember also that Dostoyevski said that the only time everything is possible is when there is no God; or when God is everything and therefore finally nothing.

And so I close this morning where our little parable of the end time closes. It ends on both a demanding and an encouraging note. The day of our relief and vindication in God will come. But it comes not by our divinations and projections, not by our gradual upward ascent, but by God's sudden descent and in God's sweet time. Nothing earthly can dictate the time or the place or the shape of God's advent among us. God cannot be manipulated. But God can use our lives for his divine purpose.

Our only true hope is in God's faithfulness above all human desires and devices, over the rise and fall of the best and worst we do. And so, until that day, watch, lest the master come suddenly and find you asleep. What I say to you, I say to all: Watch! Amen.

21. Where Have All the Angels Gone?

Dale S. Bringman

"Of the angels, God says, "Are they not all ministering spirits, sent forth to serve?"

———Heb. 1:14

Two couples from this parish sent a picture postcard of the 700-year-old Gothic, stone Voss Kirke in Norway. When they worshiped there three weeks ago, eight babies were to be baptized during the service. The baptismal font was in the arms of a wooden, carved angel suspended above the chancel. At the time for the baptisms, the acolyte went behind a screen to free a rope that would lower the angel holding the baptismal bowl to the floor level. Apparently the rope had slipped off a pulley, and the angel didn't come down. The acolyte jerked frantically on the rope but to no avail. Eventually a lady, perhaps the altar guild president, went for a stepladder, climbed up, and got the bowl for the baptisms. At that point, the angel came crashing to the floor.

Until the last incident, that episode is a good illustration of angels, whose function once was to bring God's grace down to his people, but who now remain suspended beyond our experience. That makes it necessary for people, like that Norwegian lady, to do what God wants to have done.

Dale S. Bringman is pastor of St. Peter's by the Sea Lutheran Church in San Diego, California (Evangelical Lutheran Church in America). He is the author of *Prayer and the Devotional Life* and *A Star is Born*. A graduate of Susquehanna University, Bringman received his bachelor of divinity degree from Lutheran Theological Seminary in Gettysburg, Pennsylvania. He has previously been the pastor of Lutheran churches in Harrisburg and State College, Pennsylvania.

Where have all the angels gone? Long time passing. Where have all the angels gone? Long time ago. Where have all the angels gone? Gone to Christians, every one. When will we ever learn? When will we ever learn that when the angels remain suspended beyond us, God must find others whom he can send forth to serve.

To get a God's-eye view of angels and of ourselves, let's begin with the Lord himself.

God is holy and majestic, high and lifted up, a transcendent God, and transcendent means "to stand across from, to rise above, to go beyond." God is the wholly other, the *mysterium tremendum,* as theologian Rudolph Otto has phrased it. God's ways are above our ways. His thoughts are beyond our thoughts.

One of the problems with God's transcendence is that it can separate him from us so completely that he seems not to be involved with us or to care about us. It is as if the Lord once made our world the way a clock-maker makes a clock, after which he let it run on its own. He is no longer involved.

The opposite of transcendence is immanence. A God who is totally immanent is confined only to this world and has no existence apart from it. An immanent God is a good buddy, "by our side upon the plain," but he neither rises above nor goes beyond with infinite power and measureless might.

How then can God communicate to us that he is transcendent without being separated from this world in which we live and move and have our being? Or how can God make us aware that he is immanent, involved with and concerned about us, without being limited only to this world? You and I can ask questions like these abstractly. The writers of the Bible thought concretely. To them, God was a great King above all gods, high and lifted up, the Maker and Ruler of all. Yet those writers of the Bible knew also that the Lord cared about them and was involved with them in this world. One way God conveyed this was through angels whom he sent forth to serve.

Angels visited Abraham and Lot, wrestled with Jacob, strengthened Moses, guided Joshua, and fed Elijah. Isaiah described how it worked.

> I saw the Lord sitting upon a throne high and lifted
> up, and his train filled the temple. Above him stood
> the seraphim [the angels]. Each had six wings.

[Wings made it possible for them to fly from God to
people.] Then one of the seraphim flew to me,
having in his hand a burning coal which he had
taken with his tongs from the altar. And he touched
my mouth and said, Behold this has touched your
lips. Your guilt is taken away, and your sin is
forgiven. (Isaiah 6:1–8, RSV)

The holy, and the wholly other, transcendent God communicated
his presence, his power, his forgiveness, and his guidance through
angels who were ministering spirits sent forth to serve.

Move your focus, in the second place, from God to angels themselves. About 1,400 years ago along the Via Salaria, six miles north
of Rome, a church was dedicated to Michael the archangel. He, together with Gabriel and Raphael and Uriel, had been given a special day on the church calendar. Perhaps there should have been a
special day for "Lo" since the Bible says, "Lo, the angel of the Lord
came upon them." Later the Reformers lumped all the angel days
into one festival: the Day of St. Michael and All Angels. As we celebrate that day on September 29, we preachers are expected to say
something current, cogent, convincing, and above all, correct about
angels, who seem to us archaic, ancient, anachronistic, awkward,
and unreal—suspended beyond our experience.

The word *angel* (*malachi* in the Old Testament, *angelos* in the
New) means "messenger." Angels are not people who have died
and gone to heaven. If you think you have started to sprout wings,
that's an indication, not of your goodness, but of your badness.
You've been eating too much and your clothes are too tight. No,
angels are a different order of creation—"ten thousand times ten
thousand of them," Daniel writes. They are "ministering spirits
sent forth to serve."

Edmund Spenser described the function of angels in *The Fairie
Queene:* "And is there care in heaven? And is there love? Oh, the
exceeding grace of highest God . . . who loves his creatures so . . .
that blessed angels he sent to and fro."

Some of the angels goofed. According to the Bible and tradition, one third of them, under the leadership of Lucifer, rebelled
against God and were cast out of heaven. "O Lucifer, son of the
morning," Isaiah wrote. "How you are fallen from heaven . . . you
said, 'I will ascend.' [I will take over.] I will raise my throne above

the stars of God. [I'll be the chief angel.] I will sit on the Mount of the Assembly in the far North [the place of privilege]. I will establish my throne . . . I will ascend above the heights above the cloud. [I shall take my place above God.] I shall be like the most high." Ezekiel tells us what happened: "Thus says the Lord God . . . I cast you as a profane thing from the mountain of God, and the guardian cherub drove you out . . . I cast you to the ground." The writer of Revelation put it in these words: "The great dragon was thrown down, that ancient Serpent, who is called the devil and Satan, the deceiver of the whole world."

Satan, the devil, is a fallen angel whose influence, whose "tail swept down a third of the stars of heaven." This means that one third of all created angels are now evil spirits tempting us in this world, blinding the minds of unbelievers, taking away the Word from the hearts of Christians. Evil is a terrible reality. "Stand against the wiles of the devil," we read in Ephesians, "for we wrestle, not against flesh and blood, but against the rulers of this present darkness, against the spiritual hosts of wickedness."

Satan is the adversary, leading the rebellion against God. But Michael, the guardian angel of Israel, is described in the Bible as being one of the mightiest of all angels. The name *Michael* means that he is like God, and Michael conquers Satan and all his army. God's will and work are done through angels. Thirty-four books of the Bible tell us about them. Angels are ministering spirits sent forth to serve. That's the biblical view of angels.

Then the Lord showed people a more excellent way. In the fullness of time, the transcendent God sent forth, not angels, but his Son, born of a woman. God himself became one with us in Jesus, so effectively, so marvelously, that you and I need never wonder whether the Lord loves us and cares about us. "O yes, he cares," the gospel song goes. "We know he cares." Jesus Christ came into our world, lived, died, and was raised from the dead. Fifty days after that first Easter, the Holy Spirit was poured out on all flesh, and the Holy Spirit is God alive, right here, right now. The transcendent God is immanent. The immanent God is transcendent. "Therefore with angels and archangels, we laud and magnify his holy name."

We've focused on the Lord, on angels, and now, in the third place, how do we fit into the Lord's scheme of things? Your body and mine are temples of the Holy Spirit. "I live," Paul wrote, "yet not I, Christ lives in me." Catch hold of what that means. The devil

and all his fallen angels—evil, discouragement, fear, and death—
—cannot defeat us. The Lord lives in us, and, as John puts it in his
letter, "he who is in you, is greater than he who is in the world."

But a responsibility goes with this, too. When will we ever learn
that since the angels are gone away, God must and does find other
ministering spirits and bodies whom he sends forth to serve. "You
have not chosen me," Jesus said. "I have chosen you." We Christians are to go into all the world. Could it be that what God once
expected of angels, he now expects of us?

We Christians, like angels long ago, are to communicate God's
presence to others, "sweetly singing o'er the plain." All of us are
evangelists, a band of angels coming for to carry someone home. As
an angel once provided Elijah with a jar of water and a cake baked
on coals—angel-food cake, if you will—we are to feed the hungry in
Africa and Asia, in Central America and in our land. Like Michael,
the archangel, we are to fight the hosts of wickedness—apartheid,
the proliferation of nuclear weapons, the spoiling and wasting of
natural resources, the abuse of children, the battering of women,
the neglect of the aging, the injustices to workers from Mexico, the
harsh treatment of escapees from Central America. Wherever evil
raises its head, it bruises the heel of our Savior, and we are to crush
it. The whole Christian Church on earth is to be a giant *los angelos*,
ministering people sent forth to serve. We are to be as wise as ser-
pents, lest we rush in where angels fear to tread. When someone is
sick or in need, we are to be the angels watching over them. Right
here this morning in our fellowship of believers, some are hurting.
All of us need the forgiveness, the warmth, and the strength of
God's love. An anonymous author once wrote,

> If after kirk, ye rise and flee;
> we'll all seem cold and stiff to ye;
> The one that's in the seat with ye;
> Is stranger here than you, may be.
> All here hae got their fears and prayers;
> Add ye yourself unto our prayers;
> Be ye God's angels unawares.

St. Michael and all angels had their day. Now you—and you and
you—and I are God's ministers sent forth to serve.

IV. ETHICAL

22. Prophetic Faithfulness
Allan Boesak

Num. 22:6, 28, 32

I am grateful to God that we can be here together for this very important moment in the life of this church that I have come to love so much and work with so often over the past few years.

I have decided to speak to you on the topic of prophetic faithfulness. It is not only something that Presbyterians in the United States should hear but something that we have to hear every day in South Africa, where I live and minister. We will do that by turning our attention to the story of Balaam's ass. You will see why I thought it appropriate for us Reformed people to listen once again to the story.

I will concentrate on three verses in Numbers 22:

- "Come now," Sir Balak says, "curse this people for me, since they are too mighty for me; perhaps I shall be able to defeat them and drive them from the land; for I know that he whom you bless is blessed, and he whom you curse is cursed." (v. 6)
- "Then the Lord opened the mouth of the ass, and she said to Balaam, 'What have I done to you, that you have struck me these three times.?' " (v. 28)
- "And the angel of the Lord said to him, 'Why have you struck your ass these three times? Behold, I have come forth to withstand you, because your way is perverse before me.' " (v. 32)

Allan Boesak is president of the World Alliance of Reformed Churches and serves as pastor to students at the University of Western Cape, Capetown, South Africa. Rev. Boesak also is affiliated with the Foundation for Peace and Justice in South Africa. This sermon was delivered in Louisville, Kentucky, at the dedication of the national headquarters of the Presbyterian Church (U.S.A.).

I remember three reasons why Balaam became famous—or infamous. One is that there are precious few stories in the Book of Numbers, and this is one of them. The second reason is that Balaam has become known as the prophet for hire—the one who goes out, for pay, to curse Israel, and then ends up blessing Israel against his will. The third reason, maybe the most important, is that he has this marvelous conversation with his donkey. The donkey talks to him, and he talks back, and it is the most natural thing in the world. The biblical writer doesn't even blink as he tells us this.

I think, however, there is more to Balaam's story than this. It is not just an account of an unknown prophet from that particular time who wanted to curse Israel, who got paid for it, and who then in the end had to change his tune because his donkey confronted him along the way.

The background to the story is that Balak the King of Moab sees Israel around him and is very much afraid. He knows military attack is out of the question, so he goes for the second-best thing—get someone of some reputation to go and curse the people of God. That curse will help because, it is the ancient belief, a blessing means that power has been bestowed on you and you have the special favor of the gods—somehow your enemies can fight against you but will never prevail—while a curse is just the other way around. The curse takes away the blessing, weakens your resolve, takes away the invincibility, and brings vulnerability instead. And, most important of all, the curse limits the powers of this god you pray to.

What Balak does not understand, however, is that Israel's God is not like any other god. The blessing that God has given Israel is that God has decided, "I will make this nation my own. I will tie my future to theirs. I will make a covenant with them." The blessing lies in the fact that God sees the misery and the pain and the suffering of God's people, and God says: "I have seen it. I have seen the way you have been driven by Egypt. I will come down and I will rescue you."

That is the blessing that Israel has: The promise that "I . . . will be your God, and you shall be my people" (Lev. 26:12). There are no borders for this God. He is Lord of all; he is Lord over all. There is not a single inch of life in all of this world where the lordship of this God is not to be seen and understood and celebrated.

Balak does not know this, but he is about to find it out. The curse on Israel is important not only because of what Balak wants but because God wants to use it to make this king understand exactly who God is.

So God chooses Balaam, and we're not sure why. Traditionally we see Balaam as a kind of a pirate, a prophet for hire. He is the man who early on in the Bible demonstrates what Americans have come to understand better than anybody else in the world: Everybody has their price.

Balaam is approached by King Balak: "If you go and curse Israel, I will pay you so much." When Balaam says no, the king says, "Let me make the offer a little better." More money, more gold, more silver. As the story evolves, Balaam says, "I want really only to do God's will"—and he says this a number of times. "You sleep here tonight because I want to confer with God, to know whether God really wants me to go." He is bargaining. He is going to go, he knows that in the end he is going to go, but he is not going to fall for the first offer. He uses God for his own purposes every time he says, "I want to listen to what God says."

Maybe we have misunderstood this story. Maybe Balaam is a prophet of God who knows the Lord. Three times he says, "I do not want to do anything without consulting God. I want to hear what God has to say. I will not go with you unless God tells me to do so." I propose we take the man at his word. He remains faithful even when the temptation grows and even when the price is raised. I think it is the voice of Yahweh that tells Balaam, "Go with these people and do what the king wants you to do." He has to go in order for Balak to see who this God is, in order for Balak to see on his own territory that this God will remain faithful to God's people, that God's promises will never fail, that God's covenant will remain in spite of the kings of this earth who would want to change it. That is the purpose of this story: the faithfulness of God and of God's prophet.

God says to Balaam, "If the men have come to call you, rise, go with them" (v. 20). But we read in verse 22: "But God's anger was kindled because he went." Now, how is this possible? Why can't God make up his mind here? The problem may be one of translation more than anything else. The word here that we usually translate as "anger" can also mean that God is in a state of concerned agitation. You could use the word *nervous*.

When I read this, I thought to myself: But this is amazing. Can God be nervous? And then I thought of myself as God's servant, and I thought, yes, God can get nervous. I think it is much better to say that when Balaam went, something happened along the way that aroused God's concern. God was worried about this man. Something happened to Balaam that made God say, "Something's wrong here." God got nervous for the sake of this man who was supposed to do something God wanted him to do.

Why would we have to deal here with a nervous God? I think it is because the task of the prophet is crucial. The prophet is God's voice in this world, and every time the prophet says, "Thus says the Lord. . . .," he actually speaks for God.

In this world the task of a prophet is difficult. It is risky. Ask Jeremiah, when he was locked up in that jail, when he was thrown down in that well, when he feared for his life.

The task of a prophet is dangerous. Ask Elijah how he felt when Jezebel sent him that message that "this time tomorrow you will be like one of those you have killed; I will see to it—and remember, I am not Ahab, I can do it."

Ask John the Baptist how he felt sitting in that prison, thinking: "I am the one who was called to make way for the Lord in the desert. I am the one who was called to point and say, 'There is the lamb of God who will take away the sins of the world,' and I did that, and I spoke to the king, and told him of his sins, and I said to Israel, 'Don't accept automatically that you will be children of Abraham; God can make these stones children of Abraham.' It is his truth, not mine, that I spoke, and yet I am in this prison. I don't know whether I will come out alive." And he did not. Do you blame him for sending his disciples to ask Jesus, "Are you the one who was to come, or shall we wait for another?" The task of a prophet is dangerous.

The life of a prophet is in danger every time he opens his mouth to speak God's Word.

A prophet must remain faithful. A prophet must remain alert, sensitive to hear God's voice among all the other voices—the alluring voices, the tempting voices, the threatening voices. A prophet must see what God sees although others around him cannot see it and get angry with him for seeing what God sees that they cannot see.

But a prophet is human and gets scared. The prophet says, like Elijah, "Take away my life, God, it is enough; I can't take this anymore." He says, like Jeremiah, "I am too young; I cannot speak."

A prophet fails often. He can give in to temptations. And if that happens, who will confront the Balaks of this world?

Somehow this is happening to Balaam, and he does not even notice—and that's the point. Somehow Balaam does not discern the dangers that face him. Somehow he forgets how risky his life is in his calling; somehow he forgets how easily he can be tempted. Somehow he does not see how slippery his role has become. And because he does not see, God must awaken him in some way.

A prophet who does not see the dangers will no longer be able to fulfill the prophetic calling.

It is now that God intervenes. The angel comes and stands in Balak's way. And again the point is that Balaam does not see. The donkey does. And it is now that the shameful part begins. What the prophet cannot see, what the prophet does not hear, the donkey sees and hears.

The Bible often does this to us. If the Bible wants to make clear just how incredibly insensitive we have become, how incredibly wayward we have become, how incredibly stupid we have become, how it is possible that we who have been called as God's prophets in this world fail to see, fail to hear his voice, fail to remain sensitive to our calling, fail to remain faithful, God goes to something else, something extraordinary like an ass—or a snake in the Garden. The snake speaks, and the donkey speaks.

And the point is not a nice debate about whether it is possible for God to somehow miraculously change the vocal cords of the donkey so that it can speak. The point is not whether the donkey spoke or not. The point is, what did he say? And it is because God introduces this extraordinary thing that it actually captures Balaam's attention. That is why Balaam talks back to this donkey and has this conversation. It is not strange because it is what is being said that matters.

The prophetic task of the church, my brothers and sisters, is so clear in the world today. It is our task, our main task, to say to the world: "This is the word of the Lord. Thus speaks the God who has created Heaven and Earth. Such is the word of this God who is Lord of all, Lord over all, before whom all powers shall bow."

We think the church is prophetic when we make statements. We say when we go to assemblies, the church has been prophetic because we have this wonderful resolution on South Africa and sanctions or something.

That is not being prophetic. The church is not prophetic when we make a resolution or take a decision, or even when we write a memorandum that we send to Congress or the president. That is not prophetic witness.

We really become prophetic only when we take those words and those resolutions and the meaning that they have and we give them life with our bodies, with the risks we take, with the testimony we give, and with the witness we are in the world on the streets, so that people can see what it means to be the church. Only then are we prophetic.

My church has the Confession of Belhar, which is one of the most incredible documents that we have ever produced in our country. It is a beautiful document that says God is on the side of the poor. It says apartheid is heresy, and we thought we were prophetic when we said that. But we discovered that we became prophetic only when we were willing and able by God's grace to take courage and stand in the streets and say, "This is the Confession," and go to jail and say, "This is the Confession," and face the tear gas and the dogs and the guns and say, "This is the Confession of the church." Then, and then only, are we prophetic.

And so it is true for every church. As you begin a new role, a new journey, I can ask the question. Are you really sure that the money you have spent to move from where you were to here is going to be recovered in the way that it can be useful to the Kingdom of God? I can ask that question, and I do, because I love you.

And I must ask: What are you going to do when you dedicate this new building—is it going to be an efficient machine, or is it going to be the heartbeat of a church that is beginning to understand anew in the America of today what it means to be prophetic?

Does this new beginning mean you have learned a new form of prophetic faithfulness in this country where the lot of nations far-flung over the face of the earth is being decided if your president takes up his pen and signs one bill?

Will your prophetic faithfulness be crucial to the life and the witness of this church, to the life and witness of this nation, and to the life of this world in which God has placed you? Or will it be necessary for God to get an ass to stand in our way and remind us of the things we do not see anymore, the vision we have lost, the dream we cannot dream anymore? And of the power we don't know we possess, because we think power lies in power to challenge the power of the world, and we forget that our power lies in our weakness because we love the Lord Jesus Christ?

God confronts Balaam as his adversary. And only then does Balaam see. Oh, my brothers and sisters, if only the church will see; if only our eyes will be opened to see the pain and the suffering. If only our eyes will be open to see that the task of the church is to stand where God stands against all injustice and pain and suffering and with the poor and the oppressed and the lowly and the meek. If only our eyes will be open to see the temptations facing us and see that we can get buried in so many bureaucratic things that we forget the simple rule of listening to the voice of God first and foremost, every single day as we march into our offices and climb into our pulpits.

If only we will be able to open our eyes and see what God sees, forget the temptation and the fear of confrontation in South Africa, and see the necessity of obedience of the voice of God.

It is not a matter of being brave; it is not a matter of challenging; it is a matter of obedience.

If only we will be able to open our eyes and see how we can remain faithful. Faithfulness is not fearlessness. You can be afraid sometimes. It's OK. I know I am. One day in the church where I work the police walked in, surrounded the church with police and vehicles, and posted men around it with their guns. A captain walked up the aisle and told me, "You must please be quiet because I have an announcement to make." Now, we were having a church service, praying for those in detention, and he comes in ready to arrest the whole church. I tell you I was scared—until I learned that I could say to him, "But who do you think you are? Just because you have a uniform, or just because you have a gun, do you think you can actually come into the church of God and tell us to be quiet because you want to say something?" So I said to him, "I will not be quiet. You sit down there, and you listen to the Word of God-"—which in the end he didn't do but walked out.

The point is not that I am such a fearless person. The point is that when you fear, you learn not to reach within yourself, but you know to whom to turn. And that is the secret—the One who will never let go of your hand, even as the bullets fly.

When Balaam's eyes are finally opened, he says to God, "I will turn back, I will go back," and God says, "No you don't; you go with them—go with them, but only the words which I bid you, that you shall speak."

The Presbyterian Church (U.S.A.) must not turn around, now that we have bumped against Balaam's ass standing before you to-day. You must go—go, but speak only the words that God wants you to speak.

That is the key; that is the secret of prophetic faithfulness. That is the life of the church. We see what God sees, or we do not see at all. We hear what God hears, or we do not hear at all. We speak what God wants us to speak, or we have nothing to say at all. We go where God wants us to go, or we will remain immobile. We love where God wants us to love, or we will never love at all. This is the church, or it is not the church at all.

23. Why Me, Lord?
William H. Hinson

It was a long trip for Moses from the courts of Egypt to the back side of Sinai—a very different kind of world for an ex-prince of Egypt, now a shepherd. He didn't go to Sinai that day looking for a religious experience. He had been in Midian for forty years; he had a very settled life there. But on the back side of Sinai he saw the strange sight of a burning bush that was not consumed by the burning. In that remarkable phenomenon, God got his attention. Moses' life was never the same again.

I read an article recently in which the author described our God not only as a good shepherd but said, "Just as all good shepherds have dogs, God also has dogs. When we tend to go astray and refuse to follow the Good Shepherd, those dogs will come after us biting at our heels and nudge us back into line until finally, when we get to the Father's house, we'll be able to look back and thank God that he didn't just leave us to our own whims and desires." It made an interesting article. It's just not right.

God's election of us as servants has always been related to our willingness to turn aside and our willingness to be obedient. When he found a man like Moses, who would turn aside and listen, it didn't take God long to get to the heart of the matter. He said, "Moses, I have seen my people's affliction. I have heard their cries; day and night they come up before me." He said, "I know their suffering, and I want to send you to do something about it."

William H. Hinson is senior pastor of First United Methodist Church in Houston, Texas. He is the author of *Solid Living in a Shattered World*, *A Place to Dig In: Evangelism in the Local Church*, and *Reshaping the Inner You*.

Now Moses was a man of substance in Midian. Moses had it made in Midian. He had a wife and children. He had security there. He had standing. His father-in-law was a priest of Midian. Moses was a contented man when God interrupted his life that day. He discovered then what C. S. Lewis discovered later when he called our God and his Christ a "transcendental interferer." We want him to let us alone. "Mind your own business," we say. That's the last bitter pill to go down, that God has the right to intrude and direct our lives. He goes on acting as if we are his business and he has every right to tell us what we ought to do.

When I became a Christian, I thought I'd surrendered myself to Christ, but in reality, I was giving him little pieces, a part of myself at a time, like poker chips or something of value. Every time I'd give a little bit more of myself to God, I'd wait for him to be impressed, to brag on me for surrendering a little bit more. I remember how scary it was when I came to the realization that he wasn't going to brag on me for those little pieces of myself. He wanted everything there was. He was treating me as if I were bought and paid for. He was treating me as if his name were written across me. The God who would not withhold his only Son, but gave him up to die for us on the cross while we were yet sinners, will never apologize for using us to the utmost.

Moses was a reluctant deliverer. "Why me?" he asked. "Lord, of all people, why me? I've already tried that deliverance routine one time. I killed an Egyptian back there, and my own people turned on me." He asked, "Why me? They won't listen to me. Besides that, I'm not very eloquent." You read the story, and you'll see that Moses declared, "I wasn't eloquent before I had this experience with you, God, and if you don't mind my saying it, I'm not eloquent after I've had this experience." There wasn't anything in grace that made Moses a better speaker, so he continued to plead with God about his lack of ability. But you know lack of ability is not our problem. We have worlds of ability. Our problem in the Church is not ability, and it's almost a cliche to say it. Our problem is availability.

I talked to Hal Lanier yesterday. Hal Lanier is a former manager of the Houston Astros, a friend of mine. Hal Lanier will confirm what I read in an old story about the manager's favorite player. Many times the player closest to the heart of the manager is not the regular player who gets all the publicity but the one who sits on the bench, the one who—when the score is tied, or you're one run behind in the bottom of the ninth, and you have two outs, and there's a man on base, and you desperately need a run to tie or to win—the one closest to the manager's heart is the one who, when the manager looks down that bench, doesn't turn away from him, doesn't avert his eyes or look at the floor but looks into the face of his manager and points to himself and taps the bat. It's the one who's available.

Who could ever forget the way Howard Thurman used that metaphor again and again? Howard Thurman was my professor at Boston University. Howard Thurman changed my life. He loved to tell that story about how he and his little friends were going across the sandlot one day where some older boys were playing baseball. Howard, wanting to impress his buddies, said, "You see those boys over there?" He said, "I could get an uppance with them. I could get a turn at bat." They said, "Aw, go on, Howard. They'd never let you bat, a little guy like you." But Howard knew what he was doing because one of those boys over there was dating his oldest sister. He knew he'd do anything to get in good with the family. So Howard waited until it was his turn at bat, and he walked up and pulled at his arm and said, "Let me have your uppance." The boy turned to give him the back of his hand, but he saw who it was and said, "Sure, Howard, you can have my bat." He handed him that great big old bat, and Howard choked up on it. He said he had as much bat back there as he had out front. He stepped up to the plate, and they threw a strike, and it was in the mitt before he could get the bat around. And then it was strike two, and it was strike three. Howard said, "I didn't hit a home run." He said, "I didn't get a triple, double, single; I didn't get a 'snig,' not even a foul tip." But he said, "When I walked back to my friends, I was so proud I didn't think my body could hold my heart because, you see, I'd been in the batter's box. I'd had my uppance."[1]

When we face our crucified Lord one day he's not going to want to know how many home runs we've hit. He will not want to hear a recitation of all our successes. He'll want to know, Have you been faithful? Have you stood in the batter's box? Have you made yourself available? Have you swung from your heels? Have you done the best that you could for the highest you know?

You see, our God wants to send us, too. Jesus made it plain. He said, "I want to do with you what God did with me. As the Father has sent me, even so send I you." That's the charter of the Church

under which we serve. That's Ephesians 1. We have a common ordination in our baptism—to make Christ real and visible in our world.
Why don't we do that better?

We have an amazing paradox in the Church just now. On the
one hand we have a great hunger for the Word of God. We have
people who are not yet ready to serve in the really tough positions
because they aren't familiar with all of the self-revelations of God
that form our salvation history. They're spiritual orphans, really.
They don't know how to find the Gospel of John, let alone understand what it says. Consequently, the Disciple Bible program in the
United Methodist church is such a wonderful gift to the Church. In
the church I serve, we've gone from having no Bible studies outside
of Sunday school to having fifty this fall. More that forty of them
will be the Disciple program. So, on the one hand, we have these
beginners, some of them in their fifties and sixties, just trying to get
a basic understanding of what the mission of the Church really is.

But then, on the other hand, we have this group that is almost
church alumni. They know everything, and they have an obsession
with knowing even more. They're obsessed with being fed. I get so
tired of people who only want to talk about being fed. I think sometimes they've taken the cross off the altar and replaced it with a feed
trough. I want to say to them sometimes, Don't you want to just take
off the bib and put on the apron and wash some feet? Aren't you
ready? Don't you have enough now? Aren't you ready to serve? So it
seems we have these two groups.

I think what we need to have happen in the Church is what happened to my nephew Michael. Michael, who's now in college, was
really fond of his pediatrician. Michael didn't want any other doctor. He had had this doctor since he was an infant. All his friends
had gone on and graduated to other doctors, but Michael wanted to
stay with his pediatrician. Well, he was a tall, gangling teenager.
When he was thirteen or fourteen, he was already six feet tall or
more. Michael would go and sit in that waiting room with all these
little babies wandering around the room. One day Michael was sitting there waiting to see Dr. Mazo in Savannah, and a little toddler,
just learning to talk, was going around the room touching first one
little baby and then the other, and each time he touched one of
those tiny children he would say in that delightful voice, "Ba-by. Baby." And then he came to Michael, and he touched him on the knee
and said, "*Big* ba-by!"

Wouldn't it be wonderful if our God could touch us, all of us, right at the point where we're holding back and say, "Big ba-by. Aren't you ready now to let me send you to be Christ to the world?"

Do you remember that dreadful conflict in Biafra when the people were tearing at one another in that awful civil war? There was, in a clearing in the jungle, a tent set up where a midwife was helping women bring children into the world. In the middle of all that death and destruction, babies were being born. An American reporter was leaning against a tree, seeing that midwife go in and out of the birthing tent. He watched her, having nothing better to do, and finally when he heard the feeble cry and knew another malnourished child had come into the world and when the midwife walked at last to the door of the tent, that American in a casual voice asked, "Boy or girl?" That midwife fixed him with her stern gaze and said, "It's a soldier, mister; it's a soldier."

When you're in an all-out war, it isn't clergy; it isn't laity; it isn't men; it isn't women; it's soldiers under a common ordination, bearing through our baptism the seal of Jesus Christ. We are those whom he would send into the world to give ourselves in service to the world for Christ's sake.

More than that, God would send us back to the very place we don't want to go. Moses said, "Oh, not Egypt, Lord. Don't send me there. They won't listen to me there. I've already tried it. I've already failed."

Do you remember where Jesus sent his disciples? First to Jerusalem, the place of their largest failure, where they had really messed up, and then he sent them to Judea. Do you know what Judea's like? Of course you do! You'd love it if you sell rocks. I mean Judea was the "pits." He was sending them back to Jerusalem and then to rocky Judea. Then he said, "I want you to go to Samaria. They really despise you in Samaria."

Where did we come up with this romantic notion that it's easy, that there is some kind of miraculous formula that makes serving God easy? There is nothing easy about going back to the place where they've already shown you they won't listen to you. There's nothing easy about that, not when materialism is rampant in our culture, not when we're rabid with self-interest, not when for many people God doesn't exist, and if he does exist, he doesn't matter. Or even worse than that, if God does exist, he exists to serve me! It's not easy! But Jesus leveled with them. He said, "I'm sending you out as lambs into the midst of ravenous wolves. As far as I'm concerned, you're wolf bait. You're going to get beat into nubbins but don't worry about it. I've written your name in heaven. I'll put you back together again." Paul said it so beautifully in Colossians when he declared, "We are those who are called to complete the sufferings of Christ in our world."

But it was going to be different this time when Moses went back to Egypt. People listen to God-sent men and women. They always do. Moses had not just had an attitudinal change; he had had an altitude change as well. You see, he had been up on a mountain. He had been up on the holy mountain. He had taken his shoes off in reverence and had conversed with God. His soul had been scorched by the holy fire on the side of that mountain, he had heard this God say, "I AM has sent you." I like Gerhard von Rad's translation of that. He says that the play on the Hebrew name for God, Yahweh, can mean "I am for you." Now, when Moses left the experience of discovering for himself that Almighty God, the God of all Creation, was for him and had condescended to call his name and to converse with him as friend with friend, out of that experience of regeneration there came a power he had never had before. Oh, how much we need empowerment in the Church!

I used to think when I asked people to take some of the tough jobs in the church like youth counselor or junior high teacher, or when I asked people to tithe, when I asked them to do jobs that took perseverance and endurance, and they said they couldn't do it, I thought they were just being stubborn. Now I know that's not the case. They were being sincere with me. They simply can't do it. They don't have the inner certainty. They don't have to power to rearrange their priorities and to establish their lives. There is a lack of empowerment.

It's like that man I heard about at the Memphis Open the other day. You know how some amateur golfers pay all kinds of money just to get to play with the professionals. Well, this guy at the Memphis Open shows up, and a friend told me that he was dressed to the nines. I mean total coordination. He had it all. In addition, he had a bag, a huge thing, into which all of the most expensive clubs had been placed. There, with all the fanfare of teeing off at that first tee, he stepped up there and wiggled and waggled as if he knew what he was going to do, and then he almost whiffed the ball; he just dribbled it off the tee. One of the old caddies there who was going to have to carry that awful bag jabbed his friend with his elbow and said, "All bag!"

We've got a lot of people who are "all bag." We are asking people in the Church to let their light shine when their lamp doesn't have any oil in it. They think they're all right. They're like Mary and Joseph—they're traveling along on a dusty road of life "supposing Jesus to be in their company," and then the darkness of night comes down, and they discover they've left him far behind. He isn't there at all. When that presence and that power isn't there, you can be like the priest of Baal. You can pile your altar high with anything you want to put on it, and you can dance and jump and pray and make strange noises all day and all night, but if the fire doesn't come down from heaven, nothing is going to happen in your church. If the baptism promised by John the Baptist, the baptism of fire and power, doesn't become a reality, we're going to have a church like Flannery O'Connor described in her book *Wise Blood*, when she was talking about Haze Mote's church. The church where Haze Mote preached was a church "where the blind don't see, and the lame don't walk, and what's dead stays dead." That's the kind of church we'll have without God's empowerment.

But those who have pulled off their shoes and are walking barefoot through life, knowing that this whole globe is to be made sacred, to be called to its responsibility in Jesus Christ, we know that we are to call the people out of one bondage into the next glorious bondage. For the sign of the success of the mission of Moses was that one day these ex-slaves would have a festival in the desert. On their way out of Egypt to the Promised Land, they would stop by Sinai, and they'd take on a covenant and a responsibility and a law. They'd exchange one terrible bondage for a glorious bondage. For you see, in the Bible we never hear of "freedom from," but it's "freedom for." To speak of freedom "from" without freedom for responsibility is to ignore the human problem and to take a very naive view of human nature. Do you remember Carlyle Marney? The other day I read one of his quotes in *Preaching* magazine. Carlyle Marney was talking about the naive view of human nature that Walter Rauschenbusch sometimes enunciated or verbalized (Rauschenbusch was the leader in the social gospel movement). Sometimes, at least to Marney, it appeared like a rootless social gospel. Rauschenbusch had said that if the people are ever free, they'll stop exploiting one another. In other words, we'll shape up. Marney said, "I am more impressed with what Andy Brown said to Amos on 'The Amos and Andy Show.' Andy said, 'If the smart ones in this world ever quit taking advantage of the stupid ones, it'll upset the whole level of stupidity.' "[2]

Sure, get them out of Egypt, but take them by Golgotha; send them by Sinai. Wesley said, "We don't know any salvation that doesn't include salvation from sin." We don't recognize any system that doesn't have a Savior. We don't recognize any method that doesn't have a Master. Get them out of their slavery and introduce them as a bond slave to Jesus Christ.

This common ministry to which you and I have been called is one in which our part is to make a faithful response to that which God has done for us in Jesus Christ. You will notice that God didn't make any demands upon his people until they had first been delivered. There was no law given until they had experienced his love, his mercy, and his power. Surely, those of us who live on this side of Calvary can understand that even better.

Sammy was in his late fifties when I met him. He was a member of the church I served. A very quiet man, he slipped in and out; very few knew his name. Sammy met and fell in love with a woman who had been married previously. As old as he, she had grown children and grandchildren. Sammy had never been married. They asked me to officiate at their wedding. Only weeks after that service they called to tell me of a terrible situation. It seemed that the wife had been stealing from the large company for which she worked over a period of many years. She had juggled the books; she had taken a great deal of money across the years and had sent it to those prodigal children of hers, and there was no hope of recovering it.

The president of the company called them in and said, "I have to prosecute. It's too much. She's going to spend the rest of her life in jail." Sammy said, "Would you reconsider if I could raise some money, if I could go back to work?" For you see, Sammy had leukemia; he knew he only had a few years to live. He had retired from his modest job, having paid for the little house that was located at the end of the street and had bought the one thing he had wanted for so many years. He had bought a boat. He had put it on the trailer, that new boat under the carport, and now he and his new wife were going to enjoy fishing, something he had never been able to do. The house was paid for, and they were going to have some wonderful years, and now he offers that man a package: "All of the money I can get by mortgaging my home, three-quarters of my salary. We won't even keep our telephone; we don't have to have it." The president said, "We'll try it for a while." Sammy worked seven and a half years. Nobody thought he could live that long. When he finally died, the president of that company wrote across all her debts, "paid in full."

No one knew what Sammy was doing when he sold his boat and remortgaged his home. Nobody in the church knew about that drama. I had moved away, and I watched the church bulletins as they came to my house each week. When he died, there was a single memorial and, of course, his wife gave that memorial. But then, it's easy to give a memorial for someone who's laid down his life for you, isn't it? It's easy to make a memorial of your life for someone who left his throne in glory and took the form of a servant and became obedient even unto death so that at the cross your debt was marked "paid in full." I can take off my shoes before a God like that. I can hear my name being called by a God like that. I can say with Moses, "Here am I, Lord. Here am I."

NOTES

1. William H. Hinson, *Solid Living in a Shattered World* (Nashville, TN: Abingdon, 1985).
2. Carlyle Marney, *Preaching* (July–August 1989):42.

24. Disposable People
Arleen Whitney

Gen. 1:26–27; 1 John 3:1–3

For thirty years I have been cleaning them, soaking them, and sterilizing them. For thirty years I have done everything humanly possible to prevent damaging them or losing them. I have poured out hundreds of dollars insuring them and replacing them. And finally after all these years I have become an expert in wearing contact lenses. So guess what I did last week? I took them right out of the storage case and threw them down the drain! Every two weeks from now on, I am going to throw out my contact lenses! I am now wearing the latest in disposable lenses. If I lose one, so what? It only costs five dollars to replace it.

We are living in a disposable society—a throwaway society. For the most part, we love it. It makes life easier. We use disposable diapers, plates, and soda pop cans. Vacationers this summer can snap pictures with disposable cameras. We even now have disposable wedding gowns!

I can remember, when I first started working as a nurse, when we switched from glass syringes to plastic disposable ones. It was great! We didn't have to sterilize syringes anymore, which made injections safer. There was less danger of contamination and infec-

---

Arleen Canfield Whitney is associate pastor of Geneva Presbyterian Church in Laguna Hills, California. Whitney holds two nursing degrees from Loma Linda University, the Ed.D. in higher education from the University of Southern California, and a master of divinity degree from Fuller Theological Seminary. In the past twenty years she has taught critical care nursing in a number of institutions and in 1981 led a group of nurses on a visit to hospitals and clinics in the USSR. Whitney's ministry at her present church is especially among the critically ill and those faced with life-threatening illnesses.

tion. Needles were only used once—they were never dull. So injections were less painful, and the whole process was cheaper. But now, as you are aware, plastic syringes are washing ashore along our coastlines. Over fifty miles of beaches from New Jersey to New York are contaminated with all kinds of medical debris, including contaminated vials of blood.

We are discovering that the disposable habit we love so much comes with a price. It comes with risks. Our disposable habits are not just polluting our seas, but they are destroying our land, the air we breathe, and all kinds of wildlife.

But there is another peril that lurks in our throwaway society—a more subtle problem but far more dangerous. Alvin Toeffler over fifteen years ago warned us about it in his now famous book _Future Shock_. We are living in a disposable society with _disposable people_. We are living in a society where beliefs about human dignity and human worth are slowly being eroded.

We see it in the news every day: gang shootings and freeway killings. Recently a newborn baby was abandoned in the trash can in the restroom of a 747. Another baby was left on the steps of one of our local churches here in Orange County, California.

Our relationships with people, places, and things in our throwaway society are temporary and disposable. The average American moves every five years. Half of our marriages end in divorce. Over half of our children are being reared in single-parent homes. More than half of the school population changes over every year in Los Angeles. We move. We change jobs. We are unable to develop long-term relationships. People become disposable.

Therapist Norm Wright, agreeing with Toeffler, believes we are raising a generation of people who _feel_ disposable—who feel rejected. When we feel disposable, all kinds of psychological boomerangs are set off. We feel lonely, depressed, and unloved. We feel unworthy, inadequate, and defective. We start treating ourselves as disposable. We don't take care of ourselves. We eat too much. We overwork. We neglect our needs. In essence, we are disposing of ourselves. And if it gets bad enough, if the pain becomes unbearable, some of us try the ultimate in disposing of ourselves—we attempt suicide. Now, of course, if things get this desperate we urgently need therapy and medical intervention.

But the reason I bring all this up is because I think as Christians, as God's people, we need a corrective. We need a biblical understanding of our worth as human beings to help us know how to treat ourselves and one another. We also need a biblical understanding to make increasingly complex ethical decisions in our society.

In the remarkable passage we read this morning from Genesis, we get the distinct impression that the creation of human beings was a cause for celebration. It is absolutely amazing that God created us in God's own image—in God's own likeness. The very fact that the Creator would do this tells us something of our inherent value and worth. Being in the image of God is what makes us distinctive. It is what distinguishes us from animals and from every other creature—even angels.

What it means to be in the image of God is hotly debated. Not everyone agrees. Some people believe that to be in the image of God is to be rational; to be able to think, to reason, to make choices. This is probably true—yet there is much more that makes us human. We all know rational people who are quite capable of all kinds of irrational acts.

Still others think that being in the image of God has to do with making moral decisions. Yet we know all too well that some of the most "moral people" can act immoral. The recent TV evangelist scandals are sad examples.

Many point out that part of being in the image of God is to accept the responsibility that God has given us over Creation—to look after this magnificent world that God has given us. Certainly this is part of God's expectation of us. All the more reason, then, to be concerned about our pollution and not to treat our world as disposable.

But there is so much more to being created in the image of God! Theologian Walter Brueggemann makes a fascinating observation.[1] He reminds us that Israel was never to have idols, that Yahweh was not to be cast into any molten image. For there was only one way in which God would be imaged in this world, and that is through our humanness. As Brueggemann suggests, we are the *only* part of Creation that says something about the reality of God. God has chosen to be imaged in our world through us. Frankly, that just staggers my mind.

But there is still more, much more! Our Creator made us to be in fellowship with God, to be in relationship with God. Brueggemann observes that we are the only creatures to whom God speaks and to whom God listens. There is dialogue, friendship, companionship.

We have an intimate relationship with our Creator, and creatures that communicate with God are not disposable.

I remember a patient I took care of several years ago. When Susan was in college, she went swimming in the Kankakee River, a river that runs south of Chicago. Unfortunately, Susan misjudged the depth of the river. When she dove in, she hit the shallow bottom head first, severing her cervical spine. She was paralyzed from the neck down. A new quadriplegic, she was unable to finish college. Her fiancé deserted her. She couldn't work. She was unable to afford the expensive medical treatment and rehabilitation she needed. For all practical purposes, she was treated as disposable by society. Even the nursing staff felt sorry for her—that her life had been wasted.

One would think that Susan would be bitter. But when I went into her room to give her nursing care, I found a young woman who was peaceful and serene. She had a glow on her face that I'll never forget. She had a constant flow of devoted friends in and out of her room. For Susan talked with God. She listened to God. She knew more about prayer than I will ever know. She had a ministry: a ministry of prayer for others. People to whom God speaks are not disposable.

Still there is more! The God of love realized that a human being should not be alone. We cannot be in God's image by ourselves, living for ourselves. To be in God's image is to be in community, to be in fellowship with God and with one another.[2] We can't go it alone. We have to be together. No one is disposable.

But if we *really* want to know what it means to be created in the image of God, we must look to Jesus. For Jesus is the perfect image of God. In Colossians, Paul says, "Jesus is the image of the invisible God, the firstborn over all Creation." Look to Jesus. See him touching the leper—the outcast of society. See him healing the blind, casting out demons. See him giving food to the poor, preaching hope to the discouraged, eating meals with sinners. No one is disposable to Jesus.

Jesus shows us what it looks like to be in the image of God; he treats no one as disposable. And this is what we are called to do as people created in God's image. We are to regard no one as disposable. We are to concern ourselves with those whom society has called disposable. That is why we collect food and clothing at Christmas to give to battered women and children. That is why we have an emergency care program in our church. That is why we visit our ill in nursing homes. That is why we visit and pray with Alzheimer's victims and their families. For no one is disposable.

Furthermore, when we are faced with ethical decisions, it is helpful to have a biblical perspective on the inherent worth and dignity of persons, to know that no one is disposable.

We are living in a world where sophisticated technical advances in health care, coupled with spiraling costs, have left physicians, ministers, philosophers, and families faced with complicated issues of who will live and who will die.

Last year in the Netherlands, it is estimated that physicians participated in over six thousand active euthanasia cases. They injected lethal doses of morphine. In our own state of California there is a move to make euthanasia legal. We will have to decide. We will be asked to vote.

The issues surrounding the termination of life, of when to "pull the plug," are issues that are faced on a weekly basis by members of our very own congregation. These are often heartbreaking and soul-searching times. There are no easy answers.

There are those in our society who wish to pull back on medical treatments to the very old, to those who are retarded, to those who are permanently disabled in order to give better care to the majority. And as you are aware, there is a great tension in our country between those who are pro-life and those who are pro-choice.

We are having to deal with ethical decisions in areas that were only a figment of our imagination just a few years ago: in vitro fertilization, surrogate motherhood, transplantation of organs from anacephalic babies, and genetic engineering. I cannot even begin to unravel or solve all of these ethical problems. They are incredibly complex. They are not black or white. We will all have to grapple with them together. We will have to dialogue together. We will not all agree. But we must continue to search the Scriptures together, to seek God's perspective.

For now, I can only share with you that, when I am personally in doubt, I prefer to err on the life side. I take very seriously the biblical perspective that God is imaged in us, that God delights in us, that people are not disposable.

By now you may be thinking I have painted a far too rosy picture of human beings. For when we look inside ourselves, we realize that we fall far short of what we should be. When we look at one another, we often find it hard to see the image of God. It is difficult to see God's image in a disposable world where our children's vocabulary includes *Auschwitz*, and *nuclear winter.*

The problem is that human beings do not by nature respond to God's wonderful gift, the gift of being created in God's own image. We choose to break our relationships with God and with one another. We treat God and ourselves as disposable. We are disobedient and unfaithful. In so doing, the image of God, while not completely lost, has become blurred in us.

But there is good news! The good news is that God deeply loves us, the very joy of Creation. God loves us so much that Jesus was sent to die for us—Jesus, the one who *is* the perfect image of God. Because of Jesus, we can be restored to our real humanity.

When we look to Jesus and receive him into our lives, he makes us members of God's family. We are called the children of God. As John says, "How great is the love that God has lavished on us, that we should be called the children of God. And that is what *we* are." We really *are* God's children!

When we belong to Christ, when Christ is in us, our lives are slowly but surely being transformed into the perfect image of God. We are not there yet. We are in process. But we have hope: "For we know when he appears, we shall be like him, for we shall see him as he is."

We are not disposable!

NOTES

1. Walter Brueggemann, *Interpretation: Genesis* (Atlanta: John Knox Press, 1982).
2. Ibid.

25. Your Book of Life and Mine
Hillel Cohn

The best-known image associated with Rosh Hashanah is that of a Book of Life. According to our long and rich tradition, each of us is inscribed in the Book of Life on the basis of how we have done in the past year. God is seen as the great author who writes on the pages of the book and determines whether we will live or die, who will be hungry and who will be thirsty, who shall be at ease and who shall be afflicted. And so in keeping with that imagery, we pray to God at various points in our service of this day for inscription in the Book of Good Life, for redemption, for prosperity, for merit, for forgiveness. We pray repeatedly during this holy-day season that we be inscribed for *b'racha, v'shalom, ufarnasa tova*—for blessing and peace and ample sustenance. Many of us appreciate the poetry of those words but hardly believe that somewhere in the heavens sits God with pen in hand writing in the big book or, as some prefer to see it, writing in a huge ledger as an accountant would, noting our debits and credits, with the end result being a determination of what will be with each of us. We may say the words and sing them with fervor but not take them literally. Deep down we understand that God is not a person, that the language we so often use with ref-

---

Hillel Cohn is rabbi of Congregation Emanu El in San Bernardino, California. A graduate of the University of California at Los Angeles and Hebrew Union College, Cohn received his doctor of ministry from the School of Theology at Claremont. He is the recipient of the Emanuel Gamoran Award from the National Association of Temple Educators for developing the best new religious school curriculum in the nation. Cohn is a past member of the executive board of the Central Conference of American Rabbis and has served as president of the Pacific Association of Reform Rabbis.

erence to God is our human language, and that the imagery is poetic and symbolic.

And so the symbolism of the Book of Life for many of us, myself certainly included, leads us to believe that in many ways *we* determine our destinies. While we can't determine whether there will be a natural disaster such as an earthquake nor do we have full control over whether we will live or die, we do realize that we have a great deal to do with determining whether we will be tranquil or disturbed, prosperous or poor, whether we will really be alive or walk around in a living death. When we wish one another a *L'shanah Tovah Tikatevu*, an inscription in the Book of Life for a good year, we understand that much of that inscription is the result of *our* authorship. Our appeal to God, couched in the language of God being the Author of our destinies, is for most of us, I hope, accompanied by a realization that we do the inscribing, we do the writing. There is something beautiful about the imagery of the Book of Life, and that beauty is in no way diminished by our understanding that our destinies are *ours* to create.

This morning let me suggest that the imagery of the Book of Life has an additional application. I came to that realization a while back when someone who has become a dear friend and associate was sharing with me some of her experiences as she has sought counsel for some personal problems, certainly not problems of her own making but problems nonetheless. This delightful woman has achieved a great deal in recent years, yet she has had difficulty in accepting her own achievements. For so much of her life she had been programmed into believing that she was incapable of achievement, so that when it came, as a result of hard work and determination, she couldn't really accept it. Her counselor, knowing of her interest in literature and language, was trying to help her accept her own accomplishments and achievements. And the wise counselor said to her, "Suppose someone would write a novel about *your* life and you read it. Would you like the person in that novel?" And my friend happily concluded that she *would* like that person, an important step in the development of her self-esteem.

My friends, the imagery of the *Sefer Chayim*, the Book of Life, that is so much a part of these sacred days is one that ought to be looked at just like that. Forget the notion that God is up there in the heavens writing down our destinies. Instead, think of someone writing a novel about your own life and ask yourself the question as I ask myself the question, "If you read that novel, would you like the person who is the main character of that novel?" And bear in mind that the question has to do with whether we'd just like that person—not necessarily love that person.

I believe that to be a valuable way of doing what these days essentially call for—self-evaluation, self-assessment, *heshbon hanefesh*, taking stock of one's life. And I want to suggest to you some of the things we ought to be looking for in the main character of our own books of life so as to determine whether that person is praiseworthy, likable, or even lovable. One's life doesn't have to be filled with great adventure and excitement, intrigue or escapades to be likable. Nor do we need to find that the hero of our book of life is someone who has attained great prominence in the world, who has been one of the great artists or political leaders or warriors. Our books of life deal with simpler men and women, and the qualities that make us simpler men and women likable are more easily attainable.

Will your book of life or my book of life have as its central character someone who is really sensitive? Now that word may be overused these days, but that doesn't mean that sensitivity is of no value. Unfortunately, our age has done much to stifle sensitivity. Ours is an age that promotes being cold and calculating. People who are sensitive are sometimes looked on as wimps, people who are easily hurt and therefore weak. Men, especially in our society, have been conditioned to be strong, staid, unemotional. Getting ahead in business, we are told, depends on being *in*sensitive, hard-nosed. There's no room in the marketplace for sentimentality and feelings. Women have been allowed more of the luxury of displaying their feelings, but as they increasingly make their way into the corporate jungle, they, too, are instructed to be more *macho*. And how tragic that is! So many little boys have been scolded for crying. They were told and are still being told that "boys don't do that." Fathers and sons back off from embracing one another lest they raise the suspicion that they are somehow not really men.

Our Jewish tradition encourages us, men and women, boys and girls, to be sensitive, to be feeling. That culturally sanctioned sensitivity may be the explanation, in part, for the high proportion of artists, writers, intellectuals, and thinkers that have come from our ranks. We are commanded to feel, to empathize, to put ourselves in the place of others. The *Pirkei Avot*, the Ethics of the Fathers, say, "Do not judge another person until you have reached his or her place." That is sensitivity. We are commanded to be sensitive to the plight of the suffering, the enslaved, the oppressed as time and time again the Torah tells us that we must relate to the plight of the enslaved because *we* were once enslaved, we were once the oppressed, and so we should be acutely sensitive to the plight of those who today suffer oppression of any kind.

Along with the sensitivity that we should look for in the main character of our book of life, we should also look for a cultivated sense of spirituality. We live in an age of rampant materialism. In recent years there has been a recognition that our materialism, for all the comforts it affords us, has left us impoverished. Some respond to that impoverishment by seeking out new ways of approaching life, one of which of late has been called "New Age thinking." Late last year Martin Marty compiled a list of books that are part of what is called "New Age religion" or "New Age thinking," a way that is indebted to Shirley MacLaine for much of its popularity. Listen to some of the titles: *Tales of the Sexy Snake: The Art of Healing through Touch and Language; Voyage to the New World: An Adventure in Unlimitedness;* and *Rebirthing Made Easy*. A number of months ago, curious about the phenomenon, I attended a lecture on a Sunday evening in Santa Monica. Hundreds of young people, most of whom could be identified as "yuppies," sat somewhat spellbound as the lecturer spoke. The thrust of her message was that there was something beyond the material, and she was trying to guide them to that something, and they responded as if this was a real revelation. They were clearly entranced. It was clear that they were in search of something more than the material that for so long they had been told would make them happy and content. Those who buy those books and flock to lectures are desperately in search of something to sustain them spiritually. They have had it with materialism. The New Agers rub themselves with crystals to eliminate headaches and hold conversations with those claiming to be reincarnations of people who lived long ago. For them this is the world of the spirit that replaces the disillusioning world of things.

We *do* need to develop our spiritual selves. There are ways to cultivate the spiritual if it is lacking in your life and mine, and I believe that for the most part it is. But the spirituality we need to develop is not one that requires a mystical trip, a voyage into a world of mystery. It is the spirituality that accepts solitude as constructive, that savors the peak experiences of life, and that finds the ultimate highs coming from meaningful relationships with others. Bear in mind the developing one's self spiritually does *not* require abandoning the material. One can be comfortable yet contemplative.

Is the main character in our book of life sensitive or callous, feeling or heartless, tender or ruthless, caring or calculating, and is that person—you or me—spiritual or materialistic?

Along with sensitivity and spirituality, the main character of your book of life and mine should be serious about one particular matter-—God. In his book *Where Are We?*, which came out a few months ago and which I believe to be one of the most significant explorations of Judaism of our times, Leonard Fein, the founder and former editor of *Moment* magazine, says bluntly, "One does not have to take God literally in order to take God seriously."[1] And that, my friends, is something that should be a mark of the main character of your book of life and mine. That does not mean that we have to be people of firm, unshakeable, literal belief, appropriating lock, stock, and barrel the theology of our ancestors. Leave that for the fundamentalists. But we need to take God seriously. Leonard Fein goes on to illustrate what it means to take God seriously. He tells of the old teaching that all Jews, "the living, the dead, and the still unborn, were present at the Revelation at Sinai." And then he relates how a young friend of his was once wandering around the port area of modern Haifa in Israel when he noticed a hasid, in full hasidic regalia, walking toward him from the opposite direction. Fein's young friend, a genial sort, smiled. The hasid stopped, squinted, and asked, "Do I know you?" To which the young man replied, "Yes, of course: we met at Sinai." The hasid slapped his forehead and exclaimed, "Oh dear, you must forgive me. It was so hot and crowded that day. How have you been?[2] And then Leonard Fein goes on to say that the question of whether there was a Revelation at Sinai is far less important than the question of whether or not he or you or I were there. The first question-—whether there was a moment of God revealing Torah—requires a faith and is basically an irrelevant concern. The second—whether one was there at Sinai—requires a faithfulness that is possible and is *very* relevant. Being at Sinai means associating one's self with the event, story, or idea—accepting what it implies even though one might not accept that it actually happened. Does that sound illogical or contradictory? It isn't at all!

Taking God seriously means more than believing. We often speak proudly of Judaism being a religion of deed rather than creed. That means structuring one's life on some values that were considered to be of such importance that they were spoken in the name of God, distilled through the ages, and that respect us as human beings and that are humanizing. Again, to quote Leonard Fein, "We can bypass the sterile debate over God's existence, the tedious discussion of God's attributes, and focus instead on those elements of the system that help us make order out of chaos, that induce awe and wonder, charity, justice, and all the other elements of righteousness."[3] The person you and I read about in the book of our lives should be someone who takes God seriously, who aspires to become a fulfilled person, who has a sense of awe and wonder about the universe and who does not take the greatness of nature for granted, who recognizes the need to be a sharing person and who is committed to justice. That is taking God seriously. And one who takes God seriously, who is not unctuous or holier-than-thou in his or her beliefs, is likable.

And along with being sensitive and serious about God, the main character of your book of life and my book of life should be a person who has standards. Some of those standards will be reflections of one's sensitivity and taking God seriously. Those standards call for some basic decency, some fundamental morality. Those standards do not let us buy into the prevailing ethics of mediocrity. They are obsessed with the pursuit of excellence. Not all of those standards can be appropriated from the Bible or the writings of the rabbis, as perceptive and advanced and progressive as they might have been for their day. The biblical treatment of rebellious children, for example, is hardly a standard that any of us should follow. We have other ways of dealing with rebelliousness than taking a child to the outskirts of the city and stoning him to death. The biblical attitude toward homosexuality as an abomination came out of a world that did not have the advantage of the insights of psychology that we possess. And most certainly the attitude of the biblical authors and the rabbis who followed them concerning women, despite being progressive in relation to others of those times, still consigned women to a very secondary role. That is not an attitude that we should continue to espouse. But by and large the standards of day-to-day behavior are extremely valid and worthwhile. The heroes of our books of life need to have standards of behavior that are wholesome. Among them are those that are included in the Ten Commandments: reverence for life, honesty, faithfulness, respect for the property of another. Our ethics might more often than not be at variance with the majority. We need to be on guard lest we appropriate the standards of others that hold belief to be of higher value than behavior, creed far more important than deed. Last year Ted Koppel spoke at the commencement exercises at Duke University and said, "We have actually convinced ourselves that slogans will save us. Shoot up, if you must, but use a clean needle. Enjoy sex whenever and with whomever you wish but wear a condom. 'No.' The answer is 'No.' Not because it isn't cool or smart or because you might end up in jail or dying in an AIDS ward, but 'no' because it's wrong, because we have spent five thousand years as a race of rational human beings, trying to drag ourselves out of the primeval slime by searching for truth and moral absolutes. . . . For moral absolutes we have substituted moral ambiguity. . . . What Moses brought down from Mt. Sinai were not Ten Suggestions. They are commandments. *Are*, not were. The sheer brilliance of the Ten Commandments is that they codify in a handful of words acceptable human behavior, not just for then or now, but for all time."[4] Let the main character of your book of life and mine have high standards.

Sensitivity, seriousness about God, standards of ethical conduct—these ought to be qualities easily recognizable in the hero of your book of life and mine. And there is at least one more element. The main character of our books of life should be someone who is always engaged in struggle. Some might be praying today for a lessening of the struggles and conflicts in their lives. That is understandable. But to be free of all struggle and conflict and tension is not the way either. Billions of dollars are spent right here in this country by people seeking to rid themselves of pain. A couple of months ago I was in our nation's capital for a few days and had a chance to visit some of the exhibits at the Smithsonian. In the National Museum of American History a major display dealt with "Pain and Its Relief." There were exhibits of patent medicines that have promised to get rid of various aches and pains. A surgical suite had been put together with dummies being the doctors to show one way of doing away with pain. I was struck by one poster in particular. It read, "The pursuit of painlessness has become an American preoccupation. Nostrums and patent medicines have flooded the market, succeeded by a dizzying variety of pain-relieving drugs." And I began to wonder about our desire to get rid of pain. To be sure, we ought to get rid of most pain, even though we know that pain is an indicator of something wrong in our body and that often to get rid of pain is to get rid of an important gauge. Struggle, however, is not injurious to most of us. Struggling with ideas is maturing; struggling with problems is healthy. Struggling with traditional beliefs is necessary; struggling with customary notions and ethics is essential. To live without struggle is to not really live, and the main character of your book of life and mine should not be someone who avoids struggle. On the contrary, it should be someone who deals with tension and conflict.

These are the days, indeed this *is* the day, when our tradition fills us with the imagery of the *Sefer Chayim,* the Book of Life. Each of us has already written our own book of life, and we will continue to add to its pages until we die. If you were to read the book of your life right now, and I were to read the book of my life right now, what would we think of its main character? Would we like that person? Is that person lovable? And if not, what can be done in the days ahead to make that person more likable and lovable? How can each of us, authors of our own books of life, bring about the blessing and peace for which we pray?

May we nourish our spirits, sharpen our senses, approach God with seriousness, set for ourselves high standards of behavior, and struggle courageously. For, then, indeed, will the heroes of your book of life and mine be people of achievement an worthwhileness and blessing. Then, for sure, we will be able to read our book of life and find that we like its main character and even, on occasion, love him or her.

L'shanah Tovah Tikatevu—as you continue to write your book of life may you be among the most successful of authors.

NOTES

1. Leonard Fein, *Where Are We?* (New York: Harper & Row, 1988).
2. Ibid.
3. Ibid.
4. Ted Koppel, Commencement address, Duke University, June 1989.

26. Blessed Are They Who Care
James R. Spruce

Matt. 25:31–46

Disheveled, dirty, and out of luck. Probably drunk for all I knew, and I really didn't have time or energy for another man with a bag of excuses.

It was late Saturday afternoon. I was in my study finishing a sermon when the knock came at the door. Through the glass entrance I could see him. And through the glass I pretty well sized him up: poor, uneducated, down-and-out. The community of our inner-city church attracted a lot of street people, and it was not uncommon for them to come to the church for help.

So it was that I assessed quickly and often accurately those outside the door. Another drifter, another vagrant, another beggar. But they were all the same, as I saw them through the glass panels of the church foyer.

Whatever motivated me—and at the moment, regretfully, it was not compassion—I opened the door. All my suspicions, all my prejudices were confirmed: Here was a man wanting something, stringing up his well-worn excuses like limp garments hung on a clothesline. He looked away as he spoke.

Finally our eyes met. It startled me to look into his eyes. They were beautiful eyes, full of sorrow and anguish. And as I looked into his face, I saw something I shall never forget: I saw a being every bit as human as I, a man who was once a little boy, a pilgrim whose journey brought him to my door.

James R. Spruce is senior pastor of the Central Church of the Nazarene in Flint, Michigan. He received his doctor of ministry degree from McCormick Theological Seminary and has also pastored churches in Illinois, Texas, and Washington. He has written *Come, Let Us Worship* and a small-group Bible study for the Gospel of Mark.

He said his name was Eugene.

He said he wanted a drink of water. Sweat rolled down his face. His dark brown hair belied his age, and the half-full box of apples for sale he balanced on his hip was a bit much for a man only partially sober.

It was a simple enough request—just a drink of water. It troubled me that I was interrupted from my routine, behind as I was just before Sunday. But something else troubled me even more: I was standing in the doorway between this poor man and a drink of water. I realized I had some sort of power or authority to either grant or deny him water to slake his thirst.

My emotions seesawing, I invited him in and directed him to the water fountain and the restroom, too, at his request. I waited by the door next to the box of apples.

And while waiting, I wondered: He coughed near my face when he entered—what if he had tuberculosis? He politely shook my hand—what if he had some contagious disease? He used our restroom—what if he vandalized? He had a bulge in his coat pocket——what if he had a gun?

Presently, he returned, politely thanked me again, stooped and lifted his burden, and exchanged the comfort of an air-conditioned church for the muggy heat of Houston. My eyes followed Eugene: the Eugene of baggy pants and ungainly gait, the Eugene of floppy thongs and ripe apples. Eugene, the candidate I'd vote least likely to succeed.

And so, from the security of what had become true safety-glass comfort, I was certain of my "what ifs" about Eugene and people off the street like him. Moved, perhaps, but certain.

But the Scripture was certain of something else quite different: According to the Word of God in Matthew's Gospel, Eugene was the brother of Jesus! And whatever I did for him—or refused to do for him—I did or refused to do for Jesus.

It was troubling enough to realize that all the Eugenes I knew were akin to Jesus but even more disturbing to remember that if I also claimed kinship with the Lord Jesus then I was a brother to Eugene! This drove me back again to Matthew 25, and I rediscovered some amazing things about our text.

The twenty-fifth chapter is Matthew's last statement of Christ's parables, three in number. Each parable reveals that it is the good things we fail to do, not merely the bad things we finally accomplish, that bring consequence to bear upon eternal life. Interestingly, it is not immorality but indifference that Jesus employs as the great problem. The foolish virgins were indifferent or negligent regarding their need of oil. The lazy servant was indifferent and uncaring about making an investment. The goats, representing the callous, were indifferent about human need. And all of these, disturbingly, were banished to eternal life without God—not for the presence of terrible evil but for the absence of terrible good.

This parable of the sheep and goats is strikingly balanced in its language of contrasts: There are sheep and goats; there are those on the right and the left; there are the blessed and the cursed. There are words of clear division: *come* and *depart, inheritance* and *fire,* and *life* and *punishment.* It is as if our Lord makes everything black and white. It is as if we are given only two choices. Either we are among those who care or we are among those who do not care.

I am compelled, when reading the parable, to see that Jesus is not demanding extravagant gifts to the poor, the sale of my home to house the needy, or excessive time commitment in hospital and jail ministries. This is a reasonable parable, indeed, inoffensive in what it does command.

The parable is equable, gracious perhaps, in that it does not require me to pay the same price the rich young ruler was asked to pay—everything, my all. But I am asked to give something. Just something! Not everything, just something to eat, something to drink. I am to do that much, for something is a measure, at least, of what I could do if I cared. I must be lulled neither by the parable's poetic symmetry nor by my own feelings of sentimentality. I must see the awful truth of the parable: My eternal destiny is determined by whether or not I care enough to do something. Just something simple!

I am not sure about you, but it is easy for me to build a sturdy case for a theology that rests upon faith. Yet I, too, know that James is right:

> Suppose a brother or sister is without clothes and
> daily food. If one of you says to him, "Go, I wish you
> well; keep warm and well fed," but does nothing
> about his physical needs, what good is it? In the same
> way, faith by itself, if it is not accompanied by action,
> is dead. (James 2:15–17, NIV)

So I must give attention to the weight of this parable. It is true that we are saved by faith. But we are saved for deeds.

But deeds mean interruption, a knock at the door, a disturbance of comfort. So it is that this parable unsettles the routine of convenience and calls us to the spirit of caring. Our caring may be just that: showing loving interest in some spontaneous act of mercy without thought of reimbursement or recognition. It need not be lavish; indeed, the parable speaks of caring as if it does not wear a trendy label or announce itself in advance. It is just offered—a meal, a drink, a visit.

If we are too busy with our own interests, if we are too attached to our own loves, we shall have difficulty seeing the power of the parable. But if we choose to care enough, the words of Jesus will move us to action.

The Lord calls us to assume a challenge, a risk. Any attempt at caring about someone will cost us something. Jesus gives the parable, believing we are capable of releasing just a little of our money, our security, our time. He gives it, knowing the price on our part to show compassion is not unduly burdensome. He gives it, knowing the price on our part not to show compassion is terribly costly. Costly to us.

Money, security, time: three things we are asked to give in his name. Three things that threaten our own welfare, that test our love of the Lord himself.

We are called, first, to risk the loss of money by giving essentials. "For I was hungry and you gave me something to eat, I was thirsty and you gave me something to drink . . . " (Matt. 25:35, NIV). Essentials like food and water. Not elaborate, but essentials nonetheless. Jesus makes sure there is no mistaking on our part just in case we ask, "Lord, when did we see you hungry and feed you?" (v. 37).

Suddenly the weight of the parable falls with an astounding thud: As if to answer his own question, Jesus rejoins, "The King will reply, 'I tell you the truth, whatever you did for one of the least of these brothers of mine, you did for me.' " (v. 40). Whatever is given to someone in need—a Eugene—it is as if it were given to the Lord himself! How I treated Eugene, I treated Jesus. Surely Eugene was among the least to both the church and and society at large, but he was the brother of Jesus!

The blessed people in the parable are those who unselfishly give something simple: food and water, for example. The cursed are those who hoard for themselves.

Robert Frykenberg, in an article titled "World Hunger: Food Is Not the Answer," says,

> Finding how to circumvent the individual and corporate sins of greed, complacency and ineptitude is the answer. The abject plight of the world's poorest . . . stands as an affront to the conscience of every American. It is a perpetual rebuke against Christians. Do we gorge ourselves with luxuries while the starving hungry are suffering? Can we indulge ourselves with mobile homes, summer homes, summer trips, pleasure boats, style changes, and trivial extravagances when the world is in such a sorry plight? People in America must come face to face with their own wasteful consumption and inexcusable self-indulgence.[1]

If giving a few essential things as an act of mercy involves either a personal or collective price we are unwilling to pay because of greed, whatever other reason we use, our eternity is placed in jeopardy.

Risky? Yes, it is. It will cost us a little for essentials such as food and water. What the parable really says here is "Blessed are they who care enough to risk the loss of money by giving just the basics!" The things we take for granted are life-needs to most of the world. But, you have to ask, "Why would you be so blessed for sharing a meal or a drink of water in the name of Jesus?" Only because it is given to someone in need. We must note that the opposite consequence of being blessed for doing something is being cursed for doing nothing! For the greatest risk of the parable is not cash outlay; it is failure to rise to opportunity! For indifference to need, the cursed were condemned. What we do in response to human need has great bearing upon our position in eternity.

But we are called to do more than risk the loss of money for essential things. We are called, second, to care enough to risk the loss of security by offering shelter. Jesus said, "I was a stranger and you invited me in, I needed clothes and you clothed me . . . " (vv. 35, 36).

Food is surely a tangible expression of love but no more so than shelter or clothing. Both are mandated by the parable, but both represent different ways of being involved in the revival of caring. Giving food costs money. Giving shelter may cost the security you normally feel within the sacred precinct of your home.

At about four one morning recently I received a phone call from a young man. He sounded in genuine need. He was calling from an all-night deli. He had been sleeping in the park in bitter cold weather. His father had kicked him out of the house a week before, and he was at his wits' end. After a series of questions, answers, and decisions, I agreed to buy his breakfast the next morning and put him on a bus so he could go home and attempt reconciliation with his father.

But the hero of the evening was the manager of the deli who agreed to close his store and take the young man home for some badly needed sleep. That's inviting the stranger in—into the comfort zone of home. The parable is not suggesting that all of us do the same thing, but it is suggesting that all of us care enough to show it by doing something reasonable in the name of love. Responsible personal behavior is the key.

Many years ago I heard a returned missionary address at a convention of delegates on the theme, "Don't Cut Off the Buttons." He described to his American audience, in vivid detail, the incredible anguish felt by nationals who opened boxes of clothing with great anticipation only to discover that the sender had stripped the coats, shirts, and blouses of all buttons! He then wondered aloud how full the button jars of many American churches must surely be.

The truth lodged in our hearts: In our giving, do we still cling to ourselves the last remnants of security? Jesus compels us to be as generous to the least likely as we would be if we actually gave to him.

The late New Testament commentator William Barclay tells an incisive story about Martin of Tours, a Roman soldier. Martin, a Christian, was traveling with his company through a small village one cold winter morning. He saw a beggar asking for alms. The poor man was shivering cold, lips thin and coat ragged.

Looking down from his horse, Martin had pity upon the man. He took off his own soldier's cloak and tore it in half. One half he gave to the beggar. He kept the other for himself. In his tent that night Martin slept fitfully. He dreamed that he was in heaven with the angels and Jesus. It was bitterly cold. He looked and Jesus was wearing half a Roman soldier's coat. The Lord was shivering. Suddenly an angel asked Christ, "Lord, in weather like this, why are you wearing a coat so thin and ragged as that? Who gave that coat to you, Lord?"

Jesus turned his face toward Martin and said softly, "Martin, my servant, gave it to me." Oh, the security of our warmth.

How penetrating the words of the parable! ". . . whatever you did/did not do for one of the least of these brothers of mine . . ." Blessed are they who care enough to risk the loss of money by giving essentials! Blessed are they who care enough to risk the loss of security by offering shelter!

Finally, blessed are they who care enough to risk the loss of time by doing deeds! "I was sick and you looked after me, I was in prison and you came to visit me" (v. 36).

Giving money for a food pounding or bringing garments out of the attic for a clothing drive is not so hard to do. But giving time, for any reason, is very difficult.

Strange, isn't it, that the one item truly most valuable to us personally is the one item that is the greatest blessing? It is not that food and shelter are lesser gifts but that giving time has a wonderously healing effect on both receiver and giver. Money and clothes can be sent in the mail. But time means we have to give ourselves.

I recall few times my father ever walked up to me and gave me money. But I shall never forget the day he took me to watch the Texarkana Bears play. They were only a farm team, but it was big league to me! I was in the fifth grade, and Dad was a busy pastor. But he took the whole morning just for me. Now that I have children of my own, I know that Dad got a greater blessing that day than even I.

So the parable speaks to us but not about being sentimental do-gooders. Few things would be more abhorrent to the living Christ. The parable speaks to us about caring enough to involve ourselves, deeply, authentically, in the lives of those who might seem to be the least likely to benefit.

This is a hard lesson. We have a winner-mentality that demands a high price in terms of recompense and result. We have little room for failure in ourselves, let alone others. We have a way of looking through the safety glass of our churches and judging the limit of our interest and involvement.

But this parable is a challenge whose unabridged offer comes directly to the doors of the church: Do we, who call ourselves by the name of Jesus, love the least likely? If not, be cautioned! If so, be blessed! For it is the choice of caring over indifference that distinguishes greatness from mediocrity.

Blessed are they who care!

NOTE

1. Robert Frykenberg, "World Hunger: Food Is Not the Answer," *Christianity Today* (Dec. 11, 1981).

27. An Idea Whose Time Has Come
Gordon Campbell Stewart

Luke 16:1–13

John Burroughs, the Thoreau-like American naturalist, observed in his book *Time and Change* that "nature teaches more than she preaches. There are no sermons in stones."

If only Burroughs had lived in 1988 he might have changed his mind! For if the scientists are right, nature not only is trying to teach us something; today it is thundering a sermon whose message we dare not miss. There may not be any sermons in stones, as Burroughs thought, though I wonder about that, but there surely is a sermon in the skies these days for all who regard nature as "the art of God."

When we go out under the open skies, it is what we cannot see that should trouble us. We don't see it, but we can feel it, and we read about it in *Time* and *Newsweek* and in more scientific journals like *Science* and *Science News.* I speak, of course, about the warming of the earth's climate. This warming is attributable, according to some scientists, to the "greenhouse effect": the trapping of heat by a thickening layer of carbon dioxide, methane, nitrous oxide, and, more recently, chloroflurocarbons. On top of that there's the relatively sudden break in the ozone layer of the atmosphere, which fil-

Gordon C. Stewart is senior minister of Knox Presbyterian Church in Cincinnati, Ohio, a church known especially for its music program. A graduate of Maryville College, he received his master of divinity degree from McCormick Theological Seminary and was a Charles E. Merrill Fellow at Harvard Divinity School in 1981. Stewart is a previous winner of the Best Sermons competition.

ters the sun's ultraviolet rays to keep the earth from being scorched. It's what we've been feeling in terms of heat, though we can't see it in the open skies, that we should be heeding as the sermon nature is preaching.

Our civilization has become like the person Thomas Huxley described as "uninstructed in natural history . . . [whose] seaside stroll is a walk through a gallery filled with wonderful works of art, nine-tenths of which have their faces turned to the wall." Because we have not been instructed in nature's teachings, those who have strolled along the beaches on our eastern seaboard have seen the horror. The sea we have always played in has become a dump for medical garbage—not a place for the porpoises to frolic and the sand dollars to grow, but a dump for syringes and blood bags and all kinds of medical waste.

We're in trouble, folks, whether we know it or not. We have left nine-tenths of nature's art turned to the wall, and now we are suffering the consequences of our own ignorance and the effects of our own corporate sinfulness, the results of biting the hand that feeds us.

So I propose to you a very old idea whose time has come: the old biblical idea that somehow we have never quite gotten straight—the idea of stewardship!

Because we confuse stewardship with fund-raising on "Stewardship Sunday" in October, we have turned the true picture of stewardship, along with nature's art, to the wall of the gallery. The idea of stewardship is not primarily about the giving of money. It's about the care of the planet and of one another and of life itself.

The biblical drama casts human beings as Adam and Eve whose vocation is to care for the Garden God has made. We (humankind) are there collectively in the characters of Adam and Eve. But there are limits to our behavior. We cannot eat of the one forbidden tree without terrible consequences. The Fall itself occurs in the Genesis story when the man and the woman violate the limit God has placed upon their activity in the Garden. They eat the forbidden fruit to their own peril, and we have been doing it ever since.

To be human, according to the Genesis story, is to be a steward. Stewardship is the peculiarly *human* vocation. The steward is not the owner, only the manager of what belongs to another. The biblical drama says that the earth belongs to God; we human beings collectively are the steward, the caretaker.

Stewardship time, then, is *every* time! Yes, it's our use of money. Yes, it's our care for the homeless and hungry and for the church's program. But it's even more about the whole fabric of our lives. Stewardship is our relationship to the water we drink and the air we breathe. It's about the care of people in hospitals and nursing homes, but it's also about our responsibility for the medical wastes we create in the process and how we dispose of them. It has to do with how we warm our homes in the winter and cool them in the summer and the way we transport ourselves from here to there. It has to do with whether we dream more of exploring space than we care for the space in which we are now privileged to live, the earth that now cries out to us. It has to do with how we organize ourselves in society, lest we wish to pay the consequences of missing the sermon that nature is preaching.

Which brings us finally to the parable of the unjust steward. Can you picture us as the steward who is summoned to give an account of his stewardship in Jesus' parable?

The charge against him is that he has been "wasting" the owner's goods. Word about this wasting has reached the owner, who brings the steward, the way God brings Adam and Eve in the Genesis story, to say to him, "What is this that I hear about you? Turn in the account of your stewardship. Turn over the books and give me your keys! You can no longer be steward. You're fired!"

Without jumping ahead to how the wayward steward works his way back into the owner's good graces, note for now only that Jesus ended his parable with this point: "No servant can serve two masters; for either he will hate the one and love the other, or he will be devoted to the one and despise the other. You cannot serve God and mammon." Which is to say, you cannot walk east and west at the same time! You must choose between two masters.

That stuff washed up on our beaches draws us back to the truth of what happens when the steward serves the wrong master. What struck me when I first heard of medical waste washing up on our shores—we were on vacation in New York where we had just taken the ferry over to Staten Island when we learned on the evening news that its beaches had been closed—was how unthinkably greedy it is that somebody would care so little as to treat the ocean as if it were a dump or a cesspool!

The beaches had been closed to the swimming public because of tidal pollution. A *Time* cover story depicts the horrors of what can happen when the steward in Jesus' parable wastes the goods he has been charged to care for. As of that time, "more than 50 miles of New York City and Long Island beaches had been declared temporarily off limits to the swimming public because of tidal pollution. Some of the beaches were reopened but had to be closed again as more sickening debris washed in. And the threat is far from over: last week medical waste was washing up on the beaches of Rhode Island and Massachusetts. 'The planet is sending us a message,' says Dr. Stephen Joseph, New York City's health commissioner. 'We cannot continue to pollute the oceans with impunity.' "[1] Who says nature doesn't preach!

The crisis of the closed beaches brought attention to the fact that "since March of 1986 about 10 million tons of wet sludge processed by New York and New Jersey . . . treatment plants had been moved in huge barges out beyond the continental shelf " where "sewage has been released underwater in great, dark clouds," all of it approved by the Environmental Protection Agency.

Jacques Cousteau, the marine biologist and oceanographer we have come to love and respect for his television specials on the sea, says, "The very survival of the human species depends upon the maintenance of an ocean clean and alive, spreading all around the world. The ocean is our planet's life belt" and, according to the *Time* article, "the planet's life belt is rapidly unbuckling."

Our survival depends just as much upon that thin layer of ozone and that precarious "balance of nature" that the modern Adam and Eve have disturbed by pressing beyond the limits God has placed on their use of the Garden—their abuse of their vocation as stewards, managers of what belongs to another.

What, then, shall we do? Do you remember what the steward in Jesus' parable did when he was about to be fired? When told to give an account of his stewardship, he knew he had served the wrong master. He, too, asked, "What shall I do, since my master is taking the stewardship away from me?" He decided essentially that if he couldn't repay everything he had wasted—if there was no way to make full reparations and no way back to innocence—he would begin by doing what he could.

He went to those who were indebted to his master and whose bills he hadn't collected, and he did something very crafty. He told them to pay some percentage of what they owed—50 percent in one case, 80 percent in the other example—and then presented the money to the owner. And to our shock, the owner, in turn, commended the unjust steward for his prudence.

When the steward went to the debtors and asked for only a percentage of what they owed, he did two things out of self-interest. He made friends of the people from whom he collected, who didn't have to pay the whole amount, so that if the owner really did fire him he would at least have a few friends he could turn to. Who of us wouldn't like a bill collector like that? And he took a chance that the owner would see his efforts as evidence that he was at least trying to do right and not put him out of his stewardship.

The point of the parable is not that we should be dishonest or crafty. Jesus' point is that God leaves the door open for the steward to come around, that God is gracious! Jesus may even be saying that enlightened self-interest can provide the occasion through which God's grace works.

In that case, we can rejoice that there is still something we can do about our stewardship. We can put into practice an idea whose time has clearly come. It is time to care for the earth rather than plunder it. We can act as people who take our vocation as steward seriously, no longer wasting the owner's goods through foolish neglect or willful disregard. We can act now on the clear choice, which lies so obviously before us, of leaving the world in the hands of uncontrolled greed or enacting and enforcing laws that say that some things, like air and water and the atmosphere, are too precious to be spoiled for any selfish cause.

Though the clock is running, and there is no way to restore the ozone we have depleted, so far as we know, we can decide like the unjust steward to restore at least a part of what we have wasted or stolen from God's Creation. Perhaps it is not too much to expect, given his track record, that the owner will again be gracious when we have done all we could!

NOTE

1. *Time* (August 1, 1988).

V. PASTORAL

28. The Toughest Commandment

Charlene P. Kammerer

John 15:9–17

The toughest commandment Jesus ever issued was simply stated. He told his followers and his friends to "love one another." According to John's Gospel, Jesus also was confident that this command would become a reality—"This is my commandment, that you love one another as I have loved you."

In his *Works of Love*, Kierkegaard uses a simple analogy.

> The tree is known by its fruit: a tree is also known by its leaves but the fruit still affords the essential knowledge. If you, therefore, identified a tree by its leaves as being that particular tree, but in the time of fruit, you discovered that it did not bear fruit, then you would know from this that it was not the tree that it appeared to be from its leaves. This is true also concerning the recognition of love.[1]

I remember walking down the hospital corridor with my pastor's heart in place. The family had warned me that Dad might be a little difficult when I visited him. Although his family were members of our congregation, I had never met Joe. He did not attend worship or other church activities; he was not at home when I visited; he was away a lot "on business." Little did I realize that he was often unemployed, was in and out of the local detox unit for alco-

Charlene P. Kammerer currently is superintendent, Tallahassee District, of the United Methodist Church, Florida Conference, following ministerial posts at Duke University and several United Methodist churches.

holism, and would disappear from the scene of his family life and home for weeks at a time. As I got closer to the door of his room, I heard an angry voice screaming for someone to come and help him. Because the nurses' station was immediately across from his room, I stopped there and innocently asked if there was a problem. Was it all right if I went in for a visit? The two nurses seated there looked at each other with a knowing look, and one told me, "We're tired of his constant demands on us. Sure, go ahead and visit him—*Good luck!*" So I crossed the corridor and got as far as the threshold of the room. The moment I looked in, straight at his face, there came from his mouth a string of obscenities that blew me away. He demanded to know who I was, what in blankety-blank I was doing there, and insisted that I leave him the hell alone. Some of the things he said to me I still don't understand because of their utter brutality and vulgarity. It is the first and only time I ever had a complete pastoral call clutching the door jamb for support the entire time. He continued to scream at me, especially when he found out I was his minister. He told me he was going to die and go straight to hell and wanted to, for that matter. His body appeared through the folds of the sheets, wasted; his face was yellow and sagging; his eyes were almost black and so full of hatred. He told me he didn't love anybody, that he didn't care about anything, and he wanted to be left alone. This man, a husband and father, was no longer recognizable as Joe.

It took all the courage I had to stand there and receive his verbal abuse. When he tired, I began to shout at him across the room what I believed to be true. From what I had seen, I could not understand how anyone in the world could choose to come and help him. But guess what! His wife, his son, his two daughters loved him! I knew they had to be quite sick, perhaps crazy, to love anyone who acted like this. But even if they hadn't loved him and had abandoned him, God loved him! This seemed so incomprehensible to me that I got angry at God—for having the audacity to claim through a divine love and a divine sacrifice that this man was worth dying for. No way! I told him that, and he cussed me right out the doorway. Two days later, he died, and everyone felt relieved at the hospital and in the church and in his family. I officiated at a graveside service, with his wife and three children present. As I stood over the grave, I still felt so enraged and violated with this man's awful treatment of me and anyone around him that I expected great difficulty proclaiming the love, mercy, and grace of the gospel. But in speaking the words of divine love and forgiveness, in hearing this wounded family give witness to the man they had known and loved a long time ago, and still loved, we were all comforted.

We were able to trust in and believe in a love so profound, *God's love*, that we could finally entrust this shattered fragment of a man, who knew not love, to God's eternal care and love.

A fundamental human quest is for God, for the purpose and meaning of our lives to become clear. Even in Joe's tormented quest for meaning, for rescue from hopelessness, I believe there is grace present. Although he was unable to receive it, he was surrounded by a love so profound and so deep that he could not escape it—the love of Jesus Christ.

When I read and study John's Gospel, I am aware the author is speaking to an in-house crowd. He is keenly interested in confirming the faith of the early Christians, strengthening their life together, and correcting the faith of those whose beliefs were not accurate. The writer says several times, "No one has ever seen God." But "the author and those who share his faith have experienced the eternal Word dwelling in their midst as Jesus of Nazareth. Through him they have come to know the unseen God. From him, they have received grace abundant, as well as the truth concerning God and the life of the world."[2]

It is helpful to recall that, for John, "love" is not a feeling; rather, it is being "for" the other person and acting accordingly. To love, is to be *for* another and to act for another, even at cost to oneself. The way in which love for one another is measured is God's love for the world and Christ's love, which carried out in full and final obedience that love of God.

It is curious to me that John invited the early Christians to reexamine their fruitfulness and their faithfulness. While he never went to General Conference or never imagined such an event, he lifts up for us concerns that all Christians share. The community of Christians have defaulted on their vows. Lethargic members have had enthusiasm dimmed and faded. Their devotion has cooled and relaxed. This John of Scripture has Jesus insist on the evidences of discipleship. No pat recitations of the Lord's Prayer or quoting from the Torah or the Discipline would do! No singing psalms of praise or singing hymns in the new hymnal would do it! Discipleship had to do with concrete acts of love toward others.

In John's view, Jesus has constituted the disciples as a society of friends. This type of society will run counter to the institutional, organizational understanding of the church, which was gaining the upper hand in John's day.

The disciples are friends, not first of one another, but of Jesus. Only because of that are they friends of one another. The life of this society is characterized by joy, bearing fruit, that is, keeping the commandment of love.

Jesus said, "You did not choose me, but I chose you and appointed you that you should go and bear fruit and that your fruit should abide . . . . This I command you—to *love one another*."

Recently, our son asked his father and me a question we had been anticipating a long time. Why didn't the woman who gave him birth keep him? Of course, the questions behind that question were these: Didn't she love me? Was something wrong with me? Was I a "bad baby"? Was something wrong with her?

We answered his question with our hearts in our throats: Son, she *loved* you! She made sure that you were healthy as you grew in her body. She thought you were *the most beautiful baby* born that spring day in March. (You know something? She was right!) But she was afraid—afraid she couldn't take care of you as she wanted to. She was scared and afraid that she couldn't be a good mother. And she *loved* you so much that she asked the nurse to find a good home for you. She wanted you to have a mother and a father who would love you and treasure you. She requested that you be in a family where God's love was real. She loved you so much that she turned you over to God—for God to work a miracle of love. And God did because God is love!

Friends in Christ, the gospel declares to us,

• for all the Joes of this world, that life has beaten down, that remain hidden and forgotten;
• for all the unnamed parents of this world who are separated from their children;
• for all the brokenness, sin, evil, and despair in the world;

There is a transforming love of God known to us in Jesus the Christ.

The way we bear witness to that love is *to love one another*—especially the unloveable ones from whom we might recoil.

Jesus the Christ still asks his followers and friends today to love one another—the toughest commandment of all.

For the love of God, why don't we try it? Why don't we try it? Amen.

NOTES

1. Søren Kierkegaard, *Works of Love* (New York Harper & Row, 1964).
2. Fred B. Craddock, *The Gospels* (Nashville: Abingdon, 1981), 131.

29. Love in Action
William H. Willimon

And Jesus looking upon him loved him, and said to him, "You lack
one thing; go, sell what you have, and give to the poor"
———Mark 10:17–31

Baptist prophet Will Campbell, a man who is always an uncomfort-
able guest, was asked to be a visiting preacher for a series at New
York's Riverside Church on"What Riverside Church Can Do to
Help the Future of Race Relations in America." Here is a church
with impressively activist preachers and the right sort of forward-
thinking congregation.

Campbell took as his text Mark's story of the rich young man.
"What can Riverside Church do to help race relations?" he asked at
the beginning of his sermon. "What can this church do to relate to
its next-door neighbors in Harlem?" "Nothing," said Campbell.
"Nothing . . . unless you sell your big building and give it to the
poor. Let's go out on the street and see what you can get for this big
thing. Let's see what God will do with us."

Needless to say, the host preacher and congregation were not
amused. They wanted to know what they needed to do to be liberal,
right-thinking, not necessarily to inherit eternal life. Besides, we're
not all that rich. We do a lot of good with our big building. We have
programs of community outreach, a day-care center. What good
would our drop of wealth do when plopped in the great bucket of
the world's vast need? Such are our rationalizations in response to

William H. Willimon, a Methodist, is dean of Duke Chapel and
professor of the Practice of Christian Ministry at Duke University in
Durham, North Carolina. He is the author of twenty-six books, including
Sighing for Eden and What's Right with the Church, and is an editor-at-large
for The Christian Century.

this story of Jesus and the rich young man. You can understand why, when Will Campbell visited us, I did not have him preach in Duke Chapel.

I dare say we haven't advanced far in our rationalization for why we don't go and do what Jesus so clearly tells us. The rich young man did not expect to hear of his riches. He wanted to talk about social ethics, about the great social issues of our day. And he never would have engaged Jesus in theological debate had he not been sure that his own righteousness was impeccable. He obeyed the law. He voted Democratic in the last election, was a member of the Sierra Club and ate no non-union grapes. What can I do now to advance the cause of peace with justice? Write my congressperson? Join the NAACP?

"And Jesus loved him and said, 'Go, sell all you have, and give it to the poor.' " And Jesus loved him. Oh, I've got my own resources for rationality and weaseling out of selling all I have, and giving it to the poor. But the thing that strikes me is Mark's editorial comment, not found in the other evangelists' treatment of this tale: "And Jesus loved him." He loved him. Does that seem strange to you? With people around like Jesus to love you, you don't need anyone to despise you!

"Jesus loved him and said, 'Go, sell all you have, and give it to the poor!' " He lacked "one thing needful," something beyond the bounds of conventional morality and realistic, practical ethics.

Of course, if I had been Jesus that day, that's not what I would have said. I might have asked the well-heeled young man for an endowed fund for student scholarships or a bigger pledge for the church budget, but not *everything*. This I call pastoral care, compassion. Unlike Jesus, if I had looked upon the young man, I would have been sensitive to his personal limitations, his need for some earthly security, his desire for something practical, workable. I've had courses in pastoral counseling. I know that even though this young man is well-off financially, he is still a poor, struggling beggar—spiritually speaking, psychologically speaking. He is like all the rest of us, doing the best he can.

And that's good enough for me. So my flock, when it comes to me for counseling or guidance, doesn't expect to be told something "irrational" like, "Go, sell all you have and give it to the poor." It expects to be assured that they are doing the best they can, that whatever they have already decided in their hearts is right, is fine with me.

It's more difficult to practice this sort of pastoral care than you might imagine, for the tough part, as far as the progressive, sensitive pastor is concerned, is to figure out what people have already decided to do before they ask you your opinion of what they ought to do. "What must I do to inherit eternal life?"

"Well," Jesus should have said (if Jesus had had the benefit of a seminary education), "What do you think is practical—considering your socioeconomic circumstances? What feels right to you?"

Which would confirm your opinion that preachers are cowards. But not necessarily. As a young pastor, Reinhold Niebuhr said that he first thought that pastors preach such tame, innocuous sermons because they are afraid of being fired for saying something unpopular. The longer he was a pastor, the better Niebuhr learned that preachers get tamed, not by their parishioners' ire, but through their love. "It is tough to say unpleasant things to people one has learned to love," said Niebuhr. Justice is more practical than love. Niebuhr suggested that love is the problem, not the answer.

And yet Mark says that Jesus spoke an unpleasant word to the rich young man because he loved him. I fear that I (and most of my church) in the name of "love," have decided to help make peoples' lives a little less miserable rather than a lot more redeemed. In the name of our "love" we bless all sorts of behavior. Our goal is to help people adjust, accept, affirm, and live with who they already are rather than call them to convert to someone they could never be without the gospel. Accommodation rather than conversion is the name of our game. So rich young men will be told to use their wealth responsibly rather than fundamentally to question the values on which their lives are based. Rich young women will be told to join NOW and fight for a bigger piece of the pie that rich young men have been eating for so long. It's still the same pie. People will be asked by their preachers to be a little less greedy, a little less violent (or at least, if violent, violent in the service of "peace with justice"). You don't need Jesus dying on a cross for what everyone already finds easy.

We say we do it out of love. To ask more would be to risk provoking a crisis in their lives that might blow them away. You are so morally and emotionally fragile, aren't you glad that you have a sensitive, caring, affirming pastor like me to protect you?

Of course, there is a good chance that you're smart enough to see through my claims of pastoral love and protection. You know why I don't ask more of you, call you to Abundant Life rather than mere decency—self-protection. After all, if I called you to discipleship, to responsibility, you might call me to base my life not on my things or my alleged goodness but on Jesus. And then where would you be? I'll tell you where: We might have disposed of this anemic thing we call "love" and be on our way to something like the love of Christ.

As a young pastor, I preached a sermon against the evils of materialism and greed. I don't think that my text was the story of the rich young man, but it might have been. The sermon was quite "prophetic"—which is to say that everyone felt guilty afterward. But on his way out the door, the chair of our administrative board said, "Good sermon, preacher. But I bet you'll still expect a good raise this year."

That was the last sermon I preached on the "evils of materialism." Not that I love the chairman of my board. I love me too much to try it again! Be suspicious when I tell you that I am silent out of love for you! Can we love enough to speak the truth to one another, in love?

A couple in my church has marital problems. Well actually, the problem is he got interested in another woman and said he wanted out of their twelve years and two children. A young man in my church, a lawyer, took me to lunch. (He had me for lunch.)

"I'm very upset about the situation with Tom and Janet," he said, once our meal had started. "What do you think we should do, preacher?"

I began my liberal litany. There is probably little we can do. It is their problem. We need to love them, be supportive, caring. There are two sides to every problem. These things happen. Amen.

"Well," he told me, "If that's all you, the church, have got to say, then no wonder nobody has respect for the church. I thought the church cared about justice, right and wrong. If this is the best we can do with two people in our own family, then you've got no right to tell us what to do about Central America, capital punishment, or anything else that matters. We can't have it both ways."

Do you know anyone whom you love so much that you will tell the truth and fully expect him or her to do the same for you? I'm not talking about "hanging tough," "letting the chips fall where they may," etc. I'm talking about trusting Jesus' ability to produce the sort of people his good news really demands.

The church began as a nonviolent institution. In the early days, at least until the third or fourth century, soldiers, government bureaucrats, others who made money from war, were excluded. Conversion was the order of the day. In the debate over whether or not the growing, successful church ought to relax its moral demands and become more "realistic," Maximus the Confessor wrote, "No one must distort the Word of God to indulge his moral negligence; it is better to confess one's weakness, not concealing God's truth, lest, together with transgresssing his commandments, we become guilty of intentionally misinterpreting the Word of God."[1]

Recently, a friend of mine and I wrote a book on United Methodist revitalization. A district superintendent from New York wrote to say, "Your book is unfortunate. It will do much damage to our church. Of course, much of what you criticize is true, but if you really cared about our church, you would not have said it this way."

The Christian thing to do, the pastoral, loving, enlightened thing is to sigh deeply and give a check to the United Fund.

Are you, as individuals, as a church, so fragile? Do you really need my protection? Is Jesus so powerless as to be unable to make us into the kind of disciples he demands? In my last church, we were discussing the possibility of opening up a weekday day-care center in our church. I was in favor of the idea. We had this big building which was empty most of the week. We needed more young families. At a meeting of our Christian Education committee, we discussed the proposal.

"I can't understand why the church is in the day-care business," said Gladys Smith. "I'd like to know why we're getting into this."

"Well, Gladys," I said rather exasperatedly. "Let me explain it to you again." Again I went over the reasons: the empty building, the young couples, the need for money.

"Right," said a more supportive layperson. "You know how hard it is to put food on the table these days, Gladys. Everybody must work."

"That's not true," said Gladys. "It isn't hard for anyone in this church to put food on the table. No. There are people for whom such necessities are difficult but you know as well as I, that they wouldn't come to this day-care center. Let's be honest: What's becoming more difficult is to have the two cars, the VCR, the house at the lake—all these things that our parents never expected have become necessities for us. I just hate to see the church buying into the same corrupt value system as everyone else, telling these young couples that all that junk leads to happiness or makes them better parents. I think the church ought to have the courage to tell them—'that's a lie.' "

And I, as pastor, as resident moral guardian, said, "Dern you, Gladys. Would you let me look after the ethics of this congregation?"

And Gladys loved him and said, "Father Zossima, in Dostoyevski's *The Brothers Karamazov* (Book I, part 4) comments, 'Love in action is a harsh and dreadful thing, compared with love in dreams.' "

NOTE

1. Maximus the Confessor, *Four Centuries of Love*, IV, p. 85.as quoted in *Nonviolence*, p. 79.). Translated this means: If we can't follow Jesus on his terms, at least we should care enough to confess our weakness. Rather than change the gospel to fit our inadequacies, we ought to change ourselves to fit the gospel. Alas, I am that rich young man.

30. Embracing Our Fear of Abandonment on the Way to the Promise

Donald M. Wardlaw

And the Lord said, "My presence will go with you and I will give you fullness."

————Exod. 33:14

Can you imagine yourself talking to God the way Moses did that day out in the wilderness? Can you imagine?

Moses had every reason at that moment to give up, He was worn out with moving this ragtag band of ex-slaves toward the Promised Land. He was ready to take early retirement rather than hassle with these people any more. Forty years of struggling through the wilderness of complaints, bickering, near starvation, and administrative boondoggling. Finally, a few weeks ago Moses had come down from Mount Sinai, where he had received the precious tablets of stone, only to find his people wallowing in orgies before a golden calf. It had taken all Moses' negotiating skills to talk God out of obliterating these people on the spot. So the Lord stays with these anxious refugees, pressing the tired Moses to get on with it.

"Come on, Moses. One more push. Let's move this rebellious, frightened people across the Jordan into the Promised Land where the milk and honey of rootedness and identity awaits them."

Now we tune in on a crucial conversation between Moses and God where Moses bargains with God for some assurances in this fi-

---

Donald M. Wardlaw is professor of Christian Preaching and Worship at McCormick Theological Seminary and serves as editor of *Preaching Biblically.* Dr. Wardlaw is a past president of the Academy of Homiletics.

nal push. As we eavesdrop, we are surprised by Moses' near gall.

"Lord," says Moses, "you keep telling me that a new sense of who we are is just beyond that river and that I'm your man to get us there. Fine. But I have to have some guarantee that you will be wading through those waters with us when we cross into the Promised Land."

The Lord comes through with a major guarantee. "Moses, my presence will go with you and I will give you fullness."

To which Moses responds with a cheeky declaration, "If you don't go over there with me, let's just forget about the whole deal." And on top of that nervy word Moses pushes for yet more guarantees of God's presence.

"Lord, if you say you're with us and that I'm your man, then show me your *whole glory*, show me your face right here and now."

You could almost hear the Lord's patient sigh.

"Moses, I can only give you a glimpse of my glory, for if you were to see my face, you couldn't handle that much light. You'd die."

You see, the Hebrews believed you cannot behold the face of God in all its transcendent majesty and take it all in. It's too much. You die. Now the ever-gracious God counters with a deal.

"Here's how I'll let you peek at my glory, Moses. You hide in the cleft of this boulder here, and I'll cover you with my hand. Then I'll pass by, and you'll at least feel the train of my robe brush your face."

So Moses' spunk produces some concrete assurances.

But the closer we listen to this conversation in the wilderness, the more we wonder if it isn't the fear of abandonment that fuels Moses' *chutzpah*. Don't you hear some fear in Moses' voice when he says, "If you don't go with me, then I don't go," or, "If I'm your man, then show me your face"? What's behind this push is Moses' fear that God might abandon him in the desert. Not so much the ring of gall as the sound of terror in Moses' voice at the thought of trying *by himself* to drag this people kicking and screaming across the Jordan into the promise of spiritual maturity.

You and I know something of Moses' fear of abandonment. It's like God's gone back up on the mountain and left you and me to cross the Jordan by ourselves. It's like you've always had trouble getting next to people, and now you are left on your own to learn how to trust. It's like you've always majored in finding fault with others, and now you're set out here in the desert to figure by yourself how to accept others. It's like you've always struggled with self-confidence, and now you're expected entirely on your own to come up with a large dose of confidence. It's like you've been propelled by simmering anger all your life, and now you are abandoned to conjure a whole new life-style by yourself, one based on peacefulness.

Now, suppose the Lord appears in this wilderness of yours, just as the Lord appeared to Moses and begins urging you to get on toward the Jordan? How would you, with this fear of abandonment, respond? You may be smiling to yourself now as you think about it.

"Me, I'd probably respond as I've done most of my life. 'Don't you worry, Lord. I can handle it OK. You go on back to the council chamber on Mount Sinai and worry about the mess in South Africa and the turmoil over human rights in South Korea. I'll make it to the other side, all right.' "

Then you turn toward me and confess, "As usual I'd probably work to look so cool and self-assured. I'd want the Lord to know how easily I can handle this maturing process."

But what if I were to ask you, "How do you really feel amid this striving to look so self-sufficient?"

"Well," you might say, "if I let myself admit my feelings, I'd feel like I was working overtime to fool everyone—the Lord, myself, others."

"What would you really like to say to the Lord," I ask, "when the Lord starts pressing you to keep moving toward the Promised Land?"

As you respond I can tell it comes from deep inside.

"I'd like to say to the Lord what Moses said out there. I'd like to say I wasn't about to move through those waters to new life unless the Lord was wading there beside me. Why? Because I can't bear this burden by myself. *Because I'm afraid.* I can't make it on my own."

Fascinating, how when Moses—and you and I—embrace our fears that we can't make it alone, that's precisely when God says, "My presence will go with you, and I will give you fullness." Precisely when you and I give up the myth of our self-sufficiency and face straightaway our anxiety about crossing the Jordan all by ourselves, God says, "I'm here. I've got the promise you've always longed for." And here's the good news. You and I out there in our wilderness of pride have an advantage that Moses never had. Moses had only the hem of God's robe for assurance and not the Lord's face. But you and I have help from a Galilean who comes to us today in a thousand faces. When we learn to recognize and trust those faces, we live!

In 1931, a gentleman named Roland H. stared desperately into such a face, the face of Carl Gustav Jung, the famous Swiss psychotherapist. Carl Jung had treated Roland H. for over a year for alcoholism, but Roland kept slipping back into drunkenness. Finally, Carl Jung startled Roland by suggesting that Roland was beyond any further medical or psychiatric help. Stunned, Roland asked Jung if there was any other source of hope. Jung said the only hope would be a religious conversion that could possibly remotivate him to sobriety. Jung even suggested such a route to recovery would be pretty rare for alcoholics.

Roland H. joined the Oxford Group movement, at that time an evangelical church renewal movement that enjoyed success in Europe and America. Roland H. learned prayer and meditation and soon came to embrace his fear that he couldn't go it alone. Roland came to a radical transformation of spirit and found release at last from the compulsion to drink. He began to work with other alcoholics and soon founded an organization called Alcoholics Anonymous. Today that organization has, worldwide, a million and a half members with nearly seventy thousand chapters. The first thing every alcoholic admits when joining AA is that they can never get to the Promised Land of sobriety without God wading the Jordan with them. And it all began with the face of the Galilean, as seen in the visage of Carl Jung, humbly suggesting to Roland H. that only the presence of God could give him fullness.

Which of the thousand faces around you promises to see you through the waters to new identity and spiritual fullness? Maybe a therapist or counselor who has helped you embrace your fear that you can't go it alone, that all those games of self-control you've played in your work, marriage, or friendships haven't moved you one inch toward the Jordan. Maybe the face of a parent or special colleague who sees you struggling too hard in the wrong places to look triumphant and successful, who nevertheless offers you the arms of acceptance you need. Faces of people who both call into question your self-sufficiency and wade with you through the waters. Says Canadian author and analyst Marion Woodman, the critical transition into spiritual maturity begins with a surrender to a higher power. She writes, "At the very point of the vulnerability is where the surrender takes place—that is where God enters. God comes in through the wound."[1]

My friend Sara felt stymied in her journey toward the Promised Land. For weeks she had seemed to travel in circles in her private wilderness of isolation and fear. She struggled with the depressing feeling that her woundedness was all she had for companionship on her life journey. But then God came to her through her wound; God came through a dream. Sara dreamed she was frolicking in the snow atop a mountain. And as she awoke from her dream her head was filled with that well-known melody from Dvorak's *New World Symphony*, popularly known as "Going Home." Later Sara would see through the dream that this surrender to her dark side, to her fear that she was so vulnerable, was precisely the point where God could say to her, as to Moses, "My presence will go with you, and I will give you fullness." Time now to frolic to the music of a new world. Sara was on her way to the Promised Land.

And so with you. And so with us all.

NOTE

1. Marion Woodman, "Worshipping Illusion," *Parabola 2*, no. 2 (Summer 1987):64.

31. A Festival of Hope

Brian K. Bauknight

> In the days of Herod the king . . . during the reign of Caesar
> Augustus . . . when Quirinius was governor of Syria . . . .
> —Luke 1:5; 2:1–2

"In the days of Herod the king . . ." These are not words that mean
much to any of us. Perhaps, if we know the Christmas story well, we
recognize them as part of the narrative. But even then, we don't give
the names of Herod or Caesar Augustus or Quirinius much thought.
They are simply part of the traditional way of telling the story.

We do know something *about* these people. Herod, for example,
was a puppet king for Rome. He had a huge ego and a short temper.
Most of what he accomplished, he did by bribery. And he murdered
anyone who stood in his way. He even killed one of his wives and
two of his sons. In the language of the street, Herod was "one mean
dude." He was a terrifying figure.

Caesar Augustus was simply Caesar. He ruled like a god and
probably thought he was a god. All citizens of the empire were to
treat him as a god on a regular basis.

Quirinius is not as well established historically. We only know
that he was part of the Roman hierarchy and therefore represented
all that was hated by the Jews.

"In the days of Herod the king . . . when Quirinius was governor of Syria . . ." Why are these words in the story? Why are they
included?

Brian K. Bauknight is senior minister of Christ United Methodist
Church in Bethel Park, Pennsylvania. He attended Lehigh University, the
Theological School at Drew University, and Pittsburgh Theological Seminary, where he received a doctorate in ministry. Bauknight is the founding
member of the Make-A-Wish Foundation of Western Pennsylvania and is a
previous winner in the Best Sermons competition.

Some suggest that it is merely a matter of biblical trivia. It is filler material. (Remember how we used to add "filler" to term papers to achieve the required 2,500 words?) Are these perhaps just names that happen to be there?

Others suggest that the names and references are to give historical accuracy. They bring a level of authenticity to the story, a measure of exactness. It would be like saying, "In the days when Ronald Reagan was president of the United States, and when Bob Casey was governor of Pennsylvania, and when Sophie Maslof was mayor of Pittsburgh."

Perhaps either or both of theses speculations are correct. But suppose there is more to it? Suppose Luke is saying something far more significant. Suppose Luke is saying, as a preacher and proclaimer of the good news, "In the midst of the worst possible atmosphere, in the midst of the most depressing, despairing, and defeatest of times, in the face of a ruthless tyrant like Herod and a would-be god like Caesar and a symbol of Roman oppression like Quirinius, look what happened! Look what God did in the midst of the worst possible human scenario."

Luke may be telling us that this is no "Norman Rockwell" Christmas. This is no "jingle bells, jingle bells, jingle all the way" Christmas. This is no "ho, ho, ho!" moment. This is the worst of all possible times.

Remember how Charles Dickens began his classic novel, *A Tale of Two Cities?* It began, "It was the best of times, it was the worst of times . . ." That's what Luke is saying here, except in reverse order. "It was the worst of times, but God made it the best of times."

Many of you have read Scott Peck's book *The Road Less Traveled.* You may recall the first three-word sentence of that book: "Life is difficult."

Luke is saying, "Life was difficult beyond belief in those days." And life may again be agonizingly difficult in our day. The difficulty may be from within or from the outside. But . . . look what God did then! And look what God still does! And can do!

A beautiful bit of poetry from Madeleine L'Engle was in a Christmas letter we received recently:

> That was no time for a Child to be born,
> In a land in the crushing grip of Rome.
> Honor and truth were trampled by scorn—

Yet here did the Savior make His home.

When is the time for love to be born?
The inn is full on the planet earth,
And by greed and pride the sky is torn—
Yet love still takes the risk of birth.

In the midst of the worst possible days of our lives, God gives us a festival of hope. In the days of Herod the king, of Caesar Augustus, of Quirinius of Syria, Mary and Joseph made their way to Bethlehem. There, a child was born. Angels sang that night, and a brilliant star lit up the night sky.

Christmas is our festival of hope amidst whatever would drag us down—in our lives or in the life of the world. Whatever oppression, whatever crushing burden, whatever pain and sorrow afflict your heart, the Savior can still be born. In the midst of times when life is most difficult, through tears and trauma, there is still a living festival of hope.

That is what Luke is saying! The text is a powerful witness to the majesty and care of God. It is about a festival of hope that is very real!

It is about a hope that is real for our personal lives. This is not a false hope.

A pastoral colleague tells of a phone call he received from the wife of a friend one afternoon. Her husband was just then being wheeled into the operating room for surgery on a malignant brain tumor. A few weeks later, this pastor phoned his friend at the hospital. They talked for a while. Then the recuperating friend said, "I have come to learn something about hope in all of this. I used to caution people about the danger of false hope. I have come to the conclusion, however, that there is no such think as false hope. Either there is hope or there is not hope at all."

Luke is proclaiming the great hope for our lives in this story. The angels' song is heard against the dissonant notes of sickness, strife, and suffering in our lives.

On Christmas Eve—just a few days hence—we will have a huge throng of people in our worship services. There will undoubtedly be more people here in the space of a few hours on Christmas Eve than at any other time of the year. Sometimes we are flip and casual about the Christmas Eve crowd. We talk about our "Christmas and Easter" congregations.

But I often see faces very differently in the Christmas Eve crowd. I see them from a different perspective in the pulpit than you might see them from the pews. I see people who have come as a courageous act of hope.

Scattered throughout the room are those who are sitting alone for the first time ever on Christmas Eve. Elsewhere are the broken and divorced families sitting together as a fierce testimony to their determination not to stop being a family completely. And still elsewhere sit those people who sense that it will be their last Christmas. It is not spoken aloud; but they know it.

People who come together for a personal festival of hope. They sense God's redemption in a brutal time—some, appropriately, with tears streaming down their cheeks.

I mentioned a bit of poetry by Madeleine L'Engle a few moments ago. Recently, her book *Two-Part Invention* was reviewed. It is the story of her forty-year marriage to actor Hugh Franklin. Franklin died in 1986 of a painful form of cancer. Ms. L'Engle, who is a devout Christian, is quoted with these words from her book:

> It is when things go wrong, when the good things do
> not happen, when our prayers seem to have been
> lost, that God is most present. We do not need the
> sheltering wings when things go smoothly. We are
> closest to God in the darkness, stumbling along
> blindly.[1]

This is why we sing the carols with such verve and vitality at Christmas. That is why we sing,

> There's a song in the air
> There's a star in the sky;
> There's a mother's deep prayer
> And a baby's low cry:
>
> And the star rains its fire while the beautiful sing;
> For the manger of Bethlehem cradles our King.[2]

This is a festival of hope that is real for our personal lives.

It is also a festival of hope that is real for the life of the world.

We have been numbed by tragedy so often in the days just before Christmas. This year, the tragedy came in the form of an earthquake in Soviet Armenia. A few huge plates in the earth shift unexpectedly, and 55,000 people die, 100,000 or more are homeless, and countless others are bereft of family. Yet hope remembers the Child who was born out of that One who is Lord, even in tragedy.

Even if the world should somehow come to the very edge of the abyss itself, Christmas reminds us of our hope in the One who is Lord of the abyss.

Or consider the ray of hope that arose out of the Middle East late this same Advent season when Yasir Arafat conceded gently and firmly that"Israel has a right to exist." He followed that statement with an absolute condemnation of all forms of terrorism. And the world breathed a little bit easier.

Curiously, it is a ray of hope during the festival of Christmas out of the essentially non-Christian world. It comes out of the Muslim and Jewish traditions of the Middle East.

A friend of mine cited this quotation from *Newsweek* columnist Meg Greenfield a few years ago. It is a truly remarkable statement.

> The non-Christian world envies and covets
> Christmas, wants to participate in it, is forever seeing
> just how close it can come to this particular
> experience without threatening the imperatives of
> its own religion. The non-Christian world is bent on
> universalizing the reach of Christmas.

Do you hear those words! "The non-Christian world is bent on universalizing the *reach* of Christmas." Thus does the festival of hope become real for the life of the world.

In this final week before Christmas, join your heart and your mind and your spirit to this festival of hope! Whatever darkness lies around you or beside you or even within you, wrap yourself in the warm, healthy, festive hope of the good news.

Recently, I came across this brief quote from Fra Giovanni:

> The gloom of the world
> is but a shadow.
> Behind it, yet within reach, is joy.
> There is radiance
> and glory in the darkness,
> could we but see,
> and to see, we have only to look.
> I beseech you
> to look.

I beseech you . . . look! Know the hope. Even in the darkest day of Herod the king and Caesar Augustus and Quirinius of Syria, God can enter and reenter and renew and renew again human life and history.

It is time for us, brothers and sisters, to bear a confident witness to our highest hope.

In the days of Herod the king—even those days of terrible tyranny—even in those days, Christ was born.

Thanks be to God.

NOTES

1. Madeleine L'Engle, *Two-Part Invention* (New York: Farrar, Straus & Giroux, 1988).
2. *Ibid.*

32. In a Dark Wood
Robert G. Dever

Gen. 45:1–15

Dante's *Divine Comedy* begins with these words: "Midway along the journey of our life, I woke to find myself in a dark wood, for I had wandered off from the straight path." Joseph often woke to find himself "in a dark wood." One day, he is a favored son. The next day, he is a slave. One day, he is a beloved servant. The next day, he is a prisoner. Joseph seems to travel on wings of tribulation. Circumstances seem to conspire to destroy him.

Reverberating throughout the Joseph narratives, however, are the words *the Lord was with him.* After so much trouble, finally he is recognized as a man of outstanding gifts and is given administrative authority over the nation Egypt. Joseph, at age thirty, has moved to the top. He is married to the daughter of an important priest. He is the father of two sons. He has all the things the world values. Outwardly, his life is exceedingly good. Inwardly, he dwells in a dark wood. He lacks the one thing that matters most—he lacks reconciliation with his brothers.

"Forgiveness," writes Dag Hammarskjöld in *Markings*, "is the answer to the child's dream of a miracle by which what is broken is made whole again, what is soiled is again made clean. The dream explains why we need to be forgiven, and why we must forgive. In the presence of God, nothing stands between Him and us—we are forgiven. But we cannot feel His presence if anything is allowed to stand between ourselves and others."[1]

Robert Glen Dever is a Roman Catholic serving in a pastoral role in a Louisville parish. A graduate of the University of Louisville, Dever received his master of divinity degree from Southern Baptist Theological Seminary. He was previously pastor of Grace Baptist Church in Baltimore, Maryland.

There can be no real joy and peace in our lives when there is an absence of forgiveness and reconciliation. Forgiveness and reconciliation ultimately come from God, yet there is an organic connection to our human practice. "Forgive us our debts," we pray, "as we forgive our debtors." Joseph, the dreamer, was haunted by unforgiven and unreconciled relationships. The faces of his brothers can be seen in the dark wood.

The practice of forgiveness is necessary work to accomplish if we are to remain on the straight path. Joseph sought to live his life as though he had no past. He tried to forget about his homeland and his childhood as Jacob's little boy. He suppressed the painful memories of the pit and the prison. But Joseph, like all of us, is not able to suppress the past. We live in the middle of our memories. They well up at unexpected times and in ways that are beyond our control. All that has happened to us, including the good and the bad, follows us all the days of our lives. If, by accident or disease we lost our memories, life loses much of its meaning. We see this tragedy in those people who suffer from Alzheimer's disease. We are what we have been; and until we accept our past—both the good and the bad—and practice forgiveness toward our past, we will lack real joy and peace. This is not always easy. It is, however, necessary work if we are to make progress on life's journey.

My daddy was not a perfect man, nor was he a perfect father. Our relationship was distant, especially as I grew into adolescense. There was no outward affection. I can never remember my daddy saying, "I love you." I left home when I was eighteen. He died when I was nineteen. After his death, I spent a lot of years resenting our relationship. I felt ambivalence as I remembered pleasant experiences as a little boy going fishing with my daddy. Yet always these memories were checked by the dissidence and conflict of my teen years. He was always there but was seldom fully present.

Sometime during my thirties, I came to terms with our relationship. I knew life had not always been easy for my daddy. He grew up poor and worked hard to support his family. As a young man, he fell in love, married, and had a son. Shortly thereafter, his wife and son died. During my teen years he suffered poor health. I began to realize that perhaps he was doing the best he could, even though I felt it was not enough. Then, one afternoon, I forgave him. When I did, I tasted tears flowing down my cheeks and felt peace and joy in my heart. I then remembered the day I left home. He and my mother took me to the airport on my way into military service. I shall always remember my daddy silently standing in the airport with no words on his lips but with tears in his eyes.

Through the years, there were a lot of tears in the eyes of Joseph. This is one of the important and reccurring themes in the Joseph narratives. Over and over, we read about this patriarch shedding tears. Then one day, Joseph comes face to face with the brothers who caused so many tears and so much tribulation.

The brothers come to Egypt in search of food for survival. The famine, which helped propel Joseph to the top, has reached into the land of his childhood. Jacob has sent all his sons except Benjamin down to Egypt to find something to eat. In one of the strange and synchronistic events of history, the family is united. The brothers no longer recognize Joseph, but he immediately recognizes them. Genesis records how he tricked the brothers in order to have Benjamin brought to Egypt. A second visit occurs, including Benjamin. This time on seeing his brothers, he weeps so loudly that everyone hears. He then reveals his identity by saying, "I am Joseph." Then one of the great moments of forgiveness and grace is recorded when "he kissed all his brothers and wept upon them."

This kind of forgiveness is what we need in our world and in our lives. We may have all the things the world values, including wealth, power, and health; but if we lack forgiveness, we lack the one thing necessary to move us on in our life's journey.

Forgiveness has two dimensions. One relates to our human relationships. The other relates to our God relationship. Reconciliation with others, which comes through forgiveness, is necessary if life is to achieve full meaning. Reconciliation with God, which likewise comes through forgiveness, is equally necessary. "If we confess our sins, he is faithful and just, and will forgive our sins and cleanse us from all unrighteousness" (1 John 1:9, RSV).

We do not find in the Joseph narratives a specific forgiveness event as we see after David's affair with Bathsheba and Peter's denial of Jesus. We do see, however, a life lived within a framework of faith in God's mercy. We see a man whose tears are an outward sign of the inward mercy and forgiveness of God. Joseph's tears communicate his forgiveness to others more profoundly than any words could ever do.

When Gandhi was fifteen, he stole some gold from his brother. He became overwhelmed with guilt and decided to confess his wrongdoing to his father, who was very ill. He decided to write out his confession and take it to his father. In the note, he confessed his guilt, asked for punishment, and promised never to steal again. He handed the note to his father with much fear and trembling. "He read it through," Gandhi writes in his autobiography, "and pearl-drops trickled down his cheeks, wetting the paper. For a moment he closed his eyes in thought and then tore up the note. He had sat up to read it. He again lay down. I also cried . . . . Those pearl-drops of love cleansed my heart, and washed my sin away."

Jacob, Joseph, and the brothers grew old in the land of Egypt. Jacob's last command before he died was for Joseph to forgive his brothers. Though Joseph had embraced his brothers with tears years before, they continued to doubt his forgiveness. When the message came, he again wept and reminded them that God's mercy was with him even in tribulation. He then reassured and comforted them.

God's forgiveness is available for each of us as we respond to God. God has made the first move in self-offering. "To the Lord our God belong mercy and forgiveness" (Dan. 9:9, RSV). It is up to us to respond. If you have never experienced God's forgiveness, I invite you now to confess your sin and discover the mercy of the Lord.

If there are broken relationships in your life, I invite you to seek out those people and perform the reconciling work of forgiveness. Remember also that the accepting of forgiveness can be more diffi-cult than the giving of forgiveness. Yet it is only when forgiveness is given and received that we make progress in life's journey. Forgive-ness is the way to move us from the dark wood and put us once again on the straight path that leads us into the fullness of life.

NOTE

1. Dag Hammarskjöld, *Markings* (New York:Knopf, 1964).

33. Marriage and Love's Mystery

Joseph A. Hill

Gen. 2:21–24; Mark 10:1–9; Eph. 5:25–33

First love—ah, the rapture of first love! Who cannot remember the earliest flutter of the heart? And who would not want to savor its sweet fruit in later years? But that isn't possible, for love, like everything else in life, is ever changing. Love either matures and ripens or it withers and dies. The poet's words ring true: "He that would eat of love must eat it where it hangs."[1] You cannot gather love's fruit and store it away. Enjoy it now, or you will lose it.

Yet, our love of yesteryear need not be lost forever. The simple act of remembering can help us revive the magic and mystery of early love. Reviewing our sacred vows on our wedding anniversary each year can rekindle the ardor of marital love and strengthen its bond. "I, John, take thee, Mary, to be my wedded wife; and I do promise and covenant, before God and these witnesses, to be thy faithful husband . . . as long as we both shall live." If you are happily married, the very sound of those timeworn phrases is a symphony of joy. But listening to that wedding covenant again might well strike a dissonant chord in your heart if your marriage has turned sour or lies shattered by divorce or separation.

Some of you know all too well the hurt, the disappointment, and the heartache of forgotten vows, a dead marriage, a broken home.

Joseph A. Hill is associate professor emeritus of Biblical Studies and Greek at Geneva College in Beaver Falls, Pennsylvania. A graduate of Pittsburgh Theological Seminary, he has pastored churches in Colorado, New York, and Pennsylvania. Hill was an advisor for the translation of the *New International Version of the Bible* and has written for *Christianity Today.*

You would be the first to say that life's greatest pain is felt in the wound where love once issued forth. But if faith has its way with your heart, you will instinctively sense the elemental truth about marriage: It is supposed to be for keeps.

There are good reasons for staying in a marriage, come what may. One reason is that a promise is a promise. That sounds terribly old-fashioned, I know. When we are angry and hurt, it is not easy to be civil with each other, much less idealistic about promises. Yet, it is possible, by God's grace, to rise above our deeply felt hostility and to say to each other, "We gave our solemn word to love and cherish each other today, tomorrow, and forever, and we are not free to break that promise—even if both of us want out of our marriage." Another good reason for staying married through good days and bad days is the hope, engendered by Christian faith, that things may take a turn for the better. In fact, many husbands and wives have discovered that struggling through their problems brings enrichment and closer bonding to their marriage. But the best reason for staying together in a lifelong partnership is that marriage is a holy ordinance of God. Not all marriages are made in heaven, to be sure. But the ordinance of marriage is divine; it is one of heaven's best gifts. God made us male and female, made us to be joined together in pairs, not just sexually but totally in a shared and unified life (Gen. 2:21, 24). And God's original intention was, and still is, that marriage be a permanent union held fast by cords of love.

We have that on good authority: the words of Jesus himself. More than once Jesus took the brunt of the Pharisees' antagonism. Try to imagine them huddling together and plotting to trip him, up: "Let's ask the rabbi a trick question and watch him squirm," one of them proposes.

"Why don't we ask him about divorce?" chimes in another. "I hear he's against divorce; so we'll remind him that Moses allowed divorce. If he says that it's forbidden, he'll be contradicting Moses, and we'll be able to discredit him in the eyes of his followers."

And so they challenged Jesus. "Is it lawful," they asked "for a man to divorce his wife?" The Pharisees never minced words with Jesus. But whatever their tack, they were no match for him. Returning their volley, Jesus asked *them* a question: "What did Moses command?"

"Ah, yes, what did Moses command? I'm glad you brought that up, Jesus. Moses permitted divorce. What do you think of that?"

"What I think is this: You are right; Moses did permit divorce but only because your hearts are hard and you will not listen to what God wills."

"And what does God will? Tell, us, Rabbi. That is always of great concern to us."

"A man shall leave his father and mother and be joined to his wife, and the two shall be one flesh. That is the will of God," declared Jesus.

One flesh—one life. How quaint and sentimental that must sound to couples who are used to going their separate ways and doing their own thing! But Christians believe, as C. S. Lewis once remarked, that when Jesus spoke of husband and wife being one flesh he was not expressing a sentiment but stating a fact—just as one is stating a fact when one says that a lock and its key are one mechanism or that a violin and a bow are one musical instrument. The union of a husband and a wife is not merely a physical union, as "one flesh" suggests, but one that is essentially spiritual. Obviously, the one life a married couple shares embraces more than living together, traveling together, eating and sleeping together. A man and his wife are one flesh in an intimately spiritual sense: They are soul mates.

A man shall cleave to his wife, said Jesus. The central word here is *cleave*, from a Greek word that meant "glued together." Cleaving is sticking together, for better or for worse, not for the sake of convenience or social connection but because God has joined marriage partners as "heirs together of the grace of life" (1 Pet. 3:7).

When a marriage becomes "unglued," husband and wife usually blame each other, and if their mutual faultfinding continues, they will likely end up leaving instead of cleaving. How do they explain their breakup to their astonished friends? An estranged wife will confide to her best friend, "Over the years, we grew apart. He went his way, and I went mine. In the meantime I grew, and he didn't. Then one day I realized we didn't have anything in common anymore." Or a straying husband will admit, a bit sheepishly, that he's fallen in love with someone who is "just super in every way." "She understands me," he says. "She listens to me. She's so sensitive and caring. She brings out the best in me." (That man should listen to Vronsky, the spoiled young aristocrat who became Anna Karenina's lover, saying to himself, "With a wife one has trouble, but with one who is not a wife it's worse."[2]

Then there's the ex-wife or ex-husband who confesses, "We never talked about anything important. We discussed the grocery list and what shoes to buy the kids and what's on TV tonight, but we never talked about who we were and what each of us hoped for the other. We never discussed things that really mattered." Does that sound familiar? Or this lament? "I married him with high expectations, but I soon learned that marriage isn't what it's cracked up to be. The romance is gone, and, much as I hate to admit it, our marriage is boring and dull, and I don't know how much longer I can take it." It is a sad moment when a wife bares her soul so despairingly.

Many a wife can say, quite honestly, "Once, long ago, we were deeply in love. He used to say 'I love you' every day, and I know he meant it. But he hasn't said that in many years, and I wonder if he still loves me." Well, I suppose you can love someone without saying it over and over. But I can tell you that verbalizing love is good for a marriage. If you think it's silly to talk about love to someone you've lived with, shopped with, and slept with for twenty or twenty-five years, you can still *show* love in a hundred different ways. Do you remember Tevye and Golde in *Fiddler on the Roof?* They are a married couple who live in a Russian village where everyone knows everyone else. Tevye, a dairyman, is marrying off his five daughters, one by one. Try as he may, he cannot persuade them to marry the men he has chosen for them. Each girl in turn falls in love, and the man she loves is the only husband she will have. After giving approval, reluctantly, to the second daughter, who is deliriously in love, Tevye begins to think about his own marriage. He turns to Golde, and he says, "Do you love me?"

"Do I what?"

"Do you love me?"

"What kind of question is that?" asks Golde. "Go lie down. You must have indigestion."

"Golde, I'm asking you a question—do you love me?"

"Do I love you? For twenty-five years I've washed your clothes, cooked your meals, cleaned your house, given you children, milked the cow. After twenty-five years, why talk about love right now?"

"Golde, the first time I met you was our wedding day. I was scared, I wondered if we would get on together. But my father and mother said we'd learn to love each other. And now I'm asking, Golde, Do you love me?"

"Do I love him? For twenty-five years I've lived with him, fought with him, starved with him. Twenty-five years my bed is his. If that's not love, what is?"

"Then you love me?"

"I suppose I do."

"And I suppose I love you, too."

Tevye and Golde then sing together, and this is their song:

> It doesn't change a thing,
> But even so,
> After twenty-five years,
> It's nice to know.[3]

You are right, Tevye and Golde, it's nice to know you're loved and to say you love, for love is the glue that holds a marriage together.

In every love-glued marriage there is an element of mystery, a vibrant sense of wonder, for the union of devoted mates transcends our noblest conceptions of love. The New Testament draws our attention to the mystery of marital union and likens Christian marriage to the union of Christ and the Church. Husbands must love their wives because Christ loved the Church and gave himself for her and because we are members of his Body. (Eph. 5:25, 30).

Nowhere in the life of the Church is the love of Christ for us—and our love for one another—more intimately expressed than at the Lord's Supper. Like a marital bond, the holy sacrament is a joyous communion of Christ and his bride, the Church. At each observance of the sacred supper our Lord pledges anew his love and faithfulness; he says, "I will never leave you or forsake you." And he summons us to renewed commitment to loving relationships in our marriages, our family circles, and the Church. When we commune together we affirm that we are one Body of Christ, joined in spirit and sharing a common life in Christ. And best of all, in this Holy Communion we shall receive a foretaste of the marriage supper of the Lamb, that ultimate family gathering that awaits those who love God and one another. In that day when all mysteries are unveiled, we shall at last begin to comprehend the wonder of human love—and the still greater marvel of God's love in Jesus Christ for us.

NOTES

1. Edna St. Vincent Millay, "Never May the Fruit Be Plucked," in *The Harp-Weaver and Other Poems* (New York and London: Harper & Brothers, 1923), 37.
2. Leo Tolstoy, *Anna Karenina*, ed. George Gibian (New York and London: W. W. Norton, 1970), 494.
3. Stanley Richards, *The Best Plays of the Sixties* (Garden City, NY: Doubleday, 1970), 308f. (adapted).

34. Fear of Falling

Andrew J. Good

Now to the One who is able to keep you from falling . . .
——Jude 24–25, NEB

Telling one's dreams is a bit like taking off one's psychological clothing in public. Today I will ask you to hide your psychological eyes, for I am about to disrobe!

A Terrorizing Dream

In my teen years a recurring theme disturbed my hours of sleep. The dreams usually began peacefully enough. Suddenly I would feel myself stumble or step on something insecure, and I would fall. The falling was terror enough, especially for someone like myself who suffers from a touch of acrophobia. The worst, however, was yet to come. The ground would rush toward me; I would tense every muscle preparing to smash into the soil. But then, at what should have been the moment of impact, the ground would disappear. There was nothing to break the fall. I would awake with heart pounding and sweat glands pouring.

The dreams stopped, fortunately, after additional years. A residue of them has remained—remained because they grew out of something deep and enduring in my own insecure being. The residue is there, in addition, because I am convinced the dream arose, in Jungian fashion, out of the collective psyche of the human race.

Andrew J. Good is pastor of the Community United Church of Christ in Champaign, Illinois. He has degrees from Emory and Henry College, Boston University School of Theology, Syracuse University, and Lancaster Theological Seminary. Good's articles and sermons have been published in many periodicals including *Pulpit, Pulpit Digest,* and *Christian Ministry.*

It is easy to understand, then, that one of my favorite phrases from Scripture—indeed, from any human literature—is found in an obscure, tiny book of the Bible named Jude. The "book" hardly deserves that title; it is only twenty-five verses in length. Most of it is a dry, uninspired warning against the false teachers that often infiltrated the congregations of first-century Christians. Then, at the end of the list of ways they could stumble in faith, the writer closes with a benediction that is profound in language and implication: "Now to the One who is able to keep you from falling and to set you in the presence of God's glory, jubilant and above reproach . . ." (NEB)

This text is one I have wanted to use throughout my ministry. I have hesitated, however. It seemed, somehow, too personal, its meanings deeper than any medium in which I should choose to swim. Now, in the fourth decade of my preaching, I determined it was time to try, in hopes I might share some of the meaning it has held for me.

The Lack of a Solid Floor

The deepest terror of my dream was not the falling but the fact that there was nothing of substance under me—nothing to keep the fall from continuing.

When a series of disasters has come rapidly, we are apt to speak one of the most discouraging phrases of the language: "The bottom has dropped out." Can we hear what we say? The fear is not so much that any other individual crisis will appear; the fear is that we will continue to fall and there will be no bottom to the descent.

Al Capp, cartoonist of an earlier decade, tried to deal with this serious subject in a lighthearted way. When he wanted to be rid of some character in his strip, "Lil' Abner," Capp would have the person fall into "bottomless canyon." Such persons did not die; they were never crushed on any rocks at the bottom. There was no bottom! Occasionally there would be a scene of the person continuing to drop, carrying on a casual conversation with the folks whose homes were built into the walls of that awesome crevice. It was supposedly in good fun—but it pointed to a dark streak in Al Capp's often depressed existence.

D. H. Lawrence wrote of the same reality in more somber tones.

It is a fearful thing to fall into the hands of the living God.
But it is a much more fearful thing to fall out of them . . . .

That awful and sickening endless sinking, sinking
through the slow, corruptive levels of disintegrative knowledge
when the self has fallen from the hands of God
and sinks, seething and sinking, corrupt
and sinking still, in depth after depth of disintegrative consciousness
sinking in the endless undoing, the awful katabolism into the abyss!
even of the soul, fallen from the hands of God.

Save me from that, O God!
Let me never know myself apart from the living God![1]

Lawrence and Capp describe the sensation that we live our lives in a medium without substance, that there is nothing strong enough to support us when we are upright nor able to protect us when we stumble. Others report the same fear in different forms. Charles Kingsley, an English historian, resigned his chair of history on the ground that there is no such thing as history, no dependable knowledge of past events as they actually happened, but only inaccurate accounts of them colored by prejudice and bias. Even the memories we store in our brain cells and on which we might take an oath are more fluid than we usually admit. The child we remember being is part truth, part wish fulfillment. The past, as one wag has put it, was never as good as it used to be.

If the past is not solid, what can I make of the present or the future? Is there no structure about, no firm bottom that will, when I stumble, break my fall? I would much prefer to think there was a floor hostile in its firmness, able when I strike it to break my bones and snuff out my life, than to consider that living is only, as Macbeth said, a walking shadow.

A God Who Is Able

The writer of the few verses that carry the name of Jude was aware of the problem we have been discussing. The Christians to whom he wrote were entirely new to the faith and thus vulnerable to every interpretation of doctrine that could be presented forcefully. For twenty-three verses he described the darkened, uneven landscape over which they were moving. A multitude of ways were mentioned in which their feet could misstep. Meticulously he described the traps and instructed them to take care.

The reader can, at this point, visualize the original scene. The writer has accomplished his purpose and is ready to close. For a moment he lifts his pen and looks over what he has written. "Have I been too negative? Have I dwelt so much on the problems that I have given them nothing to cling to, no reason to hope?" There is a pause, then a flood of words as if from outside him. A secular writer might describe such a moment with words about being touched by the muse. The pen returns to paper, and the writing style that had been wooden takes wings.

> Now to the One who is able to keep you from falling
> and set you in the presence of his glory, jubilant and
> above reproach, to the only God our Saviour, be
> glory and majesty, might and authority . . . now, and
> for evermore. (vv. 24–25, NEB).

The words, moving as they are in English, are insipid beside the Greek words that Jude originally used. *"To de dynameno . . ."* When scientists first learned that nitroglycerin in a porous substance could create an explosion of enormous power, they named their discovery with that same Greek root: dynamite. Perhaps we can borrow from the youth culture with a very loose translation that might go something like this: "Now to that Ultimate Being who is dynamite, and who can use that dynamic power to keep us from falling all over ourselves . . ."

However the phrases are translated, they point to the same assuring reality. Something solid surrounds us in this life, something of substance on which we can bounce. Yes, there are infinite ways in which we can stumble, and we will continue to do so, for the Divine has not used that dynamic power to take away our freedom. But the solid, strong power of God works in our favor, heals our bruises, and sets us ultimately on our feet.

Our falling will not be continuous; there are no bottomless canyons in the world created by a loving God.

Present Resources

God is able to keep us from falling and has expressed that power in the resources already instilled in us.

Of course, we will continue to stumble from time to time, and occasionally we will fall to the ground with a damaging thud. The freedom God has chosen to give us includes the possibility of doing harmful things. Being human, we continue to take advantage of that freedom in doing some very harmful things!

Included with freedom, however, is the ability to live ordered and considered lives. We have minds and consciences and wise friends to help us avoid the potholes and stumbling blocks.

Falling: we use the word in interesting ways. Mostly we use it to describe something that happened to us, as if we were puppets on the strings of some demonic power. "I fell into debt . . ." Or, "I fell in with the wrong crowd." An alcoholic exclaims, "I fell off the wagon," and even the romantic joins with, "I fell in love."

In truth, none of these things happen to us. "I fell into debt" means I made a series of conscious decisions, some over seemingly small matters, each time trying to fool myself with the rationalization "I can handle this one more payment." "I fell in with the wrong crowd" translates into "I put myself with this group of people in a secret hope that they might become my friends." "I fell in love" usually means "I structured my life so this desirable thing might happen."

Saying that God is able to keep us from falling does not mean that the Divine will intervene to clear away the clutter we put in our own paths. The words are, instead, an acknowledgment that the power of God has already been expressed in our lives. We have been offered the power of reason to weigh alternatives, values that help us choose between better and lesser ways; muscles that do the bidding of our own brains; vision to see the outcome of our activity. How, then, do we keep ourselves from falling? Not by waiting for some Divine Spirit to blow powerfully across our path, but by using the divine resources already at our disposal. We must stop hiding behind words and phrases that seem to release us from responsibility and take charge, to the best of our ability, of our own lives.

God is able to keep us from falling and has expressed that power in the resources already offered us.

A Longer Vision

God is able to keep us from falling by offering us a longer vision of life and its meaning.

The most basic statement of religious faith is this: There is a floor. We stumble. We fall for a moment, but then we strike solid Reality. The cross is a way of describing this Reality. It announces that even death is not a bottomless canyon; the cross affirms that beyond our biggest mistake, beyond our efforts to abolish the highest values, a Divine Power endures who will not be moved or destroyed. The cross says that life and death are constantly intertwined, constantly at war, but the final word is always life.

Paul Tillich, the great theologian and psychologist of an earlier decade, saw this theme of ultimate structure appearing throughout our religious tradition. " 'The world itself shall crumble, but . . . my salvation knows no end,' says the Lord. *This* is the alternative for which the prophets stood. This is what we should call *religion . . .*"

Tillich continued:

> How could the prophets speak as they did? How
> could they paint these most terrible pictures of doom
> and destruction without cynicism or despair? It was
> because, beyond the sphere of destruction, they saw
> the sphere of salvation; because, in the doom of the
> temporal, they saw the manifestation of the Eternal.[2]

Martin Luther King, Jr., knew his people could not love nonviolently until they honestly faced the dark side of human nature. In one of his sermons he referred to the "stark and colossal reality of evil in the world—what Keats calls 'the giant agony of the world,' . . ."[3]

Then King added this inspired paragraph:

> God is able to conquer the evils of history. Divine
> control is never usurped. If at times we despair
> because of the relatively slow progress being made in
> ending racial discrimination . . . let us gain new
> heart in the fact that God is able. In our sometimes
> difficult and often lonesome walk up freedom's road
> we do not walk alone. . . . God has placed within the
> very structure of this universe certain absolute moral
> laws. We can neither defy nor break them. If we
> disobey them, they will break us. The forces of evil
> may temporarily conquer truth, but truth will
> ultimately conquer its conqueror. Our God is able.[4]

There is a bottom, and the floor will never drop out entirely. For God has given us resources to control our own behavior; God has assured us that, in the broad sweep of human history, death and destruction are never the final words.

Supportive Arms

The short letter of Jude is a reflection of an earlier religious crisis. Several hundred years before the birth of Jesus the Jewish nation had gone through a time of both religious and political weakness. So complete was their chaos that the nation's leaders felt they must start fresh. A new summary of all God required of them was compiled. The act of compiling was renewing. As the editors worked, they realized they had been turned around—had "struck bottom," as it were. So the Book of Deuteronomy became more than a summary of laws and demands. It contained, also, inspired messages of hope. One brief passage has become especially helpful to every person who at night has dreamed of falling or who in the daylight despaired that the bottom had disappeared. "The eternal God is your dwelling place," the writer affirmed, "and underneath are the everlasting arms" (Deut. 34:27).

NOTES

1. D. H. Lawrence, "The Hands of God," quoted in *Modern Religious Poems,* ed. Jacob Trapp (New York: Harper & Row, 1964), 224–25.

2. Paul Tillich, *The Shaking of the Foundations* (New York: Charles Scribners and Sons, 1948), 10–11.

3. Martin Luther King, Jr., *Strength to Love* (New York: Harper and Row, 1963), 102.

4. Ibid., 105.

VI. DEVOTIONAL

35. The Drink
Eugene L. Lowry

John 4:3-19

The text seems ordinary enough.
>Jesus and his friends are taking another little trip,
>>from Judea in the south to Galilee in the north.

Of course, in between is Samaria, so they are passing through.

Well, it may *seem* ordinary,
>until you run into that part of the text that says,
>>"They *had* to pass through Samaria."

What did the writer mean: "Jesus *had* to pass through Samaria"?

Well, you say, just look at a map; it's clear. Judea is down there, Galilee up there, and Samaria in between.
>Of course, you have to go through Samaria.

Oh, no you don't.

>Not if you are a Jew in the first century.
>>You wouldn't have to pass through—
>>>and you *wouldn't* pass through Samaria.

There is a "better" way to get to Galilee.

Eugene Lowry is professor of Preaching at St. Paul School of Theology in Kansas City, Missouri. His writings include *The Homiletical Plot* and *Doing Time in the Pulpit*. The preacher suggests that this chapter be read out loud.

You would travel east, across the Jordan River,
    up the other side,
        and then back over the river.

You would go around Samaria.

You do remember, don't you, that the Jews and the Samaritans hated one another—an old family feud that had gone on for centuries?

    Neither wanted to be caught dead or alive in the other's territory—if you could avoid it.
        You didn't go through Samaria—you went around Samaria.

But the text said, "Jesus *had* to pass through Samaria."

Well, they are on their way;
    they have traveled quite a while,
        and they are hot and tired, hungry and thirsty.

They come to that famous well of Jacob . . .
    Jesus sends his friends off to a nearby Samaritan village to pick up some hamburgers at McDonald's . . .
    and he sits down next to the well to catch his breath.

Up comes a woman of Samaria with her container to draw some water.
    Jesus says hello and asks for a drink.

Now, it may seem like an ordinary text, but the truth is, it is absolutely shocking . . .

    not simply because Jesus and his friends should go through Samaria . . .
    but that they would have anything to do with any Samaritan once they were there.

You remember Jesus asking for the favor of a drink?

Surely Jesus remembered what all the Jews understood,
    that any Jew who receives help, accepts a favor from a
    Samaritan, delays the coming of the kingdom.

    And he just asked for a favor.

Jesus had to have remembered the old rabbinic saying:
    "Better to eat the flesh of swine than to eat Samaritan bread."

        And he just sent them into the Samaritan village to get
        some Samaritan brea——. Well, it's shocking!

But it is worse than that.

It isn't just that she is a Samaritan;
    it is also that she is a *she*.

I mean, you understand, Jewish males did not hate women—they
simply understood their "place."

If male, you would not speak in public to any woman—even if you
were walking down a city street and your wife passed by the other
direction.
        You just didn't bend your dignity to say hello in public.
            It simply wasn't done.

And you surely wouldn't teach them anything about the Law—as
Jesus is about to do here.
    "Better to bury the Torah"—says another rabbinic saying—
        "Better to bury the Torah than entrust it with a
        woman."   And another:

    "Better to teach your daughter lasciviousness than to teach
    her the Law."

        You say, Well, we've come a long way, baby!

Well, we have . . . but we have a bit further yet to go.

And I'm delighted to report to you that in our denomination, at

least, we no longer have that little piece in the wedding service—
  you remember it of course—

    when after the bride has helped her father down the aisle,
they come to that moment when the clergy asks,
  "And who giveth this woman to be married to this
  man?"
  —and the father says, "I do."

Now, what's going on there?

  Did you ever notice they do not give the groom away?
  Well, there's a good reason for that—
  the groom is a person.

What is really going on is that she is property—
  and for a brief moment—
  as her hand is given to the minister—
the clergy owns the bride—
  until, reaching for the hand of the groom,
  the clergy places her hand into the hand of her new
  owner.

You say, Why we never meant that.
  Of course not, but that's what we did.

It is not just that she is a Samaritan;
  it is that she is a Samaritan woman.

But, it is more shocking than that.

  It is that she is a bad woman of Samaria.

Anyone in those days would understand that, because she was coming to the well at noon.

  The good women didn't come at noontime to draw water.
  The good women came to the well in the cool of the day
  to make lighter the burden of carrying the water
  back.

But she was not welcome to come with the good women—
>who would gather around the well,
>>have a kind of circle meeting,
>>>and talk about the events of the day.

She isn't welcome, because she is an outcast among her own people.
>She has to come alone at noon to draw water—with all eyes
>>watching as she carries the jar out to the well.

And they say, "There she goes again."

Do you understand the pathos when she says to Jesus,

>"Oh, sir, give me this other drink—
>>that I may never thirst again—
>>>and never have to come here again to draw
>>>water"?

>Do you hear it?

Well, the disciples returned from the Samaritan village with some food.
>They are shocked to discover Jesus talking with her.

The text says that they start to say something about it—
>but they hold their tongue.

>I'm so glad they didn't embarrass themselves again.

Finally, the woman takes off and leaves the container next to the well.

>She hasn't drawn the water—

>>which means she is in a big hurry to get out of there
>>or she plans on coming back.

>You remember that Jesus had told her to go get her husband and come back.

Well, she goes—and very shortly comes back—and brings a whole
group with her.

I'll bet it was not the upper crust of that town.

You may be sure it was a collection of all the outcasts of the village.

Jesus and his friends stay an extra two days to visit with
these people about God, the Law, and life.

But then a strange thing happens—
or rather, it is strange that something does *not* happen.

You remember he said to return and he would give her that drink
that wells up to eternal life?

Well, when she comes back with her friends,
she never mentions the drink again.

Nor does Jesus.

Now isn't that peculiar?

That is what he had promised.

Well, you see, she did not have to mention the drink again—
because she had already been given the drink.

I mean, she was a Samaritan, and he treated her like
a human being—
that is to be given the drink that wells up to
eternal life.

She was a woman, and he accorded her dignity—
that is to be given the drink.

She was a Samaritan woman of bad reputation,
and Jesus treated her with respect—
that is to be given the drink that wells up to

eternal life.

She didn't have to mention the drink again—

she had already received the drink.

You know, a lot has happened from that day to this.

We wouldn't have to worry about having to pass through
Samaria—
we would build an interstate over it.

But one thing is the same.

We still have our Samarias, don't we?

We have those people and those places—
why, we wouldn't be caught dead or alive . . .

I mean, you know those Samaritans—
when you've met one, you've met them all.

We cluster them in groups.

The wrong political affiliation,
the wrong job,
the wrong economic ideology,
the wrong race,
the wrong sexual orientation,
the wrong this or the wrong
that.

I presume you have your own Samaritans, don't you?

I have a few myself.

And we don't want to go into Samaria;
we don't want to rub shoulders with those people.

Please understand, I do not hate them for no reason;
    I do have my standards, you know.

I don't want to go into Samaria.

    I just want to be in the presence of Jesus.

        I just want to bask in the glory of the presence of Christ.

Isn't that what Advent is about . . .
    the anticipation of our being in the presence of the Christ?

In the little church I attended as a child, we used to sing about it:
    "And He walks with me and He talks with me,
        and He tells me I am his own . . . "

        and it feels so good.

But watch out . . .

    watch out where he is walking us to . . .

    and watch out where he is talking us to . . .

because while we are basking in the glory of the presence of the
Christ,
        he is walking due north out of Judea,
            smack dab into the middle of Samaria . . .

He spends an inordinate amount of time there.

Worse than that . . . he turns to those Samaritans, and he says,

    "And *you* are my own . . ."

        It's disgusting.

I mean, you could string up somebody for a thing like that.

In fact, I'm just a little surprised the disciples went on the trip. I am sure they had no natural inclination to go into Samaria.

Maybe it was one of them who wrote, "Jesus *had* to pass through Samaria."

And even if they had the will to go through Samaria, they would have lacked the courage.

There is only one possible reason I can imagine that will account for their being *able* to go with Jesus.

Which is
that the drink that Jesus gave the woman that day—
that drink that wells up to eternal life—

that drink is the same drink that Jesus had given to his disciples two or three years before.

It is that drink that Jesus gives to anybody who gets thirsty enough.

I don't want to go to Samaria . .

I don't like them . . .

I have no intention of being there . . .

I have trouble enough getting along with my kind of folk.

In fact, I cannot think of a good reason for me to go . . .

well, I can think of only one decent reason why anyone would
go . . .

and that is

if you just happened to want to be with Jesus.

36. Life Is a Gift
David J. Randolph

1 Chron. 29:10–25

During her first term in office, British prime minister Margaret Thatcher went to Brighton for government meetings. She checked into her hotel and was going about her business when a bomb exploded that was meant to end her life. She lived, but four of her closest friends died. In a way that we have come to associate with the British, the prime minister carried on and did what needed to be done. But two days later was Sunday and the prime minister was in church. It was a situation familiar to her, as it is to us. That particular day there seemed to be a special light shining in the candles, and when the sun streamed through the stained-glass windows, she began to weep. For at last it hit her that this was a day that she was not meant to see. There were those who wanted her dead, and they very nearly succeeded. But this day was a gift, a gift that she had not been intended to receive. With sadness at the death of her four friends, but with gratitude that she was alive, the tears streamed down her cheeks.

Life is a gift. Most of the time we take life for granted. We think life is a given. It's just here, that's all. Most people's attitude is not so much that *we have it to live* but that *we have to live it*. And one day seems very much like the day that's gone before it. Life is just a given.

But then there are times when something happens, and the awful vulnerability of life is exposed, and we see that every moment of our life is suspended over an abyss—an abyss of nothingness—and

David Randolph currently is pastor of the United Methodist Church in Babylon, New York, and has held teaching, ministerial, and administrative posts. He is the author of *The Renewal of Preaching*.

that it is only by a gift that each day comes to us. And in those moments we know that life is not a given. Life is a gift.

I believe that every one of us has had experiences like that of Margaret Thatcher, if we were really aware of them. Haven't you? I know that I have. I tend to forget them and believe that you do, too, because they're too powerful for us. It's hard to handle those feelings in which we die or nearly die or wish that we were dead. But if we look at our lives very carefully, all of us have had those experiences. This I believe. It may have been through a serious illness. It may have been through an accident. And it may have been just through some chance. I remember an incident in my boyhood when I went swimming for the first time in a creek called "Old Swifty." Before I knew what was happening, I discovered where it got its name, as the swift current knocked me over, and I went under. Panic! Over my head, tossed around. Swept away. I nearly drowned before my friend got me and helped me to the surface. That was like dying and being born again. When my head came out of the water and I could see the world again, I wanted to inhale everything, take in the whole world with my first breath.

I don't think about that every day. It's not consciously in my mind. But when I heard about Margaret Thatcher I began to think about such times in my life. That's just one. When was your moment when you came closest to death? Think about it for a moment. Seriously. When in your own experience have you come so close to death that you could practically taste it? Experience that, because it's essential to remind us that our presence here today is a gift, a gift of God's grace.

That is what David felt. David, the king in that passage from 1 Chronicles. The time had come at the climax of his imperial career to make a great offering, and so the Temple was built. The Scripture lesson is about the dedication of the Temple.

And David, David the great king at the time of dedication, realizes that life is a fight and that everything that we give back to God is in response to what God has given to us.

"Who am I," says David, "and who are my people" that we should give? We are shadows, shadows, he said. For a few moments we stand in the sunlight of eternity and then we're gone. We're strangers and sojourners upon the earth but for a moment; life is given to us as a gift, and the sacredness of life floods in upon us.

It was no accident that Margaret Thatcher's awareness of the gift of life came in church. In church, in our place of worship, we realize, perhaps more acutely than anyplace else in our existence, that life is a gift, that it comes from God. So David prays, "All things come of thee, O Lord, and of thine own have we given thee." That is the moment; this is the awareness. Every breath you take is a gift of God. Every step you take is a gift of God. Every beat of your heart is a gift of God. We exist by the very grace of God. Life is a gift, and at any given moment it may be taken away from us. This is the truth about life. All that we give of ourselves is an offering back to what God has given to us.

It's very much like breathing. When we breathe in, we receive the very air that is a gift, and then we must breathe out. I believe that the meaning of life is to receive life as a gift and to offer it back as a gift. Out of much anguish and searching I have come to this conclusion.

The meaning of life is to receive life as a gift and to offer it back as a gift. It's as essential as breathing in and breathing out. How terrible it would be if we only breathed in, if we were only receivers, if we were only takers. We would soon become bloated and explode. Yes, we receive, but then we give. We breathe out. We share the gift that has been given unto us.

This is so important that it is really the basis of our life, the basis of our stewardship. I think it is tremendously important, if nothing else happens, that we really have a sense that life is a gift that God has given to us. So I want to you to ask yourselves, Am I alive? Am I alive now? Ask yourself that question quietly. Silently. Now ask it with me out loud. Am I alive? Will you say it with me? Am I alive?

Now you can say, I am alive. Can you say that? Are you saying it? Tell me again. How alive are you? I am alive! I am alive! I am alive! Feel it! Feel it! Do you feel it? I am alive!

Now, let's say, I'm alive, thank God. Do you believe that? Let's say it together. I am alive, thank God!

Thank God! That phrase comes to us spontaneously, for we sense in that moment not only that life is a gift but that God is the giver.

Some may argue that this virtually universal experience is not spontaneous but learned from those who already believe. I do not agree, because I believe that we have here an intuitive glimpse of the unconditioned by the conditioned. But even if this is a learned response, how was it learned? It was learned out of just such experience as this when life was threatened and offered back again.

God is most surely proven not by thinking but by thanking. Yet, as Martin Heidegger observed, "Thinking and thanking are closely related." When we think God, we may "prove" God as an object of thought. When we thank God, God is "proven" as a friend is "proven." They are proven true. We can trust them.

This not to disparage the proofs for the existence of God, such as the comsmological and the ontological. These proofs demonstrate a rational basis for belief in God. At the very least they show that it is as rational to believe in God as not to do so.

But God as an object of thought cannot sustain us on the journey of life. For this we seek a God who joins us on the journey. The God of biblical faith is just such a loving companion and not just a logical conclusion.

When we sense that we have such, we are tempted to cry, not "Eureka! I've found it," but "Thank God, God found me!" Life is a gift. There must be a giver. God is the giver.

We may put it this way, but there is an admitted leap from "There must be a giver" to "God is the giver." This I believe is an intuition, a direct perception into a transcendent order. Henri Bergson believed this was as valid a basis for belief as scientific deduction. I agree.

I seriously doubt whether anyone who has never had the experience "Life is a gift, thank God!" can be argued into believing in God. But I also doubt whether anyone who has had this experience can be argued out of believing.

To believe in God as the giver of life is to believe that God stands apart from, but in relation to, us. The giver is not the gift. This is implicit in the biblical doctrine of Creation. God is the creator and therefore is not identical with the Creation. Creation is a gift. But humanity is to care for this gift, and God speaks to the caretakers to guide them. The story of Noah and the flood dramatizes the way in which God creates a covenant with humanity to care for the earth.

God is therefore not a thing among other things. While we acknowledge this at a rudimentary level, we are, nevertheless, tempted to treat God as if God were an object, perhaps the biggest and best of all objects, but nonetheless an idol. But the "one, true god" is always *beyond* our concepts and experiences of God, a "king above all gods" as the psalmist put it.

To believe that God is the giver of life is to believe that God is not an object among other objects but the ground and source of that which is. The distinction between God as an object to be thought and God as a giver to be thanked is of crucial importance.

Many people claim to believe in God, yet they feel miserable much of the time. In church they may profess the words *I believe in God* who creates, redeems, and sustains, but in daily life they are often anxious and deeply unhappy as if there were no power higher and kinder than their own. How can this be? While they believe in God in some abstract sense, they do not actually trust God. To trust God means, not only to give intellectual assent to, but also to rely on the capacity of God to guide and care for us.

Now, belief in God and trust in God are related. To trust in something in which we did not or could not believe would be foolish and, indeed, dangerous. I am assuming here that there is, indeed, reason to believe in God and that God is trustworthy on the basis of Scripture, reason, experience, tradition, and other bases.

Moreover, trust in God is complementary to trust in ourselves rather than in opposition to it. To trust God means that, when faced with a decision, we gather the best data, confer, pray, make the wisest decision of which we are capable, and trust that God is at work for us. We are not to expect God to do for us what we must do for ourselves.

The problem is that we may believe in a God and have at least some confidence in our abilities but worry ourselves to death because we do not trust God. Why? Because we are divided within ourselves. With one hand we offer our lives over to God, and with the other hand we sweep them back into our own possession. We say in one breath, "God, I surrender my will to yours," but in the next we say, "God, give that back to me. Let me worry about it. Let me obsess over this. Let my stomach ulcerate on this a while longer." We do not trust God with our lives because we believe deep down that we can take care of ourselves better than God can. We are unwilling to relinquish control or what we believe to be control over our lives.

Becoming aware of this contradiction is the first step in overcoming it. If we see that this conflict is, in fact, operating in us, we can say, "This is foolish. I am working against myself. The preferable way is to do the best I can with God's help, then turn the subject over completely to God. Worry is pointless and harmful." Then we can train ourselves to trust. Yes, trust to trust—learn to trust as we earlier learned to mistrust, engraving in our consciousness the confidence, "God, I trust you. Lord, help me trust you more."

Frankly, trust comes hard for me. But my trust in God is strengthened when I look back over my life and discern a pattern of the presence of God. I have not always been aware of the will of God working in my life, yet when I reconnoiter my past I become aware of the trust of the Irish proverb, "God writes straight with crooked lines."

Here is one example. A few years ago I was in Miami Beach, Florida. I happened to sit down at a lunch counter next to a man I had never seen before. We got into a conversation over lofty phrases like "Pass the sugar, please." We soon discovered that we had some common interests. He was then considering going into the ministry. Bill shared with me. I shared with Bill. Later Bill got in touch with me. He had entered the ministry. More recently, he has shared again, and the seed idea of spiritual growth in small groups that he shared with me at that lunch counter has taken root and is growing.

I believe that in that chance meeting at a lunch counter God was present. Believing this, I am encouraged to believe that God is present in other unobserved ways. The word *trust* comes from the Old English word *tryst*, which also means "to meet."

We can trust God to tryst with us, to meet us along the way of life. I can live my life with the trust that God will be there for me.

When God spoke to Moses, he challenged Moses to go forth to a land that was nothing but a promise. When confronted, Moses was to say, "I AM THAT I AM has sent me." God called himself, "I AM THAT I AM."

The renowned scholar W. F. Albright translated the name of God "I will be there." Moses was encouraged to move into the future with the confidence that God would meet him there.

God's promise to Moses takes on flesh in Jesus of Nazareth. He is Immanuel, God with us. God is with people in their joys and sorrows. Jesus lives love. He teaches love. He is love. Jesus pours out his life in love. At last it leads him to the cross. He has given his all. And he has given it for us. That God should love us so much as to give life for us—and to give it back again—takes our breath away.

We sing the words of Isaac Watts:

> Were the whole realm of nature mine
> That were an offering far too small.

Love so amazing, so divine.
Demands my love, my life, my all.

To the person facing an illness, to the person whose loved one is dying, to the person facing a new opportunity, God says, "I will be there."

When we believe that life is a gift and that God is the giver we are able to venture into the unknown with the faith that God will be there for us.

We receive life as a gift. We offer life back as a gift. An entire program of stewardship is implicit in this. Stewardship of the church, yes, but of all of life as well.

When we believe this, we will seek peace passionately to preserve life from nuclear holocaust. We will care for the wondrous but fragile earth in every way we can. We will seek to share what we have with those in need all around the world. We will give as generously as we can to and through the church, because it is here that we celebrate constantly the life that is a gift and the God who is the giver.

Here is one example of how all this comes together. On a recent Sunday, Joe and his wife, Sue, addressed their fellow members of our congregation and told why they were supporting our church. They found it meaningful in many ways. Even though there were economic pressures, they were increasing their pledges to the church.

This conversation was more moving to me because of a conversation I had with Joe the previous week. We were at the sharing program for the homeless, at which Joe regularly helps. Joe told me about a man he met in the program who was in bad shape. But he stood out to Joe because he had a certain quality about him. One day, Joe told the man that he had a good suit he didn't wear much now and asked the man if he would use it. The man said he would, so Joe brought the suit to him. The man took the suit and disappeared. He had come regularly to the program, but no more.

Some months later, Joe was in another part of the city, Grammercy Park, when he came upon the man in the street who was well dressed, well groomed, and apparently doing pretty well. This was the man to whom Joe had given his suit. They were somewhat surprised to see each other, but they exchanged greetings, and then the man began to open up and to tell Joe about himself. He had come from a good family, had a fine education, and had done well in business. Then he had nearly ruined himself. But he was back on his feet again, working now, and doing well. He thanked Joe and walked on.

Joe does not know exactly what happened in this man's recovery, and neither do I. But I have a hunch that Joe gave that man a lot more than a suit.

With the suit, Joe gave that man a sense that someone saw in him a possibility he had lost for himself. My hunch is that the fellow realized that he was made for something better than life on the streets, cleaned himself, put on that suit, and took the first steps back to a new life.

I asked Joe where he got this zest for life he so abundantly has. He smiled and told me that he had a heart attack five years ago. His heart stopped. He was gone.

Fortunately, he was in the hospital. They got to him in time. He still remembers, vividly, coming back into consciousness and seeing the medical team around the bed. They smiled when he spoke and indicated he was really alive.

So Joe told me, "For me, every day is a bonus. That's what my father used to say, and it's true."

Every day is a bonus! Life is a gift. Every beat of our heart, every breath that we take, every step that we make is a gift!

As Joe spoke, I felt I was receiving a great gift. Like Joe, everyone of us may receive life as a gift. We may thank God, the Giver. We may offer our lives back as a gift in loving service. Thank God!

Lord, thou has suffered more for me than all the hosts of land and sea. Help me to render back again one millionth of thy gift. Amen.

37. Building Barns, Postponing Life

Martin B. Copenhaver

Luke 12:16–21

I want you to remember or imagine a time when someone precious to you has recently died. You are at a social gathering, and you are determined not to talk about your loss. Instead you resolve, as much as possible, to bob about on the surface of pleasantries along with everyone else. Nevertheless, try as you might, it is difficult to keep the conversations in focus. Someone is talking about his teenage daughter who hasn't picked up her room in weeks, wondering if she will ever learn responsibility. In another cluster of conversation someone else is going on about how crowded the roads are these days and rails against the inability of the various levels of government to do anything about it. Then, somehow, the subject turns to real estate taxes: Can they possibly keep going up? There were other days, other gatherings, when you would have joined in such conversations but not this time. Instead you keep seeing the face of the person who is now gone, and you find yourself annoyed at the small concerns that loom so large in the conversations of these friends. You ask yourself, How could they possibly think that any of this really matters?

Martin B. Copenhaver is senior minister of the First Congregational Church (United Church of Christ) in Burlington, Vermont. Copenhaver was awarded a master of divinity degree from Yale Divinity School in 1980 and was the recipient of the Mersick Prize in Preaching from Yale in the same year. Copenhaver is the author of many articles and of the book *Living Faith While Holding Doubts.* He is also a past winner of the Best Sermons competition.

And I would also ask you to remember or imagine a time when worries nagged you to distraction. The day after you finished paying for the car you got into a fender-bender, and who knows how much it will cost? Or, your son's grades at college are getting worse, and he doesn't seem to appreciate that D's are as expensive as A's. Or, you have just begun to make a list of things that must be done tomorrow, and you are already on your second page. Or, the boss asked to see you first thing in the morning, and he has never done that before. You toss in your bed, as if wrestling with your worry, and it's a match you are losing. Sleep seems ever more elusive. And then the phone rings, with that urgent, threatening ring that phones seem to reserve for the middle of the night. On the other end is a familiar voice, obviously shaken, telling you that one you have loved went suddenly that very night, without pain, thank goodness, but gone now nonetheless. And in that instant, whatever it was that was worrying you flies into the night and disappears. It no longer matters.

Death is a teacher. It can teach us many things, silently, by its very presence. When death intrudes it can add instant perspective to our lives. It helps us sort out what is truly important and what is not. The smaller concerns that so often crowd our hearts and minds can simply scurry away in the presence of death. It is then that we are prepared to see with rare clarity what it is that deserves our attention, our devotion, and our time.

I try to imagine what it would be like to pay a pastoral call on the widow of the farmer in Jesus' parable of the rich fool. That in itself is not too difficult because I have made many such calls. The farmer has just died. His wife is in shock. She asks, "What is a person to do now? No one has told me what happens next." Her talk wanders, and I follow, mostly just listening. Then we turn to the memorial service, and I ask a few questions about the man who has recently died. You see, I didn't know him too well, although on those rare occasions when I did see him for a moment or two I genuinely liked him. But now, as we anticipate a memorial service, I know that it is up to me to speak of him as a whole person, not just of those few, fleeting moments that I have shared with him.

And so I ask, "What was important to him?" And his widow answers, "His family is—was—very important to him. He was very proud of his children, although I'm not sure they really know that. But he spoke of them often. His wallet was thick with their pictures.

And when we were younger we used to love taking walks on the beach together. We talked about retiring on the shore so we could take walks like that again. And his church was very important to him, although I know you might not have seen much evidence of that in recent years. He didn't stop believing in God, I'm sure of that, but, somehow, life just got so busy."

I ask, "How did he spend his time?" She replies, "Oh, working on the farm. And he was very successful. We had another bumper crop this year. He did not want to sell it all at once because if he flooded the markets the price was sure to fall. So he tore down the barns and built larger ones to store the crops. It was a huge task and demanded his full attention. He said he even dreamed about it. It was a lot of pressure.

"As for other parts of his life, well, they were put on hold for a while. I didn't always make things easier for him either. I would frequently ask him when it would all end and we could get on with our lives. And he would always try to reassure me, mostly by using words like *tomorrow* or *soon* and phrases like *this won't last forever* and *some day* and *I promise*. And he meant it. I know he did. He often promised me and himself that as soon as he finished his work and gathered all of his goods together he could say to himself, 'You now have plenty of goods laid up for many years; now you can go to that house on the shore, take your ease, eat, drink, be merry, and do all those things you always talked about.' And now? . . ." She pauses and then seems glad to change the subject: "Well, let's get back to planning the memorial service . . ."

Death is a teacher, and among the things it can teach us is the wide and tragic gap between our answers to the questions "What is important to you?" and "How do you spend your time?" Experiencing the death of a loved one or pondering our own death can provide perspective on our lives and help us see what is truly important and worthy of our devotion and what is not.

I believe the farmer when he says that he intends to lead a different life some day soon, just as I believe myself when I express similar intentions. Some day soon I really will stay in closer touch with my friends. Some day soon I will adhere to a more complete and consistent prayer discipline. Some day soon I will give my family the time they deserve. Some day soon I will give a more substantial portion of my time to those who are without food or shelter. And, yes, some day soon I will eat, drink, and be merry, too, as soon as the barn is built, as soon as the bills are paid, as soon as the project is complete, as soon as the trees are pruned and the room is painted, as soon as things slow down, as soon as . . . well, as soon as things are different.

And I feel quite sure that the farmer and I are not alone in this tendency. I have heard so many people speak of how their lives are going to change as soon as their barns are built . . . when they retire, when the children are grown, when the semester is over, when the task is complete, and the work is done. It's not that we are incapable of doing what we want or should do. It's simply that we seem incapable of doing them now. Time is so short, and everything else seems so long. And then, in the words of the poet Dylan Thomas, "time, like a running grave, tracks you down."

In the last decade or so of my father's life he developed an interest in wine. There is more to this hobby than you might imagine. He would read about the many varieties and vintages and vineyards. He would scout out bargains by reading the newspaper ads from wine shops. When a wine was purchased, it was carefully stored and catalogued. Occasionally he would even drink the stuff. That was always an elaborate ceremony, beginning with bringing the wine to the proper temperature, uncorking it at just the right moment, smelling the cork, tasting the wine to make sure it was suitable to serve, accompanied by florid comments about bouquet and body, descriptions that no one else understood or, frankly, cared much about.

When friends learned of my father's interest in wine, they would sometimes give him a special gift of a rare and costly bottle. I never remember those wines being served. He always said he was waiting for a special occasion. The occasion never came. When my father died—"this very night your soul is required of you"—those bottles remained unopened. I believe he intended to drink them, and, oh, how he would have enjoyed the ceremony of it all. But special occasions, like tomorrow, seem never to arrive. As Ben Hecht put it, "Time is a circus that is always packing up and moving away."

Of course, the point here is not that we should eat, drink, and be merry while we have a chance, even as that is not the point of Jesus' parable. The point is that if we postpone little pleasures at our peril, how much more perilous is our tendency to put off doing what is truly important and noble in life. It may be a good idea to save money for a rainy day, but we sometimes act as if we are saving our lives for a rainy day, and what is most worth doing remains bottled in some dark corner, waiting for that rainy day, or at least another day.

Which brings me to one of the crowning ironies of our lives: The most important things in life are also the most easily postponed. Think about that. The most important things in life are also the most easily postponed. It seems to us that we cannot long postpone building that barn, doing the laundry, running the errands, paying the bills. But all those things together do not add up to much of a life. But developing a depth of relationship with one another, taking time for a person in need, learning to pray, growing in a relationship with God, giving yourself to the cause of Christ—all of those things can be postponed, put off to tomorrow.

And yet, it is precisely those things that make for a full and fulfilling life. We may know that those things are important; we may even plan to make room for them tomorrow. And so the future becomes the repository of our noblest impulses. It is to the future that we assign "whatever is true, whatever is honorable, whatever is just, whatever is pure, whatever is gracious . . .[whatever is] worthy of praise" (Phil. 4:8ff., RSV). Everyone does noble and important things tomorrow through anticipation and resolve, but it is only the great and spirit-filled people who actually do those things today.

Several years ago I saw a television program in which David Frost, the British television personality, interviewed several prominent public figures. I do not remember much about that program, what was said, or even who was interviewed. But I do remember one question that Frost asked each person. The question was this: "What would you like to have appear on your epitaph?" He could have put the question this way: "On the night your soul is required of you, what would you want to have said about you?" It was a brilliant question because it led each person to consider what was most important to them, what they were living for. And it seemed to catch them off guard to be, in their imaginations, in the sudden presence of death. Gone were the well-rehearsed statements that had been smoothed like a pebble on a beach through countless interviews. And I remember that the question prompted remarkably similar answers. Each spoke in grand terms, about love and bettering the lives of others and even about serving God and glorifying God.

I did not find myself cynical about their responses. I believed them. I believed that they desired and intended these things for their lives. And yet, here is that irony again, the irony that the most important things in life are also the most easily postponed, for I doubt very much that the day after the interview, when their aides asked what was on the agenda for the day, that any responded, "Well, today I think I must better the lives of others and make time to serve and glorify God." More likely, facing everyday tasks when the teacher death seems distant again, they probably saved such aspirations for another day so that they could focus on how to get reelected or how to advance their careers or how to make more money—all those present and consuming concerns, all those barns to build.

Jesus does not need to tell us, but we need to be reminded again and again, that our lives were made for more. Not tomorrow, because we cannot live in tomorrow, try as we might. Rather, the only day we have been given (that is, today) was made for more. Certainly we do not want to share the fate of the one who was given the famous epitaph "Born a man, died a grocer," just as we would not want any variations on that theme such as "Born a man, died with his barns completed." Or, "Born a woman, died a politician." Or, "Born a man, died a good provider." Or, "Born a woman, died with closets clean." It makes us shudder to think that our lives could be so summarized.

Death is a teacher, and from it I think we can learn important lessons. We will learn to tend to the little things today. We will savor the little things with grateful appreciation: a walk on the beach, the taste of wine, the color of leaves in a New England fall, the warm stillness of our home.

And if, in the presence of death, we are led to ponder the end and purpose of life, we will also tend to the big things today. We will not postpone the healing of our relationships with one another or the deepening of our relationship with God. We will listen and care and pray and serve.

Finally, in the end, if we have tended faithfully to the little things and the big things, on that night when our souls are required of us, we will discover that we did not build all the barns we could have but, with God's help, we did build an abundant life.

38. The Eyes of Faith

Wesley H. Hager

Mark 8:14–18a

It was the day when Jesus fed a crowd of four thousand people with several small loaves and a few fish. Everyone was satisfied, and the disciples gathered up seven baskets of the broken pieces. Jesus had blessed and dismissed the crowd, silenced the Pharisees who wanted to argue with him, and stepped into the boat with the disciples to go to the other side of the lake, no doubt for an evening of rest.

The disciples had brought only one loaf of bread with them, perhaps thinking there was enough on the boat. Discovering their mistake, they discussed it among themselves. Jesus became aware of their concern, and it was then he spoke some of the saddest lines in the Scriptures: "Why do you discuss the fact that you have no bread? Having eyes do you not see?"

Jeremiah, centuries before Jesus, spoke a similar word: "Hear this, O foolish and senseless people, who have eyes but see not" (Jer. 5:21, RSV).

It could be said that Jesus came into the world to open the eyes of people, to help them to see. In fact, he did open the eyes of many. It is the task of his Church to open blind eyes, both physically and spiritually. Never will I forget the aged missionary from China who, with his wife, worshiped with us regularly every Sunday. They sang

---

Wesley H. Hager, a United Methodist, has been pastor of Methodist churches in New York and Missouri and of the American Protestant Church in Antwerp, Belgium. A graduate of Hamline University and Columbia University, he received his bachelor of divinity degree from Union Theological Seminary in New York. Hager, the author of several books including *Mastering Life with the Master,* is retired and devotes his time to preaching and writing.

the hymns enthusiastically. But cataracts developed, making sight difficult for him. The day came when he no longer opened his hymnal. A dedicated young eye surgeon in the congregation took him into the city and operated. In a few weeks time the hearts of many of us were touched when again Mr. Alty stood beside his wife and sang from his opened hymnal, "My faith looks up to thee, thou Lamb of Calvary."

I'm sure what troubled Jesus far more than physical blindness was the fact that many people with eyes did not see. It is the special task of his Church to open the eyes of faith so that we may, like Paul, fix our eyes "not on the things that are seen but on the things that are unseen; for what is seen passes away; what is unseen is eternal" (2 Cor. 4:18, NEB).

We casually say, "Seeing is believing." But that is not the whole truth. Most of us with average eyes see just the obvious—or we see just what we want to see. Many of us miss the unseen that gives meaning to all that we do see. We are like the one Wordsworth described in "Peter Bell":

> A primrose by a river's brim
> A yellow primrose was to him
> And it was nothing more.
> . . . .
> The soft blue sky did never melt
> Into his heart; he never felt
> The witchery of the soft blue sky.[1]

A primrose is more than just a primrose. The blue sky is more than just blue sky. Did not Jesus say, "Consider the lilies"? The grass, the primrose, the clouds . . . they are all the handiwork of the Master Artist, gifts of the Father, sacraments of the divine love.

Only the eyes of faith can see the great realities—the unseen realities that give meaning and purpose to life. It is not enough to say, "Seeing is believing." It would be truer to say, "Believing is seeing." Even Dr. Bernie Siegel of the Yale School of Medicine writes in his popular book *Love, Medicine, and Miracles*, "Science teaches us that we must see in order to believe, but we must also believe in order to see."[2]

Only the eyes of faith can see love. The ritual of the marriage ceremony includes this phrase: "The wedding ring is the outward and visible sign of an inward and spiritual grace." You can see the ring, but you cannot see "the inward and spiritual grace." It is the faculty of love to see what others, who do not love, cannot see. We miss many things because we do not see.

Many will remember Thornton Wilder's play *Our Town*. Late in the play, Emily, whose short life had ended in childbirth, was allowed to return to earth to relive her twelfth birthday. In this short time, Emily really *saw* her mother and father through their simple goodness and love for her and could realize the many small details that make up our daily life. Unable to bear the loveliness and pathos of this long-forgotten day, she suddenly called out:

> "It goes so fast! We don't have time to look at one
> another. . . . Take me back—up the hill—to my
> grave. . . . Good-bye, Grover's Corner . . . Mama
> and Papa. Good-bye to clock's ticking . . . and
> Mama's sunflowers . . . and new ironed dresses and
> hot baths . . . and sleeping and waking up. Oh earth,
> you're too wonderful for anyone to realize you. Do
> any human beings ever realize life while they have it?
> Every, every minute? . . ." And the Stage Manager
> answered, "No."[3]

And he might have added, "They never learn to see."

You can see great structures, or simple ones, made of steel and stone, bricks and mortar, metals and fabrics, glass and wood, but they are not the only realities. You cannot see the greater realities—the ideas and hopes and dreams and prayers of faith that fashioned all these material things into the school buildings, libraries, temples for worship, homes, offices, and places for healing or recreation.

You can see here in this beautiful place soaring arches of stone that lift your eyes to the heights, glorious windows through which the light of day is broken into rich and magnificent colors, and an altar of finished and carved walnut on which stands a beautiful cross. Behind it you see a magnificent woven fabric of rare and wondrous beauty. You see and sit in a comfortable pew of cherry wood shaped to fit your back and made comfortable with red cushions that match the carpet you walk upon as you approach the altar. All around you is beauty visible with your physical eyes. But it is only with the eyes of faith that you can see what is really here—a place of prayer and devotion and worship—a place brought into being by devout people of faith who sought to create here a fellowship in Christ, a replica of the kingdom of love. You see here a place built by people whose faith in the Living God and whose dreams, sacrifice, hard labor, and prayer built what we see—then dedicated all of it and all that takes place here to the life of the Spirit, the glory of God, and the growth and deepening of the Christian faith.

It is the faculty of faith to see what physical eyes alone cannot see, just as it is the faculty of love to see what those who do not love cannot see.

It has been written of Francis of Assisi that

> he could never bear to put out lanterns or candles
> because they reminded him of the Light of the
> World, and when he washed his hands he chose a
> place where the water that fell would not be trodden
> by his feet, for water was to him the symbol of
> penitence. When he walked over stones he walked in
> reverence "for love of him who is called the Rock"
> and he would never allow a whole tree to be cut
> down for firewood because Christ died on a tree. He
> exulted in all works of the Lord's hands and
> penetrated through . . . to their life-giving Cause
> and Principle.

It is only with the eyes of faith—with spiritual insight—that you can really see people. Only so can you see your friends. Our physical eyes see only the bodies they live in. Jesus saw among the common people of his day: carpenters and fishermen and tax collectors and office workers and revolutionaries, people of character and strength and leadership, and he appointed twelve of them to carry his gospel to the world, and they turned the world upside down.

He always *saw* people. There was the day when Jesus was a guest for dinner in the home of Simon (a Pharisee). A woman of the streets, apparently well known as a prostitute, entered the house with an alabaster jar of precious ointment. Standing at Jesus' feet, she began to weep, and wetting his feet with her tears, she wiped them with her hair, then anointed them with the ointment. Simon, who had invited Jesus, saw this and thought to himself, "If this man were a prophet he would know who and what sort of woman this woman is who is touching him." Jesus, reading his mind, said "Simon, do you *see* this woman?" Of course Simon saw her but not as

Jesus *saw* her. Jesus looked at her with faith and love and compassion. He saw her as the Man of La Mancha saw Dulcinea and sang to her as the chaste, beautiful soul God had made, tragically soiled in the battle of life. Jesus looked on the woman before him, forgave her, and sent her away in peace (Luke 7:36ff.).

The Reverend William Sloan Coffin, when he was chaplain at Yale, used to say to a student he had come to know well, "Jeb, you're a nice guy but not yet a good man. You have lots of charm but little inner strength, and if you don't stand for something you're apt to fall for anything." Jeb was Jeb Stuart Magruder, one of those whose life was stained by Watergate, who later stood before a federal judge and said, "I know what I have done and your honor knows what I have done . . . somewhere between my ambition and my ideals I lost my ethical compass."

The physical eyes can be dimmed by money and power. Only the eyes of faith—only our spiritual eyes—can see through the glitter and the glamour to the pointer on the ethical compass.

Only through the eyes of faith can you see what is great in America. It is not our spacious skies nor our amber waves of grain nor our purple mountain majesties above our fruited plains. All lands have these. Nor is it our great stores of wealth, our huge cities with their towering skyscrapers and beautiful parks, or our scientific achievements, faster planes, larger computers, or satellites moving in orbit around the earth.

The greatness of America is seen in the noblest ideas—the greatest ideals ever to find expression in the life of a great people—the dignity of free men; the value of a human soul; the sacredness of human life; the equality of all people before God; freedom of conscience; everyone innocent until proven guilty in a court of law; liberty and justice for all.

I saw America recently, once on a playing field where teams of eight-year-old children were playing baseball with hard ball and mitts. Their fathers were the coaches and so planned the rules that every child learned the game. What impressed me was boys and girls, of all kinds of racial backgrounds, playing together as a team. They cheered one another on, and they gave encouragement to one another when a ball was dropped or a player failed to make an easy out. I came away thinking, "I've seen America today, America in the making." A second time was at a large university commencement when I marveled again as I read through the list of graduates, names that were rooted in English, Teutonic, Oriental, Slavic, Latin, Arabian, and Jewish backgrounds.

The eyes of faith must see the spiritual roots out of which everything worthwhile in our culture has sprung.

Evil forces are powerful in the world. The minds of men are oppressed and discouraged by the constant fighting in so many areas of the globe. The fact of AIDS is terrifying. The tragedy of drugs is all around us. We live again in a day of great dark fears.

There was a time in the late first century when the Christian community lived in terror. It was dangerous to be a Christian—a member of the Christian Church. The enemies of the faith were strong. Christians were hunted and persecuted. Everything looked hopeless for the Christian cause in he world. The last of the apostles was banished to a penal colony on the Island of Patmos in the Mediterranean. The outlook was dark. Rome was in the ascendancy. But John, with the eyes of faith, saw beyond the present discouraging situation to things as they really were in God's world. He rose to sublime heights in his vision and wrote in stirring words that were secretly carried to the mainland and spread among the Christians. This words steadied men and opened their spiritual eyes. Said he: "I saw a new heaven and a new earth . . . and I heard a loud voice from the throne proclaiming, 'God has his dwelling among men and they shall be his people, and God himself will be with them' " (Rev. 21:1, 3).

This was the triumphant faith of the aged apostle who had said: "The kingdom of the world has become the kingdom of our Lord and of his Christ and he shall reign for ever and ever!" (Rev. 11:15, RSV).

Those who can look on the world with the eyes of faith are never disturbed by the tumult of the world. They are aware of God's power and presence. They walk with courage and trust and sing with the psalmist:

> God is our refuge and strength,
> a very present help in trouble.
> Therefore we will not fear
> though the earth should change,
> though the mountains shake
> in the heart of the sea;
> though its waters roar and foam,
> though the mountains tremble
> with its tumult. (Ps. 46:1–3, RSV)

It was my privilege for a few years to live and preach in Belgium. In that little land, known for its fine linen, I heard an old fable that illustrates beautifully the difference between those who see with eyes of faith and the skeptics who see only with their physical eyes. The flax field with its tiny blue flowers was a beautiful sight at harvest time, but when it was cut, the blind skeptic said, "It's gone forever!" But the man who could see said, "No, its not gone. It will soon become fine linen and grace the altar of the cathedral." After long years of use the altar cloth wore out and could no longer be cleaned and kept in repair. Again the skeptic said, "Well, that is certainly the end of the flax field." "No," said the man who could see. "The old cloth will now be made into fine rag paper. Beautiful songs will be printed on it, and it will be bound into a book from which men will sing for years." After many long years however, the book disintegrated and was finally thrown into the fire. "Now," said the skeptic, "that is the end of the flax field!" But the man who could see answered, "Oh, no! Those songs will keep singing in the hearts of men forever, songs of love and brotherhood and peace!"

Having eyes, do you not see? Day after day we pray, "Thy Kingdom come, Thy will be done on earth. . . ." But can you see it?

A world where the tanks have been turned into tractors,
a world where all the bombs have been dismantled,
a world where mothers need no longer mourn over casualty lists,
where innocent men shall no longer be held hostage in foreign
     prisons,
where men shall learn war no more (Mic. 4:3),
where all politicians shall be statesmen, instruments of
     cooperation and peace,
a world where none shall know the pangs of hunger and none
     shall walk in fear.

In the great crowd that stood on the hill of Calvary outside of old Jerusalem long years ago, there were only a few who saw anything more than two thieves and an imposter dying there. But a few did see with the eyes of faith. They had walked with Jesus and had learned to look through his eyes. They had learned to see life spiritually with the eyes of faith. They saw God himself hanging and suffering and dying there, on that central cross, so that the spiritual eyes of all men might be opened.

Many years ago, after wandering around old Jerusalem and seeing most of the so-called important sights, there was one more thing I very much wanted to see. That was the Pool of Siloam, fed by water from the Virgin's Fountain flowing through Hezekiah's Tunnel into the pool. This is the site where the man born blind was healed. John tells us about him in the ninth chapter of his Gospel. We read of Jesus that "he spat on the ground and made clay of the spittle and anointed the man's eyes with the clay, saying to him, 'Go, wash in the pool of Siloam' [which means Sent]. So he went and washed and came back seeing" (vv. 1–7, RSV).

Knowing that the pool was outside the walls, I went out through St. Stephen's Gate and wandered south through the Kedron Valley and, after some difficulty, found the pool. It is still there today, about fifty feet long and eighteen feet wide. I walked the flight of steps that led to the pavement around the pool, were village girls were busy doing the family laundry. In my mind and heart and imagination I was visualizing the scene John had described. In my imagination I saw a man, perhaps in his thirties, leaning on the arm of a friend who assisted him down the steps to the pool. When he came to the edge, I saw him kneel down very carefully, then reach into the water. I watched as he dipped his hands into the pool, washed the mud and dust from his face, then kept bathing his eyes. After a little time I saw him stand, lift his eyes to the sunlight, and shout with joy, "I can see! I can *see!*"

Slowly I walked back up the steps and made my way to my room, praying then and through all the years since (with Clara Scott), "O Lord, open my eyes, that I may see glimpses of truth thou hast for me . . . Amen."

NOTES

1. William Wordsworth, *Peter Bell* (Ithaca, NY: Cornell University Press, 1985).

2. Bernie Siegel, *Love, Medicine, and Miracles* (New York: Harper & Row, 1985), 36–37.

3. Thornton Wilder, *Our Town* (New York: Coward-McCann, Inc., 1938, 1939), 83.

39. The Gift

Dan P. Moseley

Deut. 8:1–10; Luke 12:16–31

I

The air sparkled. Damp warm had yielded to crystal cool. The red-topped, orange maple had alerted everyone that the time was drawing near. When she finally dropped her leaves, the children ran through the raked piles. They knew that the time was not far off, for soon they would be leaving, soon they would be traveling over the river of concrete, converging in the little town. They and their parents would be on a pilgrimage. From impersonal cities to homey hamlets, they would bring themselves and their goodies to a place their parents called home.

Parents often dreaded it, for it was so much work to get ready: to find some place to leave the dog, to have someone pick up the mail. But once they hit the road, their hearts jumped with anticipation, for they were on their seasonal pilgrimage to the holy place where they had received life.

Every Thanksgiving, brothers and sisters gathered to laugh and to argue, to remember and reminisce, to cry and to eat. They are like shavings of iron drawn by a magnet. Following the beams of their headlights into tree-lined streets, the cars gathered around the house, looking like sucklings gathered around a sow.

Dan P. Moseley is senior minister of Vine Street Christian Church (Disciples of Christ) in Nashville, Tennessee, and is a member of the adjunct faculty at Vanderbilt Divinity School. He received his doctor of ministry degree from Vanderbilt Divinity School. Mosely has served on the general board of the Christian Church in Tennessee and is president of the Disciples Peace Fellowship.

But their anticipation was nothing like the excitement of the old man in the old house for his boys and his girls coming home. He knew his days were numbered, and thus each year there was a heightened sense of joy as he prepared his home place for the onslaught of love, as he prepared his heart for relief from oppressive loneliness.

We are pilgrim people. In wilderness and exile we long for home. We like our freedom but long for security. We are scattered and broken, seeking our fortunes alone, chasing gods of pleasure and self-fulfillment. As separated communities of faith, we bow before gods of purity and doctrine—Jews, Christians, Buddhists, Hindus, Muslims. We isolate ourselves in tight units of family and forget the household of faith from which we were created.

But there is one who waits, one who anticipates our return. There is one who suffers as creatures wander aimlessly and divided, rejecting the love that created them—leaving brother and sister to fend for themselves. The one who creates the human community yearns in anticipation for the children's return to the table of redemption.

And sometimes they do return. Sometimes the tug of memory wins out and people divided draw together in the father's house. Sometimes the wandering pilgrims pocket their pride, give up their fear, and track back to the source, and, in so doing, gladden the heart of God. Sometimes on Thanksgiving we children of God gather together, and God laughs in joy.

II

The car doors banging and children screaming, the crowd gathered at the old house. They each brought with them their favorite foods to share with the family. There were kids and grandkids and even a little great-grand heir to carry on the family name. There were pies and sweet potatoes, green beans and bread, all from different kitchens, gathered in the old kitchen, and Jane and Mary talked excitedly of yesterday and of a thousand yesterdays. The turkey was brooded over by Bob. He tried to keep the parade of nine- and ninety-year-olds from opening the oven and delaying its ripening. Each had come bringing what they had to share to prepare a meal.

We, too, bring our gifts. We bring our food to share. We talk together of life, the stuff of hope. We bring our money for the common pot, knowing that food and life merge in table and altar. And when we do, we discover the stories of yesterday that created us as one people. We remember the stories we experienced together. We share and develop our own common stories as we pass between ourselves bread and wine, punch and cookies, turkey and dressing. Our memory runs deep, nourishing our days.

III

The children were hungry, and so as they gathered around the long table, each of the offerings was brought on the family altar. The patriarch stood and began to carve the bird. The bowls peppered the table, filled with the goodness of the world. Complete loaves of bread were there to be cut. The full pitcher of tea was there among an assortment of jelly glasses. Everything was being prepared and broken.

The gathered family members began to prepare their hearts as well. They began to break their lives and lay them out on the table. That is, they began to tell stories of their lives, what had happened long before and what had happened yesterday. (It's inappropriate at a Thanksgiving meal for one person to present all of life, for one person to present a philosophical discourse on the meaning of life.) It is only appropriate at the table to break your life and to bring it in bits and pieces and stories, stories to be shared on the family altar. The face of a clock is twenty-four hours, but the face and meaning of life is minute by minute, moments of experience.

Our gathering includes children at the table, too. We pilgrim people of God always have a place for the little ones, the powerless, the weak, the minority, the outcast. In fact, the weak and helpless are cherished by the family because it is the character of the divine family to hold the helpless and carry the crucified.

We gather at this Thanksgiving service with children, with aged, and, in our minds, with the wounded and hungry of this city. We hear the broken cries, the halting tongues as they tell their stories to us. We bring offerings that reach out and spread the table of humanity for them, too. The table without enough chairs for all people is not a table spread by God.

IV

The old man took a plate, gingerly placed a slice of white meat on it, passed it to Suzy, who put on it sweet potatoes, and Billy, who put on it green beans. Each person took it and put something on it and passed it to the next person. Every time a tall arm reached across little eyes, passing the plate, the eyes got bigger with delight. But when they had finished passing the plates, there was no loaf left, there was no whole turkey left. What was on the table was broken and shared.

What we bring is broken, for that is the only way it can be shared. The rich man in Jesus' parable did not understand this. He consolidated. He brought his stuff and sought to secure it intact. He wanted it to be wholly his—wholly controlled—where he could get to it to provide his needs.

But the people of faith break bread—at Passover, at the table of communion. The people of God know that the gifts they have been given are only made whole when they are broken to be shared with others. People of faith know that we cannot make ourselves whole but are made holy by the power of God, who takes scattered and fragmented humanity.

V

As the turkey and the rolls were shared, they were devoured along with the laughter. Uncle Bill's jokes, which would have been a little bit too shady had grandmother still been living, were washed down with the tea. As they ate, the noise level got greater. Confusion reigned. The children had taken what they had been given and consumed it without tasting it, because they were anxious to get on, to get on with building their tree house in the backyard.

Suddenly someone blurted out, in the midst of all the noise, "Hey, we forgot to have the blessing! Who'll give the blessing?" And everyone stuttered, quit chewing. Sister Elaine pointed to Ronnie and said, "Make him do it." Someone else said, "No, Joe will do it." Among the chatter and in the midst of the noise, Granddad, with his voice like God's , said, "I'll do it." And Johnny knew right then and there that he should have spoken up, for he knew how Granddad prayed. He knew that the children would be antsy and the men would be fidgety because the ball game was about to start. The women would be anxious because it was time to get things cleaned up. He also knew that Granddad had no sense of time and that his prayer would wander all over Creation, and it would go on forever. But it was too late now. They had to listen. They had to pray. And out of respect or out of guilt they bowed their heads while Granddad gave thanks.

Moses commanded God's people to remember their days of emptiness—their days of wandering when only by divine grace was manna provided. We are not to forget that our life is purely and simply a gift of divine grace. Our breath and energy is given *gratis.*

And Moses told the people to then bless the Lord your God for the good land you have been given. Jesus, too, gathered with his disciples and told them that they ought always to give thanks for the bread and the wine.

Why did Moses tell the folk to take time to remember and to give thanks? Why did Jesus always give thanks before he ate? Why does Granddad spend all the time thinking about all the things for which to pray? Why is it that we sit at the table afraid to speak our thanks? Why is it that it is an appendix to the body of our lives rather than the very heart of what we are about?

I don't know why Moses called us to remember and why Jesus gave thanks first, and I don't know for sure why Granddad talks so long in prayer. Maybe it's because they all realize that they don't really deserve what they have, or maybe it's because there are just different spirits among us.

VI

But I have sometimes wondered if the reason Granddad's prayers are so long is because his memory is so long and because Granddad not only remembers a lot but he also remembers a lot that he has lost. He sits at the table every Thanksgiving, there at the end, hanging onto the little group of people who will linger and listen and talk, hanging on like the last leaf of autumn on a naked tree. It seems to me, the older I get, the longer I sit, hanging onto the moments of my children's lives as they pass by and as they move on. Maybe that's the reason Granddad talks so long; it is because he has remembered so much and because he has lost so much, because he has taken the bread of life that has been given and he has embraced it, broken it, shared it, and then he has lost it and thus was made whole.

Granddad remembers his innocence, and he remembers his innocence lost. He remembers his little girls, and he remembers losing them to marriage. He remembers his blond-headed boy, a son he lost to a war. He remembers his meaningful work, the job he lost to a younger man. He remembers what it was like to chew steak with real teeth, lost to old age. And he remembers his wife, love of sixty years, lost to the angel of death.

I can't help but think that this loss and all the losses that he remembers cause him to realize how important and precious life is, and that's why he hangs onto the end of the table, and that's why he hangs onto the end of every word. When you have languished beside the pool of grief, the streams of laughter dance more joyously. Maybe that's why he's not anxious to leave the table anymore, why he revels in relationships. He knows that they may not come again, for Alice is graduating from college, and, after all, he is eighty-four years old now, and his heart flutters more often, and the nitroglycerin is a friend more frequently, and maybe it's because of that that he gives thanks and his prayers are so long.

Maybe that's also why Granddad is more generous with his time than his son and grandson are, for he knows how temporary things are. He remembers when time was a friend, bringing on its wings moments of love and pain, and he also remembers when time was an enemy, carrying away those people who mattered much to him. Maybe he knows better than anyone else at the table the transitory moments of life. Maybe he and he alone knows the pain when the cars pull away in the empty dark. He knows that his days will follow longer and longer, and memories will be his only companion. You see, when at the daily table of your life your own breath and your own chewing are all that you hear, then reaching arms and laughing children are a symphony.

And I wondered if Granddad isn't more tolerant now than he used to be, because he remembers so much and remembers what he lost. He's tolerant because he realizes in retrospect how few things really do matter when it gets down to it. He thinks of the day he came home from college, having shaved off his moustache and beard, and how upset his father was with him. And he chuckles as decades since he has watched his children fight with his grandchildren over how much hair they had and where it was located. And he's amused as he watches his daughters complain about his granddaughters and the clothing they wear and the clothing they do not wear, and he remembers his wife and his own daughters. You see, when you stand naked before the edge of life alone with no hair, any hair and any clothing at all is adornment for royalty.

VII

I don't know why for sure some of us sit down at the table and break the bread, break the life, and eat it, pass it on, and never stop to squeeze in the blessing during the beer commercial at a ball game, and why others of us sit there and just hang onto every moment, tasting each morsel of life before we swallow it. But I suspect that it has something to do with the degree to which we remember what has been given, remember what has been lost, and realize how precious life is.

Blessed be God who is the source of our life—our memories—our bread—our hope. Praise be to God at whose table we are made whole.

Amen.

40. And Abram Journeyed On
Michael Bledsoe

Gen. 12:1–9

The brilliant nineteenth-century Russian novelist, Fyodor Dostoyevski, has described an enormously important scene, not only for his time, but for our own. In his book *The Brothers Karamazov*, Dostoyevski has Ivan Karamazov and his brother Alyosha sitting in a wretched tavern. Ivan says to his brother,

> What have Russian boys been doing till now, some of them, I mean? In this stinking tavern, for instance, here, they meet and sit down in a corner. They've never met in their lives before and when they go out of the tavern, they won't meet again for forty years. And what do they talk about in that momentary halt in the tavern? Of the eternal questions, of course; of the existence of God and immortality. And those who do not believe in God talk of socialism or anarchism, of transformation of all humanity on a new pattern, so that it all comes to the same, they're the same questions turned inside out. And masses, masses of the most original Russian boys do nothing but talk of the eternal questions. . . . Isn't it so?[1]

The eternal questions. We ask them in here, in this sanctuary, of course, and that is why I have emphasized the theme "the sacred

---

Michael Bledsoe, a two-time winner of the Clyde Francisco Preaching Award, earned his Ph.D. from Southern Baptist Theological Seminary. A native Ohioan, Bledsoe is pastor of the First Baptist Church (American Baptist) in Columbus, Ohio. He is an active member of the Baptist Peace Fellowship of North America and is a charter member of the National Museum for Women in the Arts.

journey begins here." But it is not incorrect to say that the sacred journey has begun this morning as masses of people have stepped from the hard bed of their sleep and pondered their faces in the mirror: They have stepped between Monday and Friday and looked into their faces, with no makeup, unshaven, and uncombed. And the sacred journey finds its first expression when somehow those lips form the questions of Who? and Why? T. S. Eliot cut through the daily routine of our lives when he wrote in his poem "Preludes":

> You tossed a blanket from the bed,
> You lay upon your back, and waited;
> You dozed, and watched the night revealing
> The thousand sordid images
> Of which your soul was constituted;
> They flickered against the ceiling.[2]

As a church we have often condemned those who sit in the taverns that dot our city, and we have found it easier to condemn the behavior of people than to come to some common ground of understanding. For the questions raised in the wee hours of a person's conversation with friends or acquaintances, the questions pondered as the head aches from its temporary elation at having been numbed, these are the questions of eternal significance! They are the very questions we raise, only—as Dostoyevski has noted—turned inside out!

So we enter into this place in some attempt to not only begin a sacred journey but to continue it. We come here in some attempt to define "sacred," not to be convinced we are on a journey for we know that only too well: By our going out and coming in, by our speeding circles around his city's expressways, and by the simple movement from one room to the next, we know we are journeying. But the questions still remain: Who? and Why?

With those questions formed and falling from our mouths, we are ready to observe the journey of one man who, long ago, set out from his hometown and ventured into the unknown. Faith, beloved, always contains an unknown; faith is not the language of mathematics, but it is the language of music, which depends upon silence to shape it. May we look to the father of our faith, Abraham, and hear the silence, behold the mystery, and discover the courage to make our own journey.

Abram woke up in a country that was littered with gods. Around him people worshiped the moon and the sun and any num-

ber of gods of nature. His was an age of wandering and mass migra-
tions of whole groups of people from one place to another, seeking
some resting point while at the same time engaging in tribal warfare
and bloody sacrifice. And as the story of the Tower of Babel indicated in chapter eleven, humanity was divided and broken, unable to
communicate among one another and scattered across the earth.

What was the day like when Abram heard the voice of God calling to him? Not a bright, lighted day, I think. Not a day that began
in excitement and emotional goose bumps, but a day perhaps when
he was unshaven, tired, and feeling exceptionally old. A day perhaps when he had given up on human beings for all their killing:
mothers who had stabbed their children with scissors, husbands
who had abused their wives, and powerful men who licked their
chops at the thought of war. It was within the babel and the brokenness that God spoke to Abram.

Even the words of God were not sweet, pious, or comforting.
They were words that separated. This was a call to be broken for
the sake of wholeness. "Go from your country and your kindred
and your father's house to the land I will show you." Now we cap-
ture a glimpse of how the sacred journey begins. It begins with an
acknowledgment of separation and a stepping away from the condition in which one finds oneself.

Abram was being asked to go away from that which was secure
and arranged in the world for him. He was being challenged to accept the fact that God's land is another land altogether. Not a land
of murder, but of birth. Not a land of killing, but of healing. Not a
land of war, but of peace. Not a land of gods inferior to the very
human beings who worshiped them, but a land of the One God.
Make no mistake about it, fellow travelers: The journey is costly.
Abram was asked to give up his security and his tradition in order to
begin moving toward God's land.

Does this sound too harsh, too difficult? But recall that the eternal
questions are often the questions of this world turned inside out. Jesus
said it so often, didn't he. "If you have eyes to see, see. If you have ears
to hear, listen." We are being taught from the day we are born about
having to go from our country and kindred. For in the cry of our separation from our mothers, we are acknowledging that the sacred journey is born by separation. We must depart from our mother's womb
before we can become an individual who says I. We must leave before
we can enter. We must ask before we can hear an answer.

But God's call is not devoid of any hope. In fact, it is a clarion cry of hope within our world of babel. After he told Abram to leave, God promised him, "I will bless you." For Abram, this promise was sufficient, for we read, "So Abram went, as the Lord had told him."

For many, the sacred journey is not fulfilled because the questions are impossible to ask. As religious people, we often become immobilized by the terrifying questions that confront us in our age and, for some reason, think it unholy and unsafe to ask God and to question our tradition. Secular folk have a different problem, but it is the religious question turned inside out: What if there is a God? What if my life does mean something and I have lived it with utter disregard for others and for the God who made me? These are terrifying and fearful questions. But remember: Abram was an older man when he began his journey. Remember: God calls and promises his blessing. Jesus himself assured us, "Ask and it shall be given you. Seek and you shall find. Knock and the door will be opened unto you."

Hear the silence and acknowledge it. Yes, you are alone. You have been cut off. Since your cry at birth and your crying now, the silence misunderstood as God's absence might, in fact, be God's presence, which breaks through the noise and confronts us face-to-face. Within the silence we, too, might hear his voice, "Go."

The mystery of all this is that God is one who asks, seeks, and knocks. God asked Cain after he had killed Abel, "Where is your brother, Abel?" It is God who sought out Abram and Moses . . . and you. It is God who knocks on our door. Yes, we feel abandoned and alone, but there is One who meets us there and waits for us to put on our walking shoes.

In one of my "dark nights of the soul," I discovered this truth. I had been working in a warehouse in Florida and personal circumstances had turned very bad for me. My own sense of whether I could ever be ordained was grim. I felt abandoned and utterly alone. The small, truckdriver's restroom was the only place in that big warehouse that I could close the door and cry in private. But the God who seeks us out and will not let us go, the God who dares to ask of us the questions we ourselves are afraid to ask, that God was as near to me as the vein in my neck, and I knew, as I know my own hand and face, that God had not abandoned me. You are not abandoned. Your journey is important. God calls to you, as he called to Abram.

The mystery is that, while you and I think we are so modern and we have left behind the ancients as some kind of primitive people, we face many of the same problems. The mystery is that this God of Abraham, the God of Jesus Christ, is the God who calls to you. The mystery is reading the words in the Gospel of John where Jesus says, "Before Abraham was, *I am.*"

If we stop here, however, with the promise of God, we will not get the full picture of what our journeying means. For while the journey begins within our own questioning and separation, its completion and its becoming sacred is determined by obedience. "So Abram went." Those may be the most important words. He obeyed God. He decided to pay the price. He knew deep down within the very core of his life that to disobey God would mean, not a journey, but a wandering.

We all know the difference between wandering and journeying. For three months now, I have been trying to become familiar with the city of Columbus. Nearly everytime I go out—at least when I stray from Broad Street—I get lost. It is frustrating to be lost. It is infuriating to take wrong streets and to be left with no sign as to how to get back. Such an experience is far different from getting into the car and traveling with my family to Orlando, Florida, so we can see our families. I know the way there. We know why we're going and who we will see.

Obedience is the difference between wandering and journeying. But does obedience mean this life will find its complete fulfillment? We know by only having to look at Abram that this is not the case. He did not see the Promised Land. He did not see a nation emerge out of his family. As the writer to the Hebrews has written, Abram died in faith not having received the promise.

That just does not cut it in a society dedicated to profit. Does it? Who would even think of investing in a business or a bank or whatever if the promise of profit were qualified by "you might never see it"? The language of faith is not the language of math. It is not the language of profits. The language of faith is the language of music, where silence produces rhythm and shape. For the one who has sought and found, the promise and presence of God is enough. It is enough. After describing his going and coming, Gen. 12:9 says of Abram, "And Abram journeyed on . . . "

We seek courage to continue even as Abram continued his journey. We gain such courage by recognizing that there are those who have lived in our lifetime and live even now and courageously walk the sacred journey. One such person was Martin Luther King, Jr. On Easter eve of 1963, Martin was arrested in Birmingham, Alabama, and thrown into solitary confinement for more than twenty-four hours. He wrote about that experience: "You will never know the meaning of utter darkness until you have lain in such a dungeon, knowing that sunlight is streaming overhead and still seeing only darkness below." He admitted that he was overwhelmed by worry and fear. But he also spoke of an intense awe: "I was aware of a feeling that had been present all along below the surface of consciousness, pressed down under the weight of concern: . . . I had never been truly in solitary confinement; God's companionship does not stop at the door of a jail cell."[3]

Hear the silence. Behold the mystery. Journey on.

NOTES

1. Cited in James Pain, *Sergius Bulgakov* (Philadelphia: Westminster Press, 1976), 36.

2. T. S. Eliot, "Preludes," in *The Waste Land* (New York: Harcourt, Brace & World, 1934), 14.

3. Martin Luther King, Jr., *Why We Can't Wait* (New York: Times Mirror, 1963), 74–75.

Index of Contributors

Index of Sermon Titles

Index of Scriptural Texts